The Institutional Basis of Higher Education Research

The Institutional Basis of Higher Education Research
Experiences and Perspectives

Edited by

Stefanie Schwarz

and

Ulrich Teichler
Centre for Research on Higher Education and Work,
University of Kassel, Germany

KLUWER ACADEMIC PUBLISHERS
DORDRECHT / BOSTON / LONDON

Library of Congress Cataloging-in-Publication Data

ISBN 0-7923-6613-1

Published by Kluwer Academic Publishers,
P.O. Box 17, 3300 AA Dordrecht, The Netherlands.

Sold and distributed in North, Central and South America
by Kluwer Academic Publishers,
101 Philip Drive, Norwell, MA 02061, U.S.A.

In all other countries, sold and distributed
by Kluwer Academic Publishers,
P.O. Box 322, 3300 AH Dordrecht, The Netherlands.

This publication is supported by the Volkswagen Foundation

Printed on acid-free paper

Printed in the Netherlands.

Contents

Introduction: Comparing the Institutional Basis of Higher Education Research

STEFANIE SCHWARZ & ULRICH TEICHLER
Centre for Research on Higher Education and Work, University of Kassel, Germany

Higher education praises itself as being one of the most universal sectors of society. Yet, its structures, its development, its curricula and educational thrusts, its governance and organisation vary greatly and tend to be deeply rooted in national, cultural and policy contexts.

This is even more true when it comes to research on higher education. There are countries where only a few basic statistics are available, where overviews of higher education are general and where the basis of experts' reports is not always sound. But there are some countries where institutions and agencies involved in higher education have established units which are responsible for systematic information gathering and research on higher education, where research on higher education is a stable feature of cross-discipline research in the humanities and social sciences and where teaching higher education as a field of study and research on higher education are intertwined according to common modes of linkage.

Sharing experience in the institutional basis of higher education research and discussing improvements can therefore be seen as a rather futile task, because the conditions seem too heterogeneous to promise any fruitful insight on the basis of international comparison. However, higher education tends to be considered in all countries as a field that requires reflection and systematic knowledge. Even if research on higher education is not always accepted as a possible basis for innovation, a comparison of its institutional setting may be useful.

S. Schwarz and U. Teichler (eds.), The Institutional Basis of Higher Education Research, 1–9.
© 2000 *Kluwer Academic Publishers. Printed in the Netherlands.*

Developments in higher education research

Various attempts have been made to summarize the state of higher education research in a comparative perspective. Most of them focused on the substance of research, but they often also referred to its institutional basis.

According to earlier analyses, research on higher education was still rare only a few decades ago. For example, a book on the state of higher education research in Germany published in 1984 referred in the introduction to the widespread saying that professors conduct research about everything except the university. In the last three decades, however, this field has developed and obtained remarkable results. Yet, observers often express concern rather than satisfaction.

- How can research on higher education cover more successfully the broad thematic range and bring together the various areas of expertise?
- How can research on higher education make sure that the range of heterogeneous disciplines it refers to does not remain segmented, thus leading to simplified observations?
- What kind of problems does higher education research encounter as a consequence of the lack of systematic training of higher education researchers and experts, and are there means of improvement?
- Are the highly sophisticated practitioners in higher education a detriment for research because they believe that their reflection is a sufficient basis of knowledge and information, or does a dialogue with them offer new insights?
- Does the diverse institutional basis of higher education research match heterogeneous values, paradigms and needs of those interested in the findings, or is there a need for communication and co-operation?
- Do the barriers of communication between higher education research and higher education policy and practice protect academically demanding research, or would higher education research gain from better communication?

Issues such as these are raised in many countries. As already stated, however, we note striking differences. First, higher education research is an important entity in some countries, for example in the US, Australia, and China, whereas it is more or less negligible in many others. Second, the major institutional bases of higher education research vary. Four are found very frequently:

- In some countries, many institutions have established offices that are responsible for staff development or improving teaching and learning; their staff are often involved in research as well as with students, teaching, and learning.

– In the US, the university administration runs its own office of "institutional research" in order to base its decisions on systematic information.
– Furthermore, higher education research can rely on a relatively stable academic basis if study programmes on higher education exist. Again, this is most frequently the case in the United States.
– Finally, governments and other macro-societal actors sometimes have their own offices or institutes of policy research and prepare the policies of the actors they report to.

In addition, research on higher education can be institutionalized in a variety of ways. Often, research institutes on higher education are quite visible. They were established as specialized research units within or outside institutions of higher education; but no common institutional basis can be observed for this type of institution across the countries.

Third, the major themes of research on higher education also differ between countries. It has frequently been said that in European countries it was more prone to analyse macro-societal issues of higher education, whereas in the US it tended to study the inner life of higher education institutions, students, and the teaching and learning processes.

But two elements seem to be common to all the countries where higher education research is fairly institutionalized. First, there is a multitude and heterogeneity of institutional bases. This causes problems of communication within higher education and in providing any overview of the state of knowledge. Second, the borderline between research on higher education and other activities related to information gathering and reflection on higher education issues tends to be fuzzy. For example, most conferences, journals and associations in this domain comprise "experts" from different fields: academics, applied researchers, consultants, practitioners, etc.

The impact of the institutional basis

This rapid glance suggests that the institutional basis has salient impacts on the substance of higher education research. The modes of institutionalisation of higher education determine to large extent:
– whether systematic knowledge on higher education takes the form of explicit higher education research or is predominantly generated as an integral part of the observation of the actors,
– which themes are often studied in higher education research projects and which are not,
– the theoretical and methodological standards that higher education research strives for or achieves,
– how higher education research is related to issues of higher education policy and practice and how it contributes to practical problem solving,

– whether higher education research is undertaken only occasionally or whether there is a certain degree of professionalisation in terms of accumulation of knowledge, training of researchers, and professional co-operation.

Obviously, the institutional basis of higher education research has salient impacts on its quality, on its professional identity and on interaction with higher education policy and practice.

The aims and themes of this volume

In September 1998, the Centre for Research on Higher Education and Work of the University of Kassel, Germany, invited some 50 scholars from more than 20 countries worldwide to share their experiences in the institutional basis of higher education research and to discuss possible improvements. The symposium took place during the celebrations of the Centre's 20th anniversary and was supported by the Volkswagen Foundation, the German Academic Exchange Service and the University of Kassel.

Participants were invited to reflect upon five themes:
– the ways in which the thematic and disciplinary structures of higher education research interact with its institutional setting,
– an account of the institutional setting, for example, the links between higher education research and teaching in this area, administration of both higher education institutions and governments, or the impact of the institutional basis of higher education research on the research being undertaken,
– the relationships between higher education research and higher education policy and practice: mutual expectations, commissioning of research, dissemination and impact of research on policy and practice,
– the training of young researchers in the field of higher education and their career expectations,
– possible means of communication and co-operation between research units in different parts of the world.

The main presentations were grouped around three major themes: the general issues of the institutional basis of higher education research which cut across countries; higher education research in individual countries and regions; and specific issues, such as the training and careers of young researchers.

In the framework of the first theme, Ulrich Teichler (Centre for Research on Higher Education and Work, University of Kassel, Germany) describes higher education research as it is embedded in its institutional basis. He analyses the different roles of researchers who are based in disciplines and occasionally or continuously study higher education, theme-oriented scholars in academically based research institutes, applied higher education researchers, consultants and finally reflective practitioners. He notes the dangers of an application drift of higher education research that is willing to bridge the gap between academic theory and the demands of policy and practice. But he also notes opportunities inherent to communication between experts of various institutional bases.

Maurice Kogan and Mary Henkel (Centre for the Evaluation of Public Policy and Practice, Brunel University, England) stress the different nature of the interest in knowledge, information, and the complexity of thought and problem-solving in academic and policy-oriented research, thus mapping areas of understanding and of conflict between academic research and policy-oriented analysis. They make the readers aware that the different epistemologies are not specific to the field of higher education, but rather affect communication between research and policy in various domains.

Elaine El-Khawas (University of California, Los Angeles, U.S.A.), notes three different spheres of higher education, i.e. academia, policy, and practice, which have established their own research settings and activities. As a rule, they hardly interact, but tend to converge when there are major policy reforms.

Similarly, Guy Neave (International Association of Universities, Paris, France) warns that the process of intellectual maturation of higher education research is at risk. The intellectual identity of this domain may be lost if research aimed to serve consultancy and policy, thereby expressing a skeptical view on whether a debate on organisational forms of research is useful for touching upon the most crucial issues of the potentials and dangers of higher education research.

In the framework of the second theme – higher education research: countries and cases – James S. Fairweather (Center for the Study of Advanced Learning Systems, Michigan State University, East Lansing, U.S.A.) maps the diversity of institutional settings, themes, and approaches to funding in the US. He sees an advantage in this diversity as far as responsiveness to new issues is concerned and notes a growth in the research community as one of its consequences. But he also stresses the disadvantage "of making it difficult to achieve systemic effects, to foster a shared information base, and to form meaningful linkages between policy-makers, funding agencies, and the full array of organizations carrying out higher education research".

John Brennan (Centre for Higher Education Research and Information, The Open University, London, United Kingdom) provides an analysis of the institutional basis of higher education research in the United Kingdom as it is reflected by policy, funding, and interest groups. He examines the problems and prospects of one higher education centre in a case study which raises the question of whether hybrid forms of organisation are necessary to meet the special and distinctive needs of higher education research.

Grant Harman (Centre for Higher Education Management and Policy, University of New England, Armidale, Australia) describes an impressive variety of institutional settings, funding, themes and links to policy practice in higher education research in Australia. He expresses concern regarding the future of public funding for research and sees the higher education research potentials as often being too thinly spread "to allow for multidisciplinary work and major projects".

Two contributions study higher education research in Latin America. Carmen Garcia Guadilla (Universidad Central de Venezuela, Caracas, Venezuela) shows that research on issues of higher education is undertaken in a large number of institutions and that the number of institutions and training programmes that focus on this area has grown in recent years. Many networks of scholars from different institutions and countries that share similar philosophies have been created. Pedro Krotsch (Social Science School, University of Buenos Aires, Argentina) underscores the fragmentation of relevant research. Political tensions hinder the creation of channels of communication, disciplinary barriers are not easily overcome, and research on teaching and administrative issues in higher education institutions and on governmental policies hardly interacts.

Sarah Guri-Rosenblit (Open University of Israel, Tel Aviv, Israel) describes the development of the "Rethinking Higher Education Program" in Israel. It was created to overcome the traditional marginality of higher education research. The Programme is based on the assumption that promoting higher education research across institutions of higher education rather than establishing a single major centre for research is more beneficial both for academic quality and for the relevance of higher education research.

Helena Šebková describes the need for excellent management and strategy planning for countries in Eastern Europe to meet the challenges of a successful transition of a system that has undergone profound changes in the last decade. She analyses the development, mission and collaboration activities of research centres in the Czech Republic and emphasizes that the new freedom and decentralization of higher education institutions increase the demand for higher education research.

Tamas Kozma and Imre Radacsi (Hungarian Institute for Educational Research, Budapest, Hungary) analyse and compare the increase of professionalism and research activities in two of the Central and Eastern European countries, i. e. Hungary and the Czech Republic. They argue that the conduction of research for public purposes has gained greater significance within both countries, and that collaboration of research teams has replaced the work of individual researchers.

Magda Fourie and Kalie Strydom (Unit for Research into Higher Education, University of the Orange Free State, Bloemfontein, South Africa) analyse recent developments in higher education research in South Africa. They show that in the past it had focused on inner processes in higher education institutions and on teaching and learning. With the political changes, policy issues play a more important role. Higher education research will probably face problems because of the lack of an independent disciplinary base, of experts in the field, of a sound conceptual and methodological basis, of research training and of collaboration between higher education researchers.

Akilagpa Sawyerr (African Association of Universities, Accra, Ghana) describes a programme that aims to develop capacities for higher education research in Africa. Researchers from different African countries receive research grants and individual advice and benefit from learning experiences in training seminars. It is too soon to predict whether it will succeed in promoting a continuous base of higher education research in Africa.

A new dimension on how advanced learning systems can be created is introduced by Kathryn M. Moore (Center for the Study of Advanced Learning Systems, Michigan State University, USA). Moore defines, outlines and analyses structural concepts underlying the study of advanced learning systems. In sum, she describes learning through a new lense, taking a wide range of factors into account, integrating them in a model. The main themes that have been selected for the focus of advanced learning systems are: human capacity with attention to leadership, diversity, technology, and globalization.

The training of young researchers was one of the central themes of the International Symposium. Stefanie Schwarz (Centre for Research on Higher Education and Work, University of Kassel, Germany) analyses higher education programmes in the United States and provides information on the different stages a doctoral student must follow to obtain a degree. She also reflects on changing student numbers in the course of the last three decades and on career options in the field of higher education in the US. Whereas between the 1970s and the mid 1980s most of the graduates of these programmes were male and found jobs as faculty and high level administrators, in the last decade the majority were female. Career opportunities also dropped. Most women find jobs in middle-level administrative positions.

Barbara M. Kehm (Institute for Higher Education Research, Wittenberg, Germany) describes the European Higher Education Advanced Training Course offered by the Consortium of Higher Education Researchers to young researchers and administrators in the mid-1990s. She stresses that the course had been viewed by participants as a unique and valuable experience and therefore deplores that it has not been pursued, due to lack of funds.

Cathy Perret (IREDU, Université de Bourgogne, Dijon, France) shows that doctoral training in France specifically prepares for a thesis on higher education. She points out that the thesis tends to be seen as a single thematic specialisation within education rather than a contribution to higher education as a domain of research.

In describing the situation in Finland, Jussi Välimaa (Institute for Educational Research, University of Jyväskylä, Finland) notes a growing discrepancy between interest in higher education as a field of training and career opportunities after the award of a doctorate. Expertise in higher education was seen as a career "dead end" in the past, because the university administration felt no need for specialized knowledge of higher education, the institutions of higher education had limited possibilities to decide on institutional policy and higher education research tended to be supported through individual contracts rather than through the promotion of research units. He suggests that the situation may soon change as a consequence of the Finnish higher education policy which aims to strengthen the autonomy of higher education institutions.

Jeroen Bartelse and Jeroen Huisman (Center for Higher Education Policy Studies, Universiteit Twente, The Netherlands) describe the training of higher education researchers in the Netherlands in the context of research training in general. They emphasize the difficulty of striking a balance between training that contributes to the conceptual state of the art of the discipline and training that gathers in-depth knowledge on higher education as a field of expertise.

It should be added that this volume does not document the presentations and discussions that focus on rationales and means of strengthening international communication and collaboration among higher education researchers and research institutions. The discussions showed, however, that international collaboration among higher education researchers was considered important. Although it is hampered by geographical distance, language barriers, a lack of knowledge of the different national systems of higher education, etc., it was clearly seen as a way of overcoming narrow research foci that reflect national idiosyncracies. It offered a broader base than national collaboration and an opportunity to develop a sound conceptual basis for higher education research.

The contributions in this volume reveal the constraints and opportunities that institutional setting poses for higher education research. A small field defined by its theme rather than by a single discipline which is not highly regarded by the policy actors and practitioners in that area leads one to make modest claims about its current state. However, there are many indications that the public will give greater attention to the issues of higher education research in the future. Also, collaboration and communication between various sectors of higher education research and policy will improve when stakeholders perceive the diversity of themes and institutional settings as a virtue.

We like to express our gratitude to the Volkswagen Foundation which provided us with substantial support for our conference. A special thank you to all authors who greatly contributed with their expertise, insides and ideas, and to Helga Cassidy, Dagmar Mann, and Christina Keyes, who helped to turn the manuscript into a book.

PART ONE

THE INSTITUTIONAL BASIS OF HIGHER EDUCATION RESEARCH: THEORY, POLICY, AND PRACTICE

Chapter 1

Higher Education Research and its Institutional Basis

ULRICH TEICHLER
Centre for Research on Higher Education and Work, University of Kassel, Germany

1.1   Introduction

The aim of this publication is to discuss the state of higher education research and the role of its institutional basis. The following observations are not based on a comprehensive account of available literature. Rather, they draw from the experiences the authors have acquired internationally as participant-observers. They are also based on key documents that study the state of higher education research in an international perspective and tend to focus on the state of knowledge and its theoretical base. Five documents can be quoted here:

a) In 1982, Burton Clark invited scholars from different countries to a conference at the University of California at Los Angeles (U.S.) to analyse the state of higher education research in various disciplinary and thematic areas in a comparative perspective. The contributions were published in 1984 in *Perspectives on Higher Education: Eight Disciplinary and Comparative Views*.

b) The state of *research on higher education in Europe* was analysed at the founding conference of the Consortium of Higher Education Researchers (CHER), held in Kassel in 1988. The major contributions were published by Neave and Teichler (Research on higher education in Europe, 1989).

c) Tony Becher edited a section on "Disciplinary Perspectives on Higher Education" in Burton Clark's and Guy Neave's *Encyclopedia of Higher Education* which was published in 1992. The 19 articles addressed specific disciplines and approaches, as well as higher education research in general (Fulton 1992).

S. Schwarz and U. Teichler (eds.), The Institutional Basis of Higher Education Research, 13–24.

d) *Higher Education Research at the Turn of the New Century: Structures, Issues, and Trends*, edited by Jan Sadlak and Philip Altbach in 1997, comprises 12 reports on the state of higher education research in various countries or regions of the world and three cross-cutting articles. It is based on reports which were presented to a conference organized by UNESCO and the University of Pittsburgh (U.S.A.) in 1991.

e) Various contributions presented to two annual conferences of the Consortium of Higher Education Researchers (CHER) in the mid-1990s in Enschede (the Netherlands) and Rome (Italy) were published in 1996 in a special issue of *Higher Education* on *The State of Comparative Research in Higher Education* (Teichler 1996b).

f) Many experts from all over the world analysed "The Relationships among Research, Policy and Practice in Higher Education" at a conference jointly organized by UNESCO and the Center for Research and Development of Higher Education of the University of Tokyo in 1997 in Tokyo (Japan). A report was published (UNESCO and the University of Tokyo 1997) and the major contributions are published in *Higher Education Research: Its Relationships to Policy and Practice* (Teichler and Sadlak 2000).

Other conference proceedings, essays, reports and collections have contributed to the knowledge on the state of higher education research (Nitsch and Weller 1970-1973; CEPES/UNESCO 1981; Goldschmidt, Teichler and Webler 1984; Altbach and Kelly 1985; New trends in research on higher education 1987; Altbach 1988; Neave 1991; Mitter 1992; Teichler 1992; Goedegebuure and van Vught 1994, Smith, Teichler and van der Wende 1996). The presentations at the international symposium *The Institutional Basis of Higher Education Research – Experiences and Perspectives* held in 1998 at the Centre for Research on Higher Education and Work of the University of Kassel differ from most of the previous ones, since they focus on the conditions of research rather than its substance. But the previous discussions often referred to the institutional setting when they tried to explain the various characteristics of research.

1.2   Towards a classification of higher education research

Higher education research tends to be classified according to:
– disciplines,
– themes,
– institutional settings.

Disciplinary definitions of higher education research are widely used. Economics and business studies, political science, law, history, sociology, psychology, and education are often cited as contributing to higher education as a field. There are, however, broader definitions, such as those employed by Clark (1983), according to which "organization research" could be defined as a discipline, and by Becher (1992).

Publications which aim at classifying higher education research, e.g. bibliographies, reports on research trends or handbooks, often classify it according to *thematic areas*. But there is no general consensus. Moreover, we note that experts of individual thematic domains of higher education research tend to consider their domain as being extremely broad, not to say all-embracing. Notably, experts of higher education planning – this term was more commonly used than higher education policy in the 1960s and 1970s – or of higher education policy often do not see themselves solely as experts of the planning, policy and management mechanisms in higher education, but also of all target areas of policy and planning, i.e. of nearly all areas of higher education.

Higher education research themes are often long lists. They can include higher education policy and planning, teaching and learning, higher education systems, etc.

We can identify four *"spheres of knowledge"* structured according to the logic of themes and to the disciplines or related areas of expertise of higher education researchers (see Chart 1; Teichler 1996a, pp. 440-443). Many research projects that aim at cutting across disciplines and themes remain within a single of these spheres, thus validating this typology:

– *Quantitative-structural aspects*, e.g. admission, élite and mass higher education, diversification and the relationships between higher education and employment. Economists and sociologists tend to address these areas.
– *Knowledge and subject related aspects*, e.g. disciplinarity versus inter-disciplinarity, *studium generale*, academic versus professional emphasis, acquisition and use of knowledge, relationships between teaching and research or curricula. These areas tend to interest specialists of education and of sub-disciplines that address science (history, sociology, etc.).
– *Person or teaching and learning related aspects*, e.g. communication, guidance and counselling, teaching and learning styles, students or academic staff. Education and psychology are key disciplines here, but sociology also plays a role.
– *Aspects of institution, organisation, governance*, e.g. planning, administration, management, decision-making, funding or resource allocation. Law, political science, economics, public and business administration are the major disciplines here, but one can also include the sociology of organisation.

Ulrich Teichler

CHART 1: SPHERES OF KNOWLEDGE IN HIGHER EDUCATION AND RESEARCH ON HIGHER EDUCATION

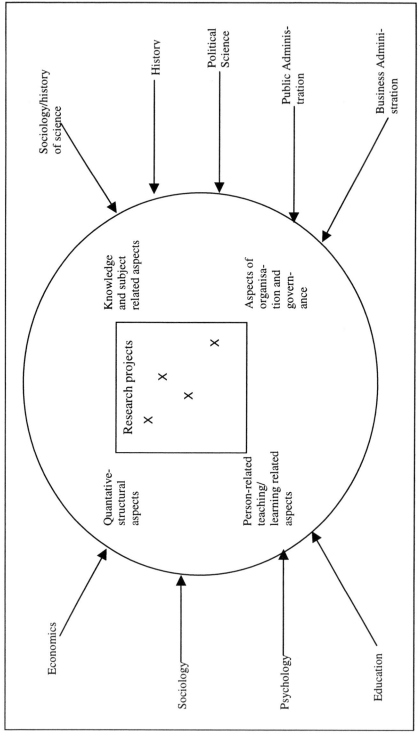

Source: Teichler 1996a, p. 441

1.3 Institutional settings of higher education research

The *institutional settings* of higher education – including their relationship to the outside world – can be described according to *five dimensions*:
- the *functional* setting: whether higher education research is only undertaken by a unit that is responsible for research, or responsible for research and teaching, or a mixture of research and administration, services, development, etc.;
- the *thematic* setting: whether higher education is the only permanent research theme or whether the researcher or the unit addresses different themes over time, or higher education as part of education, or higher education in its relationships to other areas (e.g. the links between higher education and employment);
- the *application* setting: basic research, applied research, information generation as part of evaluation, consultancy, administration, etc.;
- the *"stakeholders"*: governments, other social actors, the university administration, the academics, or the students;
- the *modes of control*: academic self-regulation, project contracting, control by a board, "reporting" to decision-makers, research by the actors themselves, etc.

This also underscores, as Elaine El-Khawas recently did, that the macro-societal and the institutional actors in the field of higher education often have their own units of research which tend to be closely linked to higher education policy and practice. El-Khawas (2000) identified research, policy, and practice as three separate bases of higher education research:
- *Research*: Higher education research often has an academic base. It can be a unit of teaching and research at a university: a professorship, a chair, an institute or a department. The academics who undertake higher education research in such settings are expected to strive for excellence and recognition by peers, for a strong theoretical and methodological basis and, to some extent, for a pursuit of knowledge for its own sake.
- *Policy*: Higher education policy research or information units are established by, or more or less permanently linked to supra-institutional agencies, notably governments. The aim of this branch of research is to enrich policy processes through information, policy-driven interpretations, policy scenarios on higher education, etc., and its success depends on anticipating or reinforcing policy agendas thematically and to provide information and possibly consultancy which are of use to the policy actors.
- *Practice*: Some higher education research and development units are linked to the management of higher education institutions, e.g. "institutional research" in the U.S. They are similar in their approach to higher education policy research because they provide information to the actors.

They differ from the former by the actors they serve and the field they analyse.

In describing higher education research in the U.S., El-Khawas stresses that these three institutional settings each have their own agenda, modes of research and communication circles and that they hardly interact. Hence, higher education research which is launched by and serves policy and management differs substantially in its rationales and approaches from academically-based research and from institutional research in its practical focus, even if it addresses the same themes.

This classification does not only apply to the U.S. For example, Frackmann (1997) classified higher education research in Western Europe according to the same three functional types, although he used different terms:
– "the national and systemwise decision support,
– institutional research and institutional management support,
– research on higher education as self-reflection".

But I believe there are also two major *interrelationships between the academically-based higher education research sector and the policy and management actors*. First, the academically-based higher education research sector can undertake *research that is contracted* by the policy and management actors. Second, the academically-based higher education researchers can conduct research *independently*. This could have *salient implications* for policy and practice.

Both could be seen as being quite similar. We could ask: Does academically-based higher education research, when undertaking contract research, proceed like consultancy firms, institutional research, research units linked to government or stake-holders, etc., or does it approach the themes differently, as far as its scope is concerned? Does academically-based research simply compete with policy and practice based research in terms of efficiency, costs, quality of methods, etc., or does it differ in its epistemology? Does it raise questions that sponsors would not raise?

It is obvious that a classification of higher education research according to the three categories cited above could be refined further. On the one hand, we note various types of settings in universities. On the other, the boundaries between the policy and practice oriented researchers and the reflective practitioners are blurred. I therefore suggest that we divide the experts into six types according to their links to academic theory, field knowledge and policy and practice (see Chart 2; Teichler 1996a).

Chart 2: Types of higher education experts

Types	Basis of expertise		
	Theory/ methodology	Field knowledge	Application development
(1) Discipline-based, occasional higher education researcher	++	-	- -
(2) Discipline-based continuous higher education researcher	++	+	- -
(3) Theme-based academic higher education researcher	+	+	~
(4) Applied higher education researcher (policy researcher, institutional researcher)	~	+	+
(5) Consultant	-	+	++
(6) Reflective practitioner	- -	++	++

(1) The *disciplinary-department based occasional researchers on higher education* often define themselves as economists, psychologists, historians, etc. They consider their peers as disciplinary-based and devote part of their academic life to different themes. In sociology, for example, many well-known scholars such as Parsons, Riesman, Lipset, Giddens, Habermas, Luhmann, and Dahrendorf devoted part of their academic life to higher education in the last few decades. This theme is of interest to them when it is *en vogue* politically. They enrich the conceptual basis of higher education research, but their research often lacks field knowledge. Most of these disciplinary-based scholars are not very concerned about the practical relevance of their research.

(2) The *continuous discipline-based higher education researchers* resemble the occasional researchers, since they are often based administratively and intellectually in university departments and disciplines. They strive for academic recognition by peers in other disciplines. But unlike the former, higher education is an important or the sole theme during the whole

or a major part of their career. They may be less well-known within the academic disciplines than the occasional scholars who regularly change themes, but they are closer to more practice-oriented scholars in their field knowledge. Therefore, they also tend to have a more salient impact on practice-oriented research on higher education. We can include Clark, Trow, Becher, and Bourdieu in this second type.

(3) The *scholars based in a higher education research institute* communicate with the disciplinary-based researchers, but they have to justify their achievements in relation to the applied researchers and in relation to their relevance for practitioners. Their way of striking a balance is influenced by the strengths and weaknesses of cooperation with other teams of higher education researchers and by the acquisition of substantial funds for large-scale projects. It is hardly surprising that those who belong to this group will help to encourage cooperation with different types of higher education researchers as, for example, Cerych, Kogan, van Vught, and Teichler have tried to do in Europe in the framework of the Consortium of Higher Education Researchers (CHER).

(4) The *applied higher education researchers* seek to establish their reputation on the utility for decision-making of their research and data collection, even though they also contribute to the academic enhancement of higher education research. They often work in an institution of higher education policy research or of institutional research, or in a unit that is responsible for research and service, e.g. a centre for staff development or teaching and learning, or the university administration.

(5) The *consultants in higher education* (who also include evaluators) could be seen as a link between the applied researchers and the practitioners. They draw from all kinds of systematic knowledge or practical experience to advise practitioners. They can be researchers who undertake consultancy activities, full-time consultants, former practitioners, or practitioners who advise fellow practitioners.

(6) Finally, *the reflective practitioners in higher education*, e.g. university presidents, administrators, scholars, and politicians, see themselves as experts. They can be part-time researchers or part-time consultants, but even if this is not the case, they often see themselves as experts and bearers of knowledge on higher education. The expert role and the blurred distinction with the reflective practitioner are publicly recognized. Associations such as the European Association for Research and Development in Higher Education (EARDHE), the European Association for Institutional Research (EAIR) or the UK-based Society for Research into Higher Education (SRHE) aim to serve a broad range of experts without making clear distinctions, and journals such as *Higher Education in Europe, Higher Education Management, Higher Education Policy* and *Tertiary Education and Man-*

agement also cater for these experts, even though only some adopt a research approach. *Higher Education* is the only recognized international journal that is exclusively devoted to higher education research.

Higher education research both *suffers* and potentially *gains* from the vague distinction between researchers and practitioners. As regards the former, the highly educated and reflective practitioners in higher education are more inclined than the actors in other fields (although we note a somewhat similar notion among various professionals) to believe that research on higher education is unnecessary. The practitioners' reflection is seen as sufficient to understand reality. This assumption is often reinforced by the fact that the practitioners know that they have greater field knowledge. Researchers note that scholarly insight is often treated by practitioners as just another opinion: "Paradoxically, the academic profession trying to persuade society that systematic scholarship and research is superior to the practitioners' experience and is essential for progress, is most sceptical about the value of scholarship, if it comes to their practical turf, i.e. higher education." (Teichler 1996a, p. 436).

It is obvious that the experts in higher education and the institutional settings are not necessarily bound to a single type. The continuous disciplinary-based or the thematically-based researchers sometimes play the same role as applied researchers and consultants. The shaky institutional and financial basis for higher education research, due to the pressures of application and practical problem-solving, leads the key researchers in this field to take over applied research and consultancy roles. Ironically, this pressure is strongest when theory-based higher education research has a certain institutional basis and resources. Whereas the individual researcher is relatively free to choose between various options, research units only have to strike a balance between pursuing demanding theoretical and methodological approach in order to offer something that applied researchers and consultants cannot offer and ensuring an overall satisfactory funding basis by providing evidence of their immediate utility for assessment and problem-solving activities.

Generally speaking, there are distinct institutional settings of higher education research, as far as the modes of control and the goals of the researchers are concerned. As a field, however, it is not defended by academics because, in most countries, it lacks the tradition of a discipline and is not closely linked to teaching. There is an application and consultancy drift in academically-based higher education.

1.4 Counteracting the biases and limitations

Pressures for application and consultancy provide opportunities for higher education research, as can be seen in the analysis of the institutional basis. They open the doors for communication and a better understanding of the problems of policy and practice and thus for designing research projects whose results are useful to the actors in the system. Theory and methodology could be improved by increasing their relevance for practice. Last but not least, involvement in applied research, evaluation or various consultancy activities could ensure a financial basis which would help to consolidate research activities that are not driven by the immediate demands of the higher education system. But these pressures are dangerous:

- Theoretical and methodological standards might drop to provide what would seem to be very useful pragmatic knowledge.
- Researchers might exaggeratedly "sell" the utility of research and hence undermine confidence in the true potentials of higher education research because the "clients" could note these exaggerated claims.
- Researchers might be pushed by the reflective practitioners into the role of data deliverers only in those areas where practitioners agree that their "arm-chair analysis" is not enough.
- Researchers might follow the political fads of thematisation and de-thematisation of issues in higher education, thus becoming completely reactive to policy and practice.
- Research that aims to be of practical relevance might consciously or unconsciously be subordinated to the prevailing norms. For example, higher education research in recent years often tended to preach the gospel of managerialism and evaluative steering.

Higher education research which neither wants to be solely recognized within its academic communities nor to copy the norms and thematic fads of the actors must be on its guard and be a strategic actor in counterbalancing the drifts, biases and pressures it is subjected to. There are different ways of counterbalancing this:

First, higher education research could engage in *meta-research and continuous reflection on its conditions*. The more higher education research is aware of the potentials and dangers to which it is exposed, the more it can develop convincing research.

Second, higher education research could embark more systematically on a *critique of research*. Its credibility is likely to grow when borderlines between acceptable and non- acceptable standards are discussed internally and made known to those who are interested in this field.

Collaborative projects of researchers from various countries are often qualitatively less satisfactory than one could have expected because language barriers, the diversity of the higher education systems, the heterogeneity of research traditions and the difficulties of communication and long distance communication often lead to a gap between high-flying ambitions and mediocre results. Yet their catalytic value of challenging the national idiosyncrasies of public debates and research traditions compensates for these deficiencies.

Research on higher education does hot have to be driven by public concerns. Higher education researchers could *anticipate changing issues* and make the key actors aware of the salient issues they are likely to face in the near future. We could give greater attention to issues which are looming but have not yet been analysed in the public debate.

The institutional basis of higher education is heterogeneous and often shaky. In countries where the stabilisation of research by a teaching function of the field is lacking, higher education research is tempted to polarize between disciplinary research that lacks field knowledge and practical relevance on the one hand and applied research which is unconsciously embedded in the prevailing policy norms on the other. Communication between higher education researchers, however, helps to see the dangers and to choose strategies which do not yield to the existing pressures but make the potential visible.

REFERENCES

Altbach, P. G. (1988). 'Comparative studies in higher education', in Postlethwaite, T. N. (ed.), *The Encyclopedia of Comparative Education and National Systems of Education*. Oxford: Pergamon Press, pp. 66-68.

Altbach, P. G. and Kelly, D. H. (1985). *Higher Education in International Perspective: A Survey and Bibliography*. London: Mansell.

Becher, R. I. (1992). 'Introduction: Disciplinary perspectives on higher education', in Clark, B. R. and Neave, G. R. (eds.), *The Encyclopedia of Higher Education*, Oxford: Pergamon Press, pp. 1763-1776.

CEPES/UNESCO (1981). *International Directory of Higher Education Research Institutions*. Bucharest: UNESCO/CEPES.

Clark, B. R. (1983). *The Higher Education System: Academic Organization in Cross-National Perspective*. Berkeley and Los Angeles : University of California Press.

Clark, B. R. (ed.) (1984). *Perspectives on Higher Education: Eight Disciplinary and Comparative Views*. Berkeley: University of California Press.

Clark, B. R. and Neave, G. (eds.) (1992). *The Encyclopedia of Higher Education*. 4 vols. Oxford: Pergamon Press.

El-Khawas, E. (2000). 'Research, policy and practice: Assessing their actual and potential linkages', in Teichler, U. and Sadlak, J. (eds.), *Higher Education Research: Its Relationship to Policy and Practice*. Oxford: Pergamon/IAU Press, pp. 37-46.

Frackmann, E. (1997). 'Research on higher education in Western Europe: From policy advice to self-reflection', in Sadlak, J. and Altbach, P. G. (eds.), *Higher Education Research at the Turn of the New Century*. Paris: UNESCO; New York and London: Garland, pp. 107-136.

Fulton, O. (1992). 'Higher education studies', in Clark, B. R. and Neave, G. (eds.), *The Encyclopedia of Higher Education*. Vol. 4. Oxford: Pergamon Press, pp. 1810-1821.

Goedegebuure, L. and Van Vught, F. (eds.) (1994). *Comparative Policy Studies in Higher Education*. Utrecht: Uitgeverij Lemma.

Goldschmidt, D., Teichler, U. and Webler, W.-D. (eds.) (1984). *Forschungsgegenstand Hochschule*. Frankfurt/M. and New York: Campus.

Mitter, W. (1992). 'Comparative education', in Clark, B. R. and Neave, G. (eds.), *The Encyclopedia of Higher Education*, Vol. 4. Oxford: Pergamon Press, pp. 1810-1821.

Neave, G. (1991). 'A changing Europe: Challenges for higher education research', *Higher Education in Europe* 16 (3), 3-27.

Neave, G. and Teichler, U. (1989). 'Research on higher education in Europe' (special issue), *European Journal of Education* 24 (3).

'New trends in research on higher education' (special issue) (1987), *Higher Education in Europe* 12 (1).

Nitsch, W. and Weller, W. (1970-1973). *Social Science Research on Higher Education and Universities*. 3 vols. Den Haag and Paris: Mouton.

Sadlak, J. and Altbach, P. G. (eds.) (1997). *Higher Education Research at the Turn of the New Century*. Paris: UNESCO; New York and London: Garland.

Smith, A., Teichler, U. and van der Wende, M. (eds.) (1994). *The International Dimension of Education: Setting the Research Agenda*. Vienna: Internationales Forschungszentrum Kulturwissenschaften 1994 (IFK Materialien, 3/94).

Teichler, U. (1992). 'Research on higher education in Europe: Some aspects of recent developments', in Frackmann, E. and Maassen, P. (eds.), *Towards Excellence in European Higher Education: Proceedings. 11th European AIR Forum*. Utrecht: Uitgeverij Lemma, pp. 37-61.

Teichler, U. (1996a). 'Comparative higher education studies: Potentials and limits', *Higher Education* 32 (4), pp. 431-465.

Teichler, U. (ed.) (1996b). 'Special issue on the state of comparative research in higher education', *Higher Education* 32 (4).

Teichler, U. and Sadlak, J. (eds.) (2000). *Higher Education Research: Its Relationship to Policy and Practice*. Oxford: Pergamon/IAU Press.

UNESCO and the University of Tokyo (1997). *Report of the Roundtable on the Relationship among Research Policy and Practice in Higher Education*. s. l. (Tokyo).

Chapter 2

Future Directions for Higher Education Policy Research
*Getting Inside: Policy Reception of Research**

MAURICE KOGAN & MARY HENKEL
Centre for the Evaluation of Public Policy and Practice, Brunel University, Great Britain

2.1   Introduction: The state of the art

The main theme of this paper is the *receptor* function in the research-policy-making-practice relationship. It is a theme not well researched in our field of study, although Anderson and Biddle's compilation (1991) contains contributions that point the way.

Educational and similar social science research, whether concerned with policy or practice issues, has no encouraging history of application. This can be blamed on practitioners and policy-makers – if they would only listen –, on the intrinsic differences between the two worlds of research and *praxis*, on the lack of relevance or of communicability of the research, or on the nature of the phenomena being researched. There are a large number of statements and explanations for a lack of take-up (e.g. Caplan 1975; OECD 1995; Sadlak and Altbach 1997) and a lot of researcher complaints about the non-receptivity of policy-makers.

So far, however, most of these accounts have failed to include any account of the nature of policy-making, and the policy-makers who might do the receiving. The issue is barely mentioned in a recent major compilation based on national reports (Sadlak and Altbach 1997). In a recent essay, Scott enumerates the types of policy-maker but goes no further into the processes in which they engage (Scott 1999). The political science categories in use in our subject area are somewhat general, and the statements about the nature of government or its likely behavioural characteristics tend to be simple dichotomies which are not untrue nor yet illuminating.

25

S. Schwarz and U. Teichler (eds.), The Institutional Basis of Higher Education Research, 25–43.
© 2000 *Kluwer Academic Publishers. Printed in the Netherlands.*

In this note we cannot remedy these deficiencies which will require sub-stantial analytic scholarly efforts to be followed by empirical studies. Instead we have to rely on studies which are largely conjectural and metaphoric or based on individual testimony. In our specific field of higher education, Re-kilä (1998) has reflected on the Finnish case. Westerheijden (1998) touches on some of the issues as they emerge in East and Central Europe. In fields other than higher education, there are, however, empirical sources which may be of help to the present discussion (e.g. Caplan 1977; Weiss 1980; Ko-gan and Henkel 1983; Bardach 1984; Premfors 1991; Henkel 1991; Buxton and Hanney 1994).

The analysis might pursue the following sequence:

a) the characteristics of government which affect its ability to relate to re-search,
b) government's mechanisms for commissioning and using research,
c) subject differences,
d) knowledge needs of policy-makers,
e) reception of research,
f) take-up for policy-making,
g) models of research-policy relationships,
h) characteristics of receptors.

2.2   The characteristics of government which affect its ability to relate to research

The governmental characteristics relevant to our theme are broadly epis-temological and social or institutional. On the epistemological characteris-tics, policy-makers depend on a wide range of knowledge – picked up from the press, or provided by their own evaluative creations, or from enquiries that they commission or, to a lesser extent, provided by independent re-search. They may be affected by percolation of deeper and critical knowl-edge, but essentially policymaking needs knowledge which is applicable to discrete problems, which are capable of solution. The word "decision" means to cut away; policy-making involves a reduction of interests and value positions so that the world can go forward. As Mrs. Thatcher said of one of her ministers, Lord Young, "The others bring me problems; he brings me solutions".

Rekilä (1998), basing her discussion on experience as both a central gov-ernment and university administrator, points out that Ministries are expert organisations, depending on the expertise of officials allowed to use in-creasing discretion but that their expertise has to be balanced by its meeting its bureaucratic necessities. They use their own kinds of expertise in "devel-oping the whole education system", in preparing decisions made by the government and implementing those decisions. They are "expert in steering and developing its own administrative system".

In all, positivist modes of research are more useful to policy-makers than critical, interactive and independent modes. That is why in government at large social research has lost much of its precarious hold on policy in favour of knowledge created by inspectors, other evaluators and consultants who start with the premises of policy-makers in a clear and pre-structured way (Henkel 1991). Perhaps, however, a move forward from instrumental and short-term perspectives can be found in the Foresight Initiatives in various countries which demand relatively sophisticated analysis of likely trends of demand and knowledge application (Martin and Irvine 1989).

Knowledge creators such as evaluators, inspectors and auditors have grown in power. There are also Think Tanks whose work is primarily that of policy analysis, that is to say, they take largely existing knowledge and re-shape it towards meeting problems that are perceived to be on the policy agenda. How far they reflect and how far they help to shape the *Zeitgeist* is a matter for contemplation. In another decade, Trow invested hope in the then new breed of policy analysts (Trow 1984). Their influence depends more on their ability to provide alternatives to policies than to create new knowledge deriving from the traditional academic ideal of the disinterested search for truth.

By contrast, research, that is enquiry based on demonstrated methods and adding to knowledge, can be used for praxis, but that which is most highly prized assumes that all questions are open and are likely to remain so after the research is completed. The idealised version is that of "the disinterested search for truth" responding not to policy-makers' criteria but to those of the Republic of Science (Polyani 1962). Applied research of repute tries, of course, to have it both ways. This involves negotiating the objectives of research with sponsors but retaining freedom over methods and to reach and publish conclusions.

If research is bound by criteria of demonstrated method and openness, policy-making and practice are related to criteria of relevance and in that pursuit will take account of Ordinary Knowledge (Cohen and Lindblom 1979).

Government has to be convergent, so that policies are consistent with each other. It must be reductionist if it is to act decisively in the face of complexity, turbulence and conflicting interests and it is concerned with order and control. At the same time, to meet any kind of democratic mandate, it must support development. Because it is concerned with a wide universe of concerns, it must view any single policy concern within a trans-policy context. Thus, higher education policies will be scrutinised not only in terms of their own logic, and in terms of financial, legal and organisational criteria that may be common to all government policies, but also in terms of e.g., schools policy, employment and economic policy and even foreign policy (on internationalisation). Because government works on a broad and often unmanageable canvass, the reduction of interests, and the search for simple and elegant solutions are a major preoccupation. Otherwise it cannot meet the political agendas of ministers, or produce workable programmes that can be rendered into priorities and actions. Yet, because it must face many interests, including professions whose claims on policy-making are based on knowledge its very organisation is tribal and multi-modal (Kogan and Henkel 1983, p. 3). It must act through a range of modes which include both persuasion and negotiation and the coercion of law; rational discourse based on research must compete with these.

The assumptions made about governmental processes start with the schematic models of Easton and others who assumed that there would be values and interest inputs from the social and political environment which government would reduce ultimately into "an authoritative allocation of values", or policies. This was challenged by Lindblom, Wildavsky and others for whom policy-making was incremental, disjointed, episodic, and incapable of leading to a synopsis of wants and needs on which to act. Schon (1971) raised the issue of how policy systems can become learning systems enabling knowledge and ideas from outside government to enter the policy arena. Others (e.g. Rein, 1983) depicted the policy process as having no clear beginning or ending and the way in which power is exercised as being as decisive as the purpose for which it is exercised. The interaction between policy-makers and their environment has been described (Linder 1981) as being either situationist, in which such environments as the constraints created by budgetary processes predominate (Wildavsky 1964), or individualist where the heroic policy-maker struggles through established norms and interests or interactionist, where the environment imposes constraints upon individuals who themselves constitute the environment for other individuals.

Those who have to seek support from policy-makers would prefer processes to be more predictable and rational than they are, but the complexity of government's tasks affects its ability to tolerate the uncertainty and complexity introduced by research. At the same time, and working in the opposite direction, the internal tribalism of government affects any potential homogeneity of the knowledge frames that government might adopt (Kogan and Henkel 1983). Also, the knowledge frames used by government are unlikely to be related to academic disciplines but are more related to policy area and client groups (Kogan and Henkel 1983). There is a necessary tension, and sometimes it seems an unbridgeable gap, between policy and research, because they represent "two different cultures with different requirements" (Caplan 1977). It is not surprising, given these characteristics of government, that it uses many other forms of knowledge.

In attempting to make sense of this area of activity it is tempting to look for simple correspondences between the nature of the problem area, the nature of the knowledge generated, and the forms of transmission and implementation that might then emerge. We must seek such correspondences but there are also assumptions which question, although do not fully destroy, them. The first assumption is that it is less the nature of the knowledge that is generated than the social and institutional characteristics of main players that constitute the primary factors in determining transmission and transfer. Secondly, it is assumed that all principal kinds of knowledge – positivistic, theoretical-critical and applied/action research – have a part to play in illuminating policy and practice. While there might be some inherent conflict between them they might, in the best possible world, constitute a virtuous and reinforcing cycle in which global statements about the macro characteristics of systems could lead to critique of existing policies and practices and both test and extend the scope of existing theories. There are paramount needs for "useful" knowledge, but has as its descant the need to ensure that the knowledge and concepts on which it is based are strong. Thirdly, it is assumed that whilst these three kinds of knowledge may seem to relate separately to linear, illuminative and collaborative forms of transmission and use, there are no absolutely contingent relationships between, for example, positivistic knowledge and linear forms of transmission. Dichotomies would be too facile a depiction of the relationship between modes and transmission. Finally, there are, again, propensities for certain kinds of knowledge to be particularly useful at particular levels of systems. But, again, such associations should not be regarded as iron clad.

Moreover, the stage of development of higher education research may well affect the issue. Van den Daele, Krohn and Weingart (1977) identify three phases of discipline development: the exploratory, pre- or polyparadigmatic phase, the phase of paradigm articulation and the post-paradigmatic phase. In the first and third phases problem orientation and discipline development are compatible. Before paradigms are established functional research can be an input into the discipline. But at the point where work is beginning to crystallize on the development of key theoretical models, the research programme is usually dictated by "internal" needs incompatible with external problems. At the third stage, when the basic explanatory models have been tested, it may be possible to coordinate the elaborations with problem-oriented research. From this time onwards such research may instead be carried out by application of the basic theory. Higher education research may generally be assumed to be at a pre-paradigmatic stage if, indeed, it is ever likely to create paradigms. At the least, this may make researchers less eager about collaboration with policy-related sponsors.

2.3   Government mechanisms for commissioning and using research

The interactions within government are decisive for its relationship with the world of research. Many governmental systems have internal brokerage mechanisms which commission and promote the assimilation of research and other forms of knowledge (Kogan and Henkel 1983; OECD 1995). Characteristically, a policy division is regarded as the "customer" for research and, in theory, should identify policy or practice problems for research. Our study of the British Department of Health and Social Security depicted a maximal system in which customer divisions were encouraged to lead research liaison groups consisting of policy-makers and researchers. The customer, then commissioned, received and, in theory, made use of the research.

In both this system, and the system run by the Swedish Board for Universities and Colleges (and no doubt many more), the role of research managers was critical. They were in a position to encourage customers to identify research to be commissioned, and took on the principal role of monitoring and advising researchers. Some interviewed in the UK had taken on the perspectives of the researchers and were critical of the short-terminism of customers, and, in effect, took on an advocacy role on researchers' behalves. There was a concern to establish a competent policy-useful research system that could be supported separately from the academically led research and funding council system. In the case of Sweden, this role was far more than brokerage, and there is no doubt that Eskil Björklund identified new approaches and themes which he mounted largely on his own initiative (Trow 1991; Björklund, 1991). To some extent these helped create new areas for independent and critical enquiry as much as policy-led concerns. At some points on the horizon, then, two cultures seem capable of enjoying friendship, if not marriage.

A particularly British bureaucratic phenomenon – their extreme mobility – made it possible to observe (Kogan and Henkel 1983) the extent to which the policy-makers became associated with particular policy stances. On shifting jobs, they were capable, and such was the ethic that this was required of them, of picking up the immediate interests of the job in hand. This applied not only to shifts between policy zones, but also to shifts from the brokerage to the policy-maker customer role. This may not apply to other systems where the policy-makers are specialist professionals.

2.4   Subject differences

There are observable differences between subject areas in the motivation for the commissioning and take-up of research. For example, in one area, nursing policy, there was a small, stable and coherent group of professionals of the Department of Health and Social Security (DHSS) who shared the preoccupations and values of the researchers. Elsewhere, as in social security research, the customers were constrained by general government policies on social equity and preserving public resources and whilst often prepared to commission work on impacts could not always be tolerant of the results.

In higher education, the UK government has, at least in the receding past, commissioned work on e.g. the relationship between higher education and the world of work, but has shown no inclination to assess the impacts of recent reform policies. Funding councils have, however, commissioned several short studies of the impacts of quality assurance, partly in order to more confidently face its critics.

2.5   Knowledge needs of policy-makers

There are several levels of knowledge which are relevant to policy-making. They are: knowledge directly relevant to macro-decisions, on the overall objectives and structure of the system; and knowledge concerning the processes and outcomes of work at the practitioner level. In between, there are several intermediate kinds of knowledge, for example, about the ways in which governing bodies work.

Social science research may have political and expressive functions beyond its instrumental and critical uses. It is important for politicians and policy-makers to demonstrate a democratic belief in the critical testing of ideas and of the policies and practices that they create and that they are responsive to political, cultural and social movements. Creative policy-making requires the testing of accepted wisdom.

2.6   Reception of research

There is little systematic evidence of the ways in which higher education research is taken up. Before considering the evidence on national policy take-up, we will briefly glimpse at the evidence on institutional and academic take-up.

There is a great deal of tacit knowledge used by higher education system and institutional leaders and administrators. A glance at the plethora of promotional literature for conferences and workshops and at those journals which are primarily produced for their use will show how the field has moved from dependence on personal recollection towards sometimes, but not wholly, instrumental renditions of the assumptions and findings of applied forms of organisational sociology and economics. Input-output models drawn from economics underpin official evaluation, and organisational constructs of hierarchy provide the modelling of institutional structures in the managerial model. But awareness of new and less boundaried organisations for the generation and dissemination of knowledge (Gibbons et al. 1994) may increasingly put some of these assumptions to test. The most recent example is that of the burgeoning literature on quality, much of it normative, but some of it exploratory, critical, and empirically based which informs events and publications directed at practitioners.

In education research in general, it is in application to teaching and learning that policy-makers feel the strongest lack in the knowledge base provided them (OECD 1995). As far as higher education practitioners are concerned, whilst in the past researchers have been able to lay claim to some success in affecting higher education practice that optimism seems to have largely gone. There are now determined attempts in UK teacher education towards teacher-involved and evidence-based learning from research (Cordingley 1997). We are told that such concepts as deep and surface learning are found useful in teacher education.

As far as academics are concerned, Teichler has noted the difficulty of persuading experts to take notice of research on their activities (Teichler 1999). At the practitioner level, research is likely to encounter the intellectual self-confidence of academics and the autonomy assumed over the curriculum and its modes of production within most systems. Although higher education's curriculum and its modes of transmission have been the subject of a great deal of reflective and normative thinking, partly under the pressure of reforms, the research evidence is that UK academics, whilst concerned about the relevance of their teaching to students, do not attend much to the research and scholarship based discussions of the subject (Gibbs 1995, Henkel and Kogan 1996). There is, however, some interest in social learning from and with peers.

2.7   Take-up for policy-making

Many countries have tried to create systematic policy analysis systems. Some do rely to some extent on HE research, whilst others do not conform to a knowledge based model, but to the heroic or individualistic model which relies on value setters who know what they want, and set out to get it without recourse to supporting or opposing evidence. As one recent British minister for higher education put it, "we don't need research to tell us what to do, we know that already". And the nuisance from the researchers' point of view is that that is a legitimate point of view in a democracy: election legitimises the weakest and craziest of policy beliefs. They derive from value preferences that can, but need not be, affected by knowledge. "Research can help you achieve your objectives (...) but it can't tell you whether to go comprehensive. That's a basic value judgement" (Kogan 1971).

A strong UK example of take-up, dating from the optimistic early 1960s, was that of the research for the Robbins Report (1963) which legitimised the expansion of higher education. It demonstrated, by using evidence from Douglas and others, that able people were leaving school at 15, and thus weakened the assumption that there was a limited pool of ability. It also used research which demonstrated the importance of human capital and the link between educational investment and the economy. Quite similar impacts of research on the expansion issue was noted for Sweden.

A second major, contemporary, example is the influence on current social and employment policies and practices by reflective thinking on gender and ethnic issues. Some of this work is rooted in sociological, psychological, anthropological and legal studies. But it would be fair to say that its initiation, take-off and impact result as much from its connection with the remedy of perceived injustice as to its research qualities and content.

Another example posits the use of critical and theoretical research which operated in a percolative and illuminative fashion. In this case scholarship changed paradigms or "assumptive worlds" and then lent force, albeit indirectly, to the democratisation of higher education. The critique of knowledge production and power relationships advanced in the sociology of knowledge – a field in which interpretative scholarship rather than empirical or analytic research has been most evident – must have done much (we cannot be sure because it has never been researched) to reduce the status of the university as a protected and specialist institution and the sapiential authority of the professariat. From the argued positions thus set up it was easier to give a stronger place for junior staff, students and external client groups in the governance of the university.

Another example is that of the French Faure reforms on 1968 which aimed to move away from the "inexistence" of universities by endowing them with autonomy and self-governing structures (Musselin, forthcoming). These were the product not so much of new research as of research-based expertise acting through government-appointed committees and the two formative conferences in Caen in 1956 and 1960. In these reforms, the scholarly critiques of the existing structures played their part. Another example from Hungary (Setényi 1997) is of how research findings affected the policy discussion, if not the outcome, of consideration of policy on student fees. In this case, the official committee depended upon academic research findings to move away from old public sector deficit assumptions towards academic research findings, from both Hungary and the West, that free education may block expansion and that a distinction must be made between public and private benefits.

These are examples rather than confirmation of strong relationships over the full range of policy and practice. In France and the UK it cannot be said that, in spite of examples to the exception, higher education research, scholarship and policy analysis have had any clear impact on either policy or practice. The recent Dearing Report (1997) on higher education in the UK notably avoided reference to either UK or international research on its main themes. Instead it depended upon mainly official reports on the nature of higher education in other countries and on short-order enquiries from consultancies and policy institutes.

The generalisations to be drawn from these examples is that it need not be the content of the research, or even its truth, that counts – we abandoned and have only now begun to return to the human capital position taken up by Robbins – but the *Zeitgeist*. The "successful" research well matches the intelligent wisdom of its time. If it is wisdom that accords with the views of those currently in power then it will certainly be listened to. If our kind of knowledge, which is largely indeterminate, unlike clinical research within health studies, addresses macro-policies it has to wait for the political agenda to move in its favour. Social and distributive issues are bound to depend on political evaluations for their pursuit in action. So much of the knowledge needed for policy planning is probably taken for granted or generated by government's own staff or derived from what Cohen and Lindblom (1979) call "Ordinary Knowledge". At the same time, is it possible that the research not only responded to but also reinforced or helped to disseminate the effects of the *Zeitgeist* which favoured expansion?

Some systematic analysis of policy and practice impacts come from the fields of health and social services where researchers (Buxton and Hanney 1994) identified payback from research from a study of eight cases ranging from heart transplants to social care management. They concluded that a number of the studies appeared to have had a direct and significant impact on policy and executive decisions, for example in care management legislation and funding of heart transplants. Other studies became part of a body of evidence that led to clinical guidance. But the case studies also identified research that was largely ignored in the policy debate. The list of factors identified as being associated with high pay-back emphasised the importance of recruiting user interest. They included: continuing support from customers; liaison with stakeholders; appropriateness and quality of research; brokerage; appropriate dissemination, ongoing programmes in their own right and as a context for specific projects. These conditions are not to be found in the current conditions of short order commissioning and they are not the conditions for fundamental, independent research. And we still finish up with pessimistic messages. One former Permanent Secretary who had been instrumental in advancing the use of research remarked, "I know of no strategic issue with which Ministers were concerned which was illuminated by the Health Services Research Programme".

2.8 Models of research-policy relationships

Turning to models of the relationship, there is first the empirically based modelling by Bardach (1984). He assumed individual rationality on the part of policy-makers. He showed how research reaches those for whom its utility exceeds the disutility of obtaining it. An example would be that of British policy-makers who complained that they lacked the time and other resources to act as efficient receptors of commissioned research (Kogan and Henkel 1983). Bardach notes that cooperative relationships grow up with consumers when producers try to reduce the cost to them of obtaining information. Bardach argues, too, that the natural sciences model of rapid and authoritative dissemination is inappropriate to the social sciences and to professionals. The penetration of the social sciences is "shallower" than that of the natural sciences. They have difficulty in getting much below the surface of the phenomena they study. And "the contextual component of the policy-making craft generally far exceeds that of the general principles component", important in identifying the type of evidence associated with good uptake.

Caplan et al. (1975) outline three theories which may explain a possible gap between policy and research: policy-constraint theory: policy is unable to handle the "rational" findings of educational research; knowledge-specific theory in which research is limited within a small framework of theories and empirical variables; and "two-communities" theory in which policy-makers and researchers adhere to different cultures, each with its own language, norms and values. Caplan et al. advocate the usefulness of the third of these theories, and are thus led to conclude, unsurprisingly, that good communication is necessary.

Caplan (1977), again, in a study of 204 federal policy-makers, noted how the decision making orientations of 70 percent of them could be divided between clinical, academic, and advocacy modes. Whilst the first group gathered information so that they could make an unbiased diagnosis of the policy issues, of both the internal logic and from the external logic, of political and social ramifications, of the problem, the academics were concerned mainly with the internal logic whilst those with an advocacy orientation used research opportunistically and sometimes to substantiate a case primarily based on political considerations. Their perspective was almost wholly external.

The relationships between the producers and users of research have been described as follows: "The underlying power relationships can be various. Some researchers work within a managerial hierarchy in which they are subordinate to policy-makers; those working within government departments are obvious examples. Others work within a market in which the knowledge is purchased on the basis of competition with other researchers. For the most part the relationship is that of a market in which exchange and negotiation are the styles adopted. In such cases knowledge is exchanged for resources and legitimacy. Some market arrangements, however, allow for quite substantial tenurial rights which weaken the pull of the market and emphasise the need for well constructed negotiation and exchange." (OECD 1995)

The notion of "established tenurial rights" is particularly relevant to higher education research. In spite of the massification of higher education the power of established academic groups remains strong (Kogan and Hanney 1999). It is thus likely that the best-established groups will concern themselves with issues and depend on methods which derive from and can feed back to established disciplines. These exercise a normative as well as an institutional pull, it being academically desirable to advance conceptualisation in an established field of work. At the same time, a second culture, sponsored not only by governments and the EU but also by research councils in some countries, asserts the primacy of operational relevance. The science-relevance tension is evident in all areas of policy study.

The range of relationships has been categorised several times and most recently synthesised into seven models which range from linear knowledge-driven or problem solving to interactive and illuminative models (Buxton and Hanney 1994). An overselling of the researchers' products (Husén and Kogan 1984) associated with the belief of researchers, but also many policy-makers, in the 1960s and 1970s, in a linear relationship between quantitative research, reform planning, and improved practice (Åasen 1993). Work conducted by policy analysts later discredited this perspective (Nisbet and Broadfoot 1980; Weiss 1982; Weiss 1989; Husén 1989). As a recent OECD Report (1995) suggests: "The view most widely held today is that the linear model of research utilisation is fundamentally flawed, and that educational research findings can only very seldom be applied directly in practice." It is assumed that while research can have instrumental effects, directly influencing decisions, it more often shapes policy-maker perceptions and agendas. But getting funding for doing that is not easy.

If there are difficulties arising from difference in values and knowledge styles in securing the relationship, other more humdrum obstacles have been noted. In some countries where bureaucratic mobility is high (as in the anglophone systems) officials commissioning the research move on, and there is no continuity of reception of the findings of research that they had commissioned. Research commissions are often poorly conceptualised. The receptor function is not well established. We have already noted that there are conflicting policies and "tribalism" at work within single government departments (Kogan and Henkel 1983). Yet in the UK attempt in the 1980s to install the Rothschild customer-contractor system, it was seen as possible to get scientists and policy-makers together (in research liaison groups), to make a study of the current pattern of research, the gaps in research that is required for practice and policy, and to commission work directed to filling the gaps. Eventually it failed because of the opposition of the medical establishment. They believed that research should be guided primarily by scientific or curiosity imperatives, or medical need as perceived by clinicians, rather than by the perceptions of health needs generated by policy-makers. Such an experiment has never been tried in education.

The reception of research depends on the national political and administrative culture and of the point in the cycle of positivism-exploratory-managerialist research at which a system is. In the 1970s in the UK, as elsewhere the system still had faith in the utility of research. Some customers took an instrumental view, while others hoped it would enhance the general understanding of problems faced by policy. Many bureaucrats surveyed wanted sound research that would be directly helpful to policy while other views were summed up by one customer as valuing it "for the depth of theoretical and historical understanding that ... is brought to bear ... and the critical but not unfriendly involvement in its business" (Kogan and Henkel 1983).

In that UK case, there were different accounts of feed-back on research. In one study (Gordon and Meadows 1981) 51 percent of the researchers interviewed claimed to have received feedback, but all the liaison officers interviewed could demonstrate that they had given fairly detailed feed back on research projects. As to the nature of the impact, some thought the research made them think and that it influenced them unobtrusively and cumulatively. A departmental study in the late 1970s based on over 200 cases of usable research "could detect useful elements in the commissioned projects", and listed an impressive number of studies that had contributed to policy. But whilst the instrumental value of the work was plain from the examples, it could not be generalised for all as could not its more percolative effects. An adequate time scale and collaborative relationships were evidently essential (Kogan and Henkel 1983)

In Sweden, the evidence of take-up is impressive for the earlier post-war decades. Research fed policy on expansion, on forms of governance and on teaching and learning. But Premfors (1984) reflected that it was not so much the research studies as the more general intellectual activity connected with them that might have affected attitudes. "...The use in policy-making in

Swedish higher education has been relatively marginal. (...) I have observed no major instance where research has made a difference, an instance where similar policy measures could not or would not have been taken in the absence of research." The two classic prerequisites of Swedish policy-generation, the Royal Commission and the remiss (or elaborate consultation) procedures often incorporated researchers and their thinking in policy consideration, but this applied more obviously to school than to higher education policy, and by the 1990s research based consideration was somewhat displaced by intuitive ministerial decisions.

2.9   Characteristics of receptors

Whether or not the research has an impact, there is national variation in bureaucratic and political approaches to it and the receptivity of policy-makers seems to depend in part on bureaucratic recruitment and other characteristics. Countries differ greatly in the backgrounds of policy-makers and other research users and in the extent to which links are institutionalised. In the countries where the connections are strongest, for example, Sweden, Norway, Finland and the Netherlands, that relationship has been enhanced by the fact that quite a few of the senior administrators have had research experience. Many have taken degrees that contain a strong element of individual research.

In Sweden (Premfors 1991), two-thirds of a sample of senior bureaucrats (in a range of public policy fields) stated that research knowledge was of great or very great importance for the accomplishment of their own work tasks. Of those in education policy work 75 percent thought research knowledge of great or very great importance. Whilst 70 percent agreed that research results aimed at being utilised in government activities were rarely used, more than half of the top bureaucrats and two-thirds of research and development managers considered that obstacles to effective research utilisation were primarily located within decision making whilst only about one in ten blame the research. They did not believe that research was irrelevant, poorly developed, trivial or over-ideological.

Even when the Swedish Board for Higher Education's research programme moved away from an emphasis on pedagogics and policy application towards funding research on historical and philosophical issues and on the theory of science (Trow 1991; Björklund 1991), this did not weaken the close ties of social research to powerful central bureaucratic and political authority and it was considered that researchers should be ready to place their competence at the service of building a better society, "but only on the condition that they themselves would continue to be in complete command of their methods and results".

A further example of mutual institutionalisation can be found in the Netherlands where a major centre at the University of Twente (CHEPS) was inaugurated because a minister of the time, an education policy academic, wanted new perspective on higher education. As in Sweden, central administration has been characterised by open relationships and easy access between researchers and bureaucrats, many of who have been researchers. There are twice annual forums between CHEPS and the Ministry. A bureaucrat is quoted as remarking that "at least you have influenced the terms the Ministry uses". The Ministry uses international comparisons on the basis of policy-making and CHEPS has produced these on access, student funding, diversity and other subjects. The two-year government HE plan is based on international comparisons.

No doubt these relationships always depend upon the wishes of individual ministers as well as on the educational backgrounds of bureaucrats. But many of these institutional relationships are now long standing. In Norway, over the last 20 years, the Institute for Higher Education and Research Studies can point to many policy issues upon which researchers have had an influence.

We can only describe and not account for these international differences in receptivity, any more than we can explain the striking differences in research styles between sponsored research in such countries as Norway and Sweden (Eide 1993).

2.10 Main points made in this paper

The main points made in this paper are:
1. The receptor function in the research-policy-making-practice relationship is not well researched in our field of study.
2. The governmental characteristics relevant to our theme are broadly epistemological and social or institutional.
3. On the epistemological characteristics, policy-making needs knowledge which is applicable to discrete problems, which are capable of solution. Positivist modes of research are more useful to policy-makers than critical, interactive and independent modes. Hence they may favour knowledge created by inspectors, auditors and consultants who start with the premises of policy-makers.
4. The research most highly prized by academics assumes that all questions are open and are likely to remain so after the research is completed. Applied research of repute involves negotiating the objectives of research with sponsors but retaining freedom over methods and to reach and publish conclusions.

5. Government has to be convergent and reductionist if it to act decisively in the face of complexity and conflicting interests and yet support development. Because it works on a broad canvass, the reduction of interests is a major preoccupation. At the same time, to face many interests, it is tribal and multi-modal. Its ability to make determinant policies have been put in doubt by those for whom policy-making is incremental, disjointed and episodic.

6. Policy-makers are the "customers" for research. Governmental arrangements for commissioning and using research include brokerage mechanisms. The role of research managers can be critical to reception, and they may act as internal advocates for researchers.

7. Differences in receptivity lie in the political frames within which research is to be received and the extent to which the researchers' paradigms accord with the perceived "reliability" of the methods employed by those who are the object of the research. The determinacy attributed to an area of study will also affect reception.

8. Particular and instrumental forms of knowledge are used by institutional leaders and administrators. But awareness of new and less boundaried organisations for the generation and dissemination of knowledge may put some of these assumptions to test. Not much use is made by academics of higher education research on curriculum and its modes of transmission.

9. There are several examples of the take-up for policy-making in higher education but these substantially depend on how far the research accords with the political and social *Zeitgeist* of the time. It also depends on the national political and administrative culture and of the point in the cycle of positivism-exploratory-managerialist research which a system has reached.

10. In other areas of study, the list of factors identified as being associated with high pay-back emphasise the importance of recruiting user interest. They include: continuing support from customers; liaison with stakeholders; appropriateness and quality of research; brokerage; appropriate dissemination, ongoing programmes in their own right and as a context for specific projects.

11. The models of the researcher-receptor relationship include Bardach on the individual rationality of policy-makers in which research reaches those for whom its utility exceeds the disutility of obtaining it. The range of relationships has been synthesised into seven models which range from linear knowledge-driven or problem solving to interactive and illuminative models.

12. There are national variations in bureaucratic and political approaches to research. Receptivity depends in part on bureaucratic recruitment and other characteristics. In the countries where the connections are strongest,

the relationship has been enhanced by the fact that quite a few of the senior administrators have had research experience. This makes mutual institutionalisation of the relationship easier to secure.

2.11 Conclusion

Although the general picture drawn in this paper is not wholly discouraging in terms of research receptivity, the potential lessons for researcher behaviour that might lead to a more positive receptor function are not easy to identify. The broad conclusion is in fact virtually a tautology – that attempts to secure a mutually fruitful relationship might produce a better relationship. Where reception is good it may also depend upon the accident of whether the research chimes in with the *Zeitgeist* and whether the receptors are recruited from those who are likely to be predisposed towards research.

The relationship of systematically and publicly funded research to government may, however, not hold completely true for other forms of research and scholarship. Private foundations still remain capable of funding independent research, and there is no evidence that that is less or more effective in influencing policy than that funded by government. Bodies such as the OECD in effect domesticate research findings in a form that had an effect in perhaps less sceptical days on governmental acceptance of the findings of the relationship between higher education and the economy or the capacity of education to advance social ends such as equality. And percolative or contaminative effects of research can be assumed, if not demonstrated.

NOTES

* A substantial part of this paper is contained or foreshadowed in Maurice Kogan *Higher Education,* a paper given at the OECD-CERI Conference, May 1998, Paris, on Production and Use of Knowledge in the Education and Health Sectors. An earlier version was delivered at the Annual Conference of the Consortium of Higher Education Researchers, Kassel, 1998.

REFERENCES

Åasen, P. (1993). 'Evaluation of Swedish educational R&D'. *Research Programme 1992-1995/6*. Stockholm: National Agency for Education.

Anderson, D. S. and Biddle, B. J. (eds.) (1991). *Knowledge for Policy. Improving Education Through Research*. London: Falmer Press.

Bardach, E. (1984). 'The Dissemination of Policy Research to Policymakers' *Knowledge*, 6 (2).

Björklund, E. (1991). 'Swedish research on higher education in perspective', in Trow, M. A. and Nybom, T. *University and Society. Essays on the Social Role of Research and Higher Education*. London: Jessica Kingsley Publishers, pp. 173-192.

Buxton, M. and Hanney, S. (1994). *Assessing Payback from Department of Health Research and Development*. Brunel University Health Economics Research Unit.

Caplan, N. (1977). 'The use of social research knowledge at the national level', in Weiss, C. H. *Using Social Research in Public Policymaking*. Lexington, DC Heath. Reproduced in Anderson and Biddle, pp. 183-197 (see above).

Caplan, N., Morrison, A. and Stambaugh, R (1975). *The Use of Social Science Knowledge in Policy Decisions at the National Level*. Ann Arbor: University of Michigan Press.

Cohen, D. and Lindblom, C. E. (1979). *Usable Knowledge*. Yale University Press.

Cordingley, P. (1997). 'Constructing and Critiquing Reflective Practice' (unpublished paper).

Dearing Report (1997). *Higher Education in the Learning Society. Report of the National Committee*. London: HMSO. Main Report and Four Appendices.

Eide, K. (1993). 'Educational Research Policy in the Nordic Countries. Historical Perspectives and a Look Ahead'. Unpublished paper presented at OECD Conference, Sunne.

Gibbons, M. et al. (1994). *The New Production of Knowledge. The Dynamics of Science and Research in Contemporary Societies*. London: Sage Publications.

Gibbs, G. (1995). 'The relation between quality in research and quality in teaching', *Quality and Higher Education* 1 (2), 147-158.

Gordon, M. G. and Meadows A. J. (1981). *The Dissemination of DHSS Funded Research*. Leicester: Primary Communications Research Centre, University of Leicester.

Henkel, M. (1991). *Government, Evaluation and Change*. London: Jessica Kingsley Publishers.

Henkel, M. and Kogan, M. (1996). 'The Impact of Policy Changes on the Academic Profession'. Presented to the Society for Research in Higher Education, Cardiff.

Husén, T. and Kogan, M. (eds.) (1984). *Educational Research and Policy: How Do They Relate?* Oxford: Pergamon Press.

Kogan, M. (1971). *The Politics of Education*. Harmondsworth: Penguin Books.

Kogan, M. (1997). 'Learning from other areas of study', in S. Hegarty *The Role of Research in Mature Educational Systems*. Slough: NFER.

Kogan, M. and Hanney, S. (1999). *Reforming Higher Education*. London: Jessica Kingsley Publishers.

Kogan, M. and Henkel, M. (1983). *Government and Research*. London: Heinemann Educational Books.

Martin, B. and Irvine, J. (1989). *Research Foresight: Priority Setting in Science*. London: Pinter Publishers.

Musselin, C. (forthcoming). Chapter in forthcoming book about development of French higher education policy.

Nisbet, J. and Broadfoot, P. (1980). *The Impact of Research on Policy and Practice in Education*. Aberdeen: Aberdeen University Press.

OECD (1995). *Educational Research and Development. Trends, Issues and Challenges*. Paris: OECD.

Polyani, M. (1962). 'The Republic of Science: Its Political and Economic Theory.' *Minerva*, 1(1).

Premfors, R. (1984). 'Research and policy-making in Swedish higher education', in Husén, T. and Kogan, M. (eds.). *Educational Research and Policy: How Do They Relate?* Oxford: Pergamon Press.

Premfors, R. (1991). 'Scientific bureaucracy. Research implementation as Swedish civil servants', in Trow, M. A. and Nybom, T. (eds). *University and Society*. Essays on the social role of research and higher education. London: Jessica Kingsley Publishers, pp. 88-98.

Rein, M. (1983). *From Policy to Practice*. New York: Macmillan.

Rekilä, E. (1998). 'Dialog in University Management: A Study of Bureaucratic and Academic Organisations'. Presented to IMHE Conference, Univerity of Tartu.

Robbins Report (1963). *Higher Education*. Report of the Committee appointed by the Prime Minister under the Chairmanship of Lord Robbins, 1961-63. Cmnd 2154.

Sadlak, J. and Altbach, P. (1997). *Higher Education Research at the Turn of the Century*. New York: Garland Press and Paris: UNESCO.

Scott, P. (2000). 'Higher education research in the light of a dialogue between policy-makers and practitioners', in Teichler, U. and Sadlak, J. (eds.). *Higher Education Research: Its Relationship to Policy and Practice*. Oxford: Pergamon/ IAU Press.

Schon, D. (1971). *Beyond the Stable State*. New York: Random House.

Setényi, J. (1997). 'Policy development and educational research: The Hungarian experience.' *Tertiary Education and Management*, 3 (3) 237–247.

Teichler, U. (2000) 'The relationships between higher education research and higher education policy and practice: The researchers' perspective.', Teichler, U. and Sadlak, J. (eds.). *Higher Education Research: Its Relationship to Policy and Practice*. Oxford: Pergamon/ IAU Press.

Trow, M. A. (1984). 'Researchers, policy analysts and policy intellectuals', in Husén, T. and Kogan, M. (eds) (1984). *Educational Research and Policy: How Do They Relate?* Oxford: Pergamon Press.

Trow, M. A. (1991). 'Introduction: Swedish research on higher education: an appreciation of a research program and its director', in Trow, M. A. and Nybom, T. (eds.). *University and Society*. Essays on the Social Role of Research and Higher Education. London: Jessica Kingsley Publishers.

Van den Daele, W., Krohn, W. and Weingart, P. (1977) 'The Political Direction of Scientific Development', in Mendelsohn, E., Weingart, P. and Whitley, R. (eds.). *The Social Production of Scientific Knowledge*. Dordrecht and Boston/USA: Reidel Publishing Co.

Weiss, C. (1980). *Social Science Research and Decision-Making*. New York: Columbia University Press.

Weiss, C. (1982). 'Policy research in the context of diffuse decision-making', in Kosse, G. (ed.). *Social Science Research and Public Policy-making*. London: NFER-Nelson.

Weiss, C. (1989). 'Congressional committees as users of analysis', *Journal of Policy Analysis and Management* 8(3), 411-431.

Westerheijden, D. 'Researchers and policy-makers in higher education in East Central Europe', in Leitner, E. (1998). *Educational Research and Higher Education Reform in Eastern and Central Europe*. Frankfurt: Peter Lang.

Wildavsky, A. (1964). *The Politics of the Budgetary Process*. Boston: Little Brown.

Chapter 3

Patterns of Communication and Miscommunication between Research and Policy

ELAINE EL-KHAWAS
University of California, Los Angeles, USA

With the approach of a new century, the demands on higher education appear to be growing, not declining. As reports from several multinational organizations have shown (World Bank 1994; UNESCO 1995; OECD 1998), higher education in both industrialized and developing countries is facing heightened expectations for increased access, improved performance and greater relevance to workplace needs. For systems of higher education, traditional approaches are being questioned, and pressures are mounting for new, more cost-efficient and responsive practices.

In such a challenging context, systems of higher education could benefit greatly from the insights of scholars who have acquired special expertise on higher education and its accomplishments, shortcomings and possibilities. The context is right for expert knowledge to be heard, and to be a resource for shaping a vision for higher education's role in the future.

However, in two recent meetings – one held in Tokyo, Japan (Jones 1997) and another in 1998 in Kassel, Germany – a range of international participants stated that the relationship between research and the world of higher education policy is considered to be problematic in a number of countries. Concerns have been raised by observers and researchers in the United States as well. Terenzini, reflecting on the place of academic scholarship in US policy debate, has recently described a pattern of considerable distance and disconnection (Terenzini 1996).

Such criticism is especially troubling in view of the fact that higher education study is an "applied" field of inquiry. As with other applied or object-oriented fields that are linked to areas of professional practice (e.g., engineering, medicine), researchers who are in the field of higher education have an explicit mandate to investigate and understand higher education for the

45

S. Schwarz and U. Teichler (eds.), The Institutional Basis of Higher Education Research, 45–56.

purpose of improving it. If the relationship between research and praxis is poor, then serious efforts are needed to understand the reasons for this disconnection and to seek ways to develop a better relationship between the two.

This paper offers a perspective on the relationship of policy and research in higher education by focusing especially on communication patterns among them. It suggests some reasons that relatively poor communication persists between research and policy settings in higher education, and offers some suggestions for improving communications. The paper draws on an earlier analysis (El-Khawas 2000) of the three "homes" of research on higher education and builds on some insights about the policy process that were developed some years ago by John Kingdon (1984). It also incorporates a number of the perspectives offered by participants in the Tokyo and Kassel meetings, both of which considered the relationship between research, policy, and practice and sought ways to improve the interface among them.

3.1 Structural aspects of the relationship

To consider communication patterns and problems affecting higher education research, it is useful to begin by regarding research, policy, and practice as separate functional spheres (Figure 1).

FIGURE 1

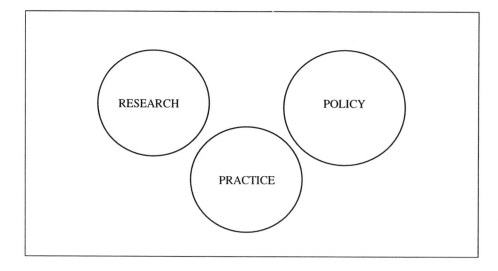

On questions related to higher education's functioning or effectiveness, a variety of different relationships might occur between and among these spheres. Relationships might be close, or distant. Two of these spheres might work together closely, with another being at some distance. Teichler has argued, for example, that most European countries have recently exhibited a pattern in which there are quite close ties between research and policy, as implied by figure 2 (Teichler 1996 and 1998).

FIGURE 2

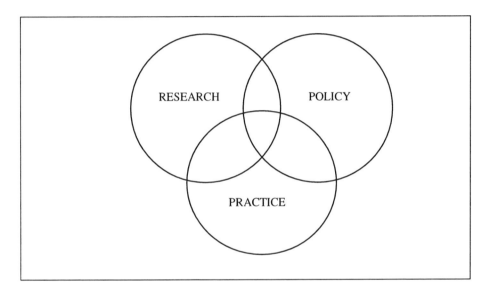

Other configurations are also possible. Kaneko has suggested that, in Japan, research has undergone steady development recently, but has not had a strong relationship to policy and practice. Citing an example relevant to other countries, he notes that recent policy initiatives to spur self-evaluation by universities and to strengthen university management have not been informed by objective and reliable research (Kaneko 2000). In still another pattern, Jayaram (quoted in Teichler and Sadlak 2000) has argued that policy makers in South Asia pay attention to academic research on higher education only if it has been sponsored by or conducted for policy-makers.

The general point is that, functionally, research, policy, and practice are different spheres of activity and, in any particular country, the three functions can be related in quite distinctive ways. Thus, too, identifying the major actors in each sphere of activity, and understanding who the major actors are and how often they are in contact with each other, help clarify some of the dynamics among research, policy, and practice settings. Academic researchers, for example, are but one of many actors who may wish to influence policy formation (Urzua 1997, p. 6). Kaneko has suggested that relevant actors, all with different perspectives and interests, include students, parents, and the general public, as well as media, employers, and the government (Kaneko 2000). Sawyerr (1998) usefully notes, too, that today's young academic researchers may well move into policy or practice positions in the future.

Research functions can be carried out entirely by civil servants in government agencies who issue reports and memoranda on a frequent basis. At the other extreme, the task of research might be delegated entirely to academics in universities who release their study results rather infrequently and direct their attention primarily to scholarly audiences. Variations between these two approaches are also important and seem to be growing in prominence. Thus, Tan has described another model, in which the Chinese government has established several research institutions affiliated with the government; they collect research results, organize advisory mechanisms, and in other ways function as formal links between higher education research and policy making (Tan 1997). Arimoto (1998) has documented, on the other hand, the growing importance of university-based research centers in Japan. In a blended model, the Australian government has often called upon both research centers as well as university academics to conduct research on policy-relevant matters (Harmon 1998). Still another alternative is the use of independent organizations that contract with government agencies to conduct research. This latter category, currently seeing use in many countries, may include quasi-academic organizations – possibly, a group of former academics who have created their own research firm – but it also can include multinational consulting firms, "think tanks", or other multipurpose contracting organizations (cf. Urzua 1997). Arimoto (1998) has described a diversity of such "quasi-academic organizations" that currently offer research on higher education in Japan.

Another aspect of the relationship between research and policy involves the degree to which there is an overlapping of functions. In the United States and in some other countries, there are quite fluid boundaries between the spheres in terms of who conducts research studies. Research on US higher education takes place in academic settings, in policy settings, and in practice settings as well. However, the nature of the research in each setting is often quite distinctive, each having developed according to different concerns and opportunities. As a consequence, individuals tend to work in one of these areas, while having limited interaction with researchers in the other settings. Teichler (2000) has noted that the research done in such different settings often parallels the differing ideological perspectives and concerns of various policy actors. Harman (1998) has noted that, in Australia, a further division of research activity takes place, with three different research communities that focus, respectively, on matters of academic practice, policy and management, and vocational education.

So too, the type of research may differ by setting. Policy-related research in the US, conducted in response to questions raised by policy-makers in state or national government, is usually small-scale and specific, designed to answer certain questions and not others, and directed toward the development of policy options, not toward comprehensive understanding. It includes the work of legislative aides and government staff but also the work of consultants and analysts in various organizations. In contrast, "institutional research", conducted in university settings, is a style of research that is problem-focused and context-oriented, usually directed to one institution's problems or to those of a small set of institutions.

Academic research, as conducted by those holding professorial positions, differs from these other types of research. Academic research often works in the framework of large-scale, multiyear research projects, aimed at uncovering general explanations rather than detailed solutions for policy dilemmas. Its results are most often reported in annual scholarly conferences or in books or journals in which a year or more may elapse between manuscript preparation and release of the final publication. Krotsch (1998) reminds us, however, that the precise nature of the academic research community varies from country to country and, indeed, that changes have occurred in several Latin American countries over the last two decades.

3.2 Sources of miscommunication

Based on this recognition of different research settings and different ways that the settings can approach their work, the problems of communication between research and policy can be better understood. First, there are problems that arise among the actors in each setting. Many observers have commented, for example, about the impatience of policy-makers, who want quick answers to complex questions or who consider policy alternatives as much for their political appeal as for their general effectiveness. So too, academic researchers can be criticized for an inward-looking, overly analytic style. Critics say they give greater attention to ambiguities of definition, methodological weaknesses or their theoretical models than to the pressing need for practical ideas (Sadlak and Altbach 1997).

Attention can also be directed to the policy environment and its distinctive characteristics. Some insights in the policy studies literature offer useful perspective on aspects that contribute to miscommunication between academic researchers and those they might interact with in policy settings. Specifically, John Kingdon (1984) has described the policy process as involving three largely unrelated "streams" of activity:

- a *problem stream*, consisting of researchers and other experts with information about the actual status of a problem area, whether it's worsening or improving, and what measures exist to address it;
- a *policy stream*, consisting of advocates and other specialists who analyze problems and formulate possible alternatives; and
- a *political stream*, consisting of legislative and elective leaders and the rules by which they operate.

In this view, major policy reforms take place when the three "streams" converge: when a problem is recognized as serious and requiring a new solution; when the policy community develops a financially and technically workable solution; and when political leaders find it advantageous to approve it. The disparate elements and interests must come together if new policies are to emerge. Political interest alone, or policy formulations alone, cannot bring about effective policy change.

Kingdon's tripartite description of the policy process emphasizes a number of useful points, especially the prospect of significantly different perspectives held by the various actors. Thus, capable and responsible professionals in each sphere often interpret events, problems, and possible actions from quite different lenses. Kogan (1998) has offered a detailed and insightful analysis of some of the dimensions which give rise to these different perspectives. One consequence, for communications, is that the research and data that seem to offer compelling evidence to one set of actors may not be persuasive to those with different perspectives. This insight also implies that, despite a lengthy public record of what policy advocates and political leaders intended with a new reform, practitioners may have still another view of what is intended and what should be done.

In the United States, the researchers who work in policy settings in state or national government often pay attention both to the policy stream and the political stream, trying to be responsive to a varying array of issues raised by policy officials. Their communication with academic researchers is limited, however, and when it does occur, often frustrating for both sides. As Kingdon has emphasized, analysts in the policy setting look for solutions and specific ideas that will fit into existing policy frameworks; yet, academic researchers tend to focus on the broad issues and their underlying causes, looking for complex and multi-factor explanations of a problem.

In addition to differences in purposes, the two different settings differ in communication style. In policy settings, communication is brisk, expecting participants to understand the many assumptions and constraints of a situation. Comments focus on only the issues that are "on the table" at the time. Memos and briefing papers are the main written communications, sometimes with a limited number of illustrative statistical tables or graphs. The typical communication style of academic researchers offers a strong contrast. Most academics prepare scholarly studies. They give lengthy and detailed explanations of their results, requiring a familiarity with their theoretical concepts or methodological approaches. Most academics find it difficult to abstract parts of their research or to make inferences from their research evidence to the very different context offered by actual policy options.

In brief, the two worlds operate with different purposes and modes of communication. The result has been a major disjunction between the worlds of research and policy, with costs to both sides. One such cost is seen in narrowly conceived reports and minimal use of relevant concepts that could provide a link with enduring themes in the research literature (Harman 1998). To be sure, there are notable exceptions where academics have served effectively as advisors to government leaders, have given thoughtful and well-timed testimony in government hearings or in court cases, or have introduced academic insights to the policy community in other ways. As Kogan (1998) has noted, the Robbins report in the UK marked a significant example of a way in which research evidence paid a significant role in influencing policy directions. Similarly, in the US, infrequent instances can be cited where the policy agenda was influenced by research; in the 1980s, for example, a widely influential report, titled "Involvement in Learning," was prepared by a study group comprised of academic researchers and published by the US Department of Education. In general, however, the dominant pattern in the US has been one of substantial gaps in communication, a pattern that has persisted for many years.

3.3 Toward improved communications

With a recognition of the different worlds of policy and research in higher education, improved communication must begin with all parties acknowledging these differences and agreeing to develop a strategy for better communication. If new, more useful modes of communication are to be constructed, they must respond to the specific circumstances of each setting while still allowing room for the separate interests, perspectives, and preferred communication styles of policy makers, practitioners, and researchers.

The following pages outline three steps researchers might take to help develop better communication with those who work in policy settings. In turn, these steps may help policy analysts and policy officials to make more effective use of the important insights that researchers have about the problems currently facing systems of higher education.

3.3.1 Choose the best "modes of delivery"

Academic researchers could have a major role in helping to define a policy issue, i.e., contributing to the problem identification or "enlightenment" function in policy development (cf. Weiss 1977). Their in-depth knowledge of an area allows them to explain the nature of a problem, for example, or to document whether a problem is worsening or taking on new dimensions over time. They also bring strength in being able to critique proposed approaches to dealing with a problem area. To do so, however, researchers must choose effective ways to communicate their understanding.

Rather than limiting themselves to academic journals and conferences, they can turn to policy-relevant forums and publications. This may involve preparation of "opinion" pieces for newspapers or participation in briefings arranged with policy officials. Following Maassen's suggestion (1998), it may require academic researchers, possibly with the leadership of policy research centers, to create new mechanisms – public forums, annual legislative briefings, etc. – that are crafted specifically to allow researchers to speak to policy makers. Sawyerr (1998) has noted several useful precedents in research conferences recently held in Africa that drew the participation of ministers of education, vice-chancellors and other senior academic officials.

Under this approach, researchers would need to adapt their writing and communication styles to fit approaches more familiar to journalists than to scholars. Well-prepared stories and anecdotes, for example, are effective ways to succinctly present the importance of complicated research studies. The specifics of cases and illustrative situations communicate well with solutions-oriented practitioners and policy officials, far better than the details of statistical tests or comprehensive project histories. Researchers could also benefit by using appropriate and persuasive communication devices, such as developing slogans, policy platforms, or other formal public statements. In a recent example in the United States, a single phrase – "one-third of a nation" – was repeatedly given prominence in different policy settings, cumulatively raising awareness of the future importance of ethnic diversity to the United States.

3.3.2 Pay attention to the audience

For many researchers, contributions to what Kingdon called the "problem" stream – the identification of a problem and its key dimensions – will be their most appropriate activity. Others may wish to be involved with the "policy" stream as well, that is, the analysis of alternative ways to address a problem or, sometimes, to design a new policy. Because the analytic tasks involved with these efforts can contrast sharply with the usual work of academic researchers, researchers must adopt a flexible approach as they embark on discussions over policy development.

Policy is never developed in a vacuum, or under controlled laboratory conditions. Sabatier (1986) has emphasized that policy formation is highly dependent on situational constraints, current political moods and strategies, and other context factors, including recent successes or problems that policy makers have before them.

For academic researchers, therefore, effective participation in discussions designed to fashion new policy solutions must often begin with listening, rather than explanation. While the researcher may have background and depth on a problem, he or she must also become informed about the relevant aspects of the setting in which policy might be made. In essence, the researcher is facing a diagnostic task: to listen, and recognize existing constraints; to observe the specific concerns of policy makers; and to listen for the gaps and opportunities for shaping new directions. What are possible solutions, from the point of view of the policy officials who, in this context, are the "client" or "audience" that the researcher needs to understand? What level of resources can be directed to a problem? What are the micro-level issues that simply cannot be addressed, whether for practical or political reasons, and what are the best options for taking new direction? A specific research agenda or a proposed new policy direction may emerge from open discussion and from the "informed listening" that academic researchers can bring to such discussions.

Crafting policy options is, in large part, a negotiation among individuals; personality differences count. Some policy officials are analytically trained and want to hear detailed arguments about the pros and cons of a proposal. Other policy officials do not wish to understand a problem in depth but may want to hear about solutions, described in practical steps and with tangible results. Researchers who understand their policy audience are better equipped to select a particular aspect of information that has good prospects of acceptance. Researchers who have taken the time to hear the concerns of policy makers and to learn about the constraints they face have typically gained a certain level of confidence or trust among policy makers, allowing their suggestions to be received more openly.

3.3.3 Accept the random aspects of policy formation

For researchers whose own intellectual worlds give high priority to the ability to think logically and to prepare coherent arguments, it can be confusing to become immersed in the world of policy formulation. Such settings are fluid, with new constraints abruptly introduced or certain ideas judged differently as circumstances change. Government leadership may change, and new leaders may drop earlier initiatives that were underway, instead pressing for dramatically new directions (cf. Harman 1998). Policy formation is dynamic, responsive to changing contexts. Typically, too, there are several groups trying to influence policy, each with different ideas offered at different times. Groups differ in their purposes: some push for a new approach, others wish to prevent or weaken any new proposal. Also, most policies are formed in settings in which there is no single "client" or "stakeholder". Even if an agency head, or minister, is formally in charge, the views of many elected officials must also be weighed. If one approach to an issue seems to be the best when all other approaches are initially compared, a wider set of circumstances can tip the balance toward an option that, on first analysis, seemed unsuitable.

For researchers, it is important to be aware of the various ways that policy development is subject to change, if not reversals. This suggests, for example, that ideas that are not well received at one point in the discussion may well find better reception at a later point. These realities also suggest that researchers may be better able to make a specific contribution to policy formulation when they offer their ideas as separable components, rather than as a single, multi-step plan or approach. No matter how logically well-crafted an idea, there is a certain randomness to how ideas and approaches get picked up in policy settings. Researchers may limit their prospects of making a contribution by bundling their ideas too tightly together.

3.4 Conclusion

Surprisingly little systematic attention has been given to the question of how to improve the relationship between research, policy, and practice. Attention to this issue may be increasing, however, linked to the growing salience of higher education in many countries and to the growing sense of resource constraints facing systems of higher education. The Tokyo Roundtable, the International Symposium in Kassel, and the recent UNESCO World Conference all offer signs that serious attention is being directed to the possibilities of improved communication.

More discussion, including clarification of terms and purposes, is needed. Academic researchers, on their part, could benefit from closer attention to policy-relevant issues rather than to their own, more comfortable but typically more generalized themes (cf. Teichler and Sadlak 2000) and from integrated, coordinated studies rather than individualized, unconnected studies. Policy formation, whatever its actual constraints, could benefit from systematic attention by academics to the long-term issues that need to be understood from multiple disciplinary perspectives (Harman 1998). Future efforts should be directed both toward the task of arriving at general propositions about the relationships among the spheres and also toward the separate task of building up a literature that offers case studies and other analyses of specific policy initiatives. This literature, in turn, will help to test and refine the general points.

REFERENCES

Arimoto, A. (1998). *The Institutional Basis of Higher Education Research*. Presented to the International Symposium, Kassel.

El-Khawas, E. (2000). 'Research, policy and practice: Assessing their actual and potential linkages', in Teichler, U. and Sadlak, J. (eds.). *Higher Education Research: Its Relationship to Policy and Practice*. Oxford: Pergamon/IAU Press.

Jones, G. A. (1997). *Report of the Roundtable on the Relationship among Research, Policy and Practice in Higher Education*. Tokyo: The University of Tokyo and UNESCO.

Harman, G. (1998). *The Institutional and Funding Basis for Tertiary Education Research in Australia*. Presented to the International Symposium, Kassel.

Kaneko, M. (1999). 'Higher Education Research, Policy and Practice: Contexts, Conflicts and the New Horizon', in Teichler, U. and Sadlak, J. (eds.). *Higher Education Research: Its Relationship to Policy and Practice*. Oxford: Pergamon/IAU Press.

Kingdon, J. (1984). *Agendas, Alternatives, and Public Policies*. Boston: Little, Brown and Co.

Kogan, M. (1998). *'Getting Inside: Policy Reception of Research'*. Presented to the International Symposium, Kassel.

Krotsch, P. (1998). *'Studies in Higher Education: A Reflection in the Context of Argentina and Latin America'*. Presented to the International Symposium, Kassel.

Maassen, P. A. M. (2000). 'Higher Education Research: The Hourglass Structure and Its Implications', in Teichler, U. and Sadlak, J. (eds.). *Higher Education Research and Its Relationship to Policy and Practice*. Oxford: Pergamon/IAU Press.

OECD (1998). *Comparative Report, The Thematic Review of the First Years of Tertiary Education*. Paris: OECD.

Sabatier, P. (1986). 'Top-down and bottom-up models of policy implementation: A critical analysis and suggested synthesis', *Journal of Public Policy* 6 (January), 21-48.

Sadlak, J. and Altbach, P. (eds.) (1997). *Higher Education Research at the Turn of the Century: Structures, Issues and Trends*. Paris and New York: UNESCO/Garland Publishing.

Sawyerr, A. (1998). *Study Program on Higher Education Management in Africa*. Presented to the International Symposium, Kassel.

Tan, S. (1997). *Development of and New Issues in Higher Education Research in China*. Presented to the Roundtable, Tokyo.

Teichler, U. (1996). 'Comparative higher education: Potentials and limits', *Higher Education*, 32, (4), 431-465.

Teichler, U. (1998). *Themes and Institutional Basis of Research on Higher Education*. Presented to the International Symposium, Kassel.

Teichler, U. (2000). 'The Relationship between Higher Education Research and Higher Education Policy and Practice: The Researchers' Perspective', in Teichler, U. and Sadlak, J. (eds). *Higher Education Research: Its Relationship to Policy and Practice*. Oxford: Pergamon/IAU Press.

Teichler, U. and Sadlak, J. (eds.) (2000). *Higher Education Research: Its Relationship to Policy and Practice*. Oxford: Pergamon/IAU Press.

Terenzini, P. T. (1996). 'Rediscovering roots: Public policy and higher education', *Review of Higher Education*, 20, (1) 5-13.

UNESCO (1995). *Policy Paper for Change and Development in Higher Education*. Paris: UNESCO.

Urzua, R. (1997). *Academic Social Science Research and Policy-Making*. Presented to the Roundtable, Tokyo.

Weiss, C. (1977). 'Research for policy's sake: The enlightenment function of social research', *Policy Analysis* 3 (Fall), 531-45.

World Bank (1994). *Higher Education: The Lessons of Experience*. Development in Practice Series. Washington, D.C.: World Bank.

Chapter 4

On Fate and Intelligence: The Institutional Base of Higher Education Research

GUY NEAVE
International Association of Universities, Paris, France
CHEPS, Twente University, Enschede, Netherlands

4.1 Introduction

Not all historians subscribe to the cyclical theory of human affairs, though it has to be admitted that Marx in his more acerbic and despairing moments did precisely that. Even if one does not believe in this interpretation, it is, of course, well within the bounds of human ingenuity to impose such a perspective. History as cycles is, perhaps, the ultimate expression of the conservative view on the development of humanity since what it says is that there is virtually nothing wholly new under the sun. Yet, there is a certain tidy satisfaction in being able, like the Salmon, to come back to where it all started. There is a good deal of comfort in being back in familiar waters. More to the point, such a return journey makes us very much aware of the distance we have travelled in the meantime. Aquatic patho-neurology has yet to determine whether Salmon have thoughts at all, let alone whether on such occasions they indulge in the nostalgic and the metaphysical. By contrast, the evidence over the past ten years of CHER's ability to think about our fields and to do so creatively, remains unimpaired. If it were not, something – to use the obvious *jeu de mots* – would indeed be very fishy! Still, after ten years, if a little nostalgia befits the occasion, we should not allow it to cloud our judgement of what we have done in the intervening period.

Almost ten years ago, though not to the exact day, we held our first meeting. Our purpose was to map out the fields of higher education research and more specifically to plot out the state of the art in our various countries, beginning with Western Europe. The ensuing decade has been both fruitful

S. Schwarz and U. Teichler (eds.), The Institutional Basis of Higher Education Research, 57–71.
© 2000 *Kluwer Academic Publishers. Printed in the Netherlands.*

and frustrating. It has been exceedingly fruitful in the international ties, links, exchanges, joint research, cross national studies. Those involving multi-system comparison have been considerably strengthened outside the more usual international agencies and inter-governmental forums. That many amongst us are individually and severally engaged in common research projects of a medium term nature is witness to the strength of this trend. In short, the trans-national and international dimension of our collaboration is no longer a rare and somewhat exotic activity. On the contrary, it stands as a natural extension to the work we pursue within our own respective systems. And the analyses we make of our own systems, or those in which we live or work – which is not always the same thing – and the issues they face, is increasingly enriched by the insights cross national studies provide.

4.2 Disciplinary dynamic or claim to "professional" status?

As with any field of enquiry, the splitting off, sub division and emergence of new areas of attention has been particularly vigorous over the course of the past ten years. In the earlier part of the decade, scholarly attention identified some 20 disciplines and domains contributing to the study of higher education. They ranged from anthropology through to women's studies (Becher 1992).

Today, other perspectives are emerging. And one sign of this is the emergence of new journals specifically to give an outlet to the writings of adepts, specialists, and practitioners. Amongst them, quality and evaluation studies, cooperation studies, studies on the relationship between university and industry, and finally, as they would have themselves be known, international relations – not the minutiae of diplomatic manoeuvrings between the powers, great and less, so much as the study of cross national links, ties and flows of students, administrators, dons and students between institutions of higher education. To be sure, founding a journal is somewhat of a dialectical point since it can just as well be one sign of the intellectual maturation of a perspective, as it is also a prime indicator of that uncontrollable disciplinary dynamic inherent to the modern university (Clark 1995). It provides an outlet for publications which otherwise would not find a home, just as it can create "an intellectual market" where none existed before. Yet journals, above all in the domain of higher education, have a certain ambiguity about them. They stand at the crossing point of two separate but very different processes, the one research driven, the other having more to do with what may be described as the "definition of professional (sic) identity".

4.3 Contrary motivations

Founding a journal in the case of the former may be construed as part of that process which involves primarily the scholarly definition of a perspective, the laying down and refining of its methodology the ultimate purpose of which is to move a inchoate body of disorganised knowledge on towards coalescing around a "domain", a formally recognised field of study, and in doing so, conferring a precision to its intellectual shape, form and content. In the case of the latter, however, the process involved is indeed a very different kettle of – fish. Rather than having as its prime purpose the definition of a field, the main consideration is to reinforce – if not to make an initial claim to – particular consideration and status on behalf of a group of individuals. The claim to intellectual specificity is not so much an end *per se*. Rather, it stands as a means to an end. That end is to secure conditions of employment, career, particular influence or responsibility by asserting the claim of being master of a particular type of knowledge. The latter aspect of journal founding is, in short, part of a broader intent which one might qualify as motivating various strata within the world of practitioners or administrators, that of staking a claim to the status of professional where earlier neither the task nor the level of qualification, still less the tasks discharged by the persons involved, stood the remotest chance of successfully asserting such pretensions.

There are many points one might make in connection with this dichotomy in the processes which underlie the areas of activity and study grouped under the general heading of "Higher Education Research". The first is that whilst they take place in an overall setting which is itself without precedent – namely, the massification of higher education – they are, in point of fact, very old and abiding features of the university *qua* learning society. Their origins can be traced back to that distinction which the mediaeval world drew between the acquisition of knowledge in general, and which consisted in dividing it between *amor scientiae* and *amor pecuniae* (Ruegg 1992). Transposed into contemporary language, they are best rendered as "love of learning", that is, learning driven by the internal evolution of knowledge, the "disciplinary dynamic" as against "love of the fruits of learning", that is, learning for what it may bring in material reward, standing, advancement or, in this instance, "recognition as professionals".

The second point which follows has already been made elsewhere, namely the equally abiding tension in the field of higher education between the adepts of the former and those who subscribe to the latter. In a masterly essay on why higher education research appears not to have the weight one might expect upon practitioners, administrators and those taken up with the running of higher education, Teichler (2000) noted that one characteristic of practitioners was their relatively high level of sophistication in matters of higher learning. This, he argued, tended to blunt the impact research might have upon policy. But his analysis also extended to different levels of interest and concern within the world of higher education's administration and particularly at the institutional level. This gives us an additional clue to one element which lies behind the "professional dynamic" as one influence upon the evolving spectrum of fields that have emerged in the course of the last decade.

4.4   Transfer of functions: their significance for our field

Yet, administration is far from being a uniform entity and, moreover, its degree of sophistication varies in keeping with the type of responsibilities it exercises. These may range from the strategic to the routine, from administering multi-million pound budgets to overseeing the provision of lecture theatres, overhead projectors, and keeping the lawns mown. In short, administration is multi-layered, just as it discharges multiple functions. It is not without coincidence that those areas of study newly emerging in the course of the nineties – evaluation, quality studies, mobility studies, international cooperation – are precisely those which are, in effect, migrating from being amongst the range of responsibilities, once exercised as part of the general and unspecified residual functions within the academic estate. In many European universities, they are being "relocated" within the administrative nexus, either as specialised activities, as a specific sub-set of upholding an institutional mission. They are driving towards acquiring occupational specificity and specialised career paths rather than being one in a range of ancillary tasks which academics fulfilled in addition to teaching and research (de Groof, Neave and Svec 1998).

Two features stand out in this transfer of functions. The first is that such a development reflects one of the Leitmotifs in European higher education for the best part of the past decade and a half – in effect, the drive towards managerial rationalisation, sometimes alluded to as the "Managerial Revolution". As such, it stands as one particular aspect of the further complexity which market rationality and competition place upon the university. At another level, however, such a displacement of functions brings with it new claims to status by those who take them over, demands in keeping with the rationalisation and concentration of responsibility such new functions entail. The second point must be that amongst certain sectors of institutional administration, the desire for recognition as self-standing "professionals" is no less a powerful element in the de facto "disciplinary" dynamic of our field than is the research-driven quest for better understanding. And this motive is important on its own account. It puts a new light entirely on the basic question of the physical, institutional and administrative location or siting in the organisational chart of higher education studies. It also makes our task more complex and for that matter, demands a far more nuanced analysis than if we were to confine ourselves simply to the world of classically-defined operational research units, Centres of Higher Education Studies or sub sections of graduate programmes dealing with higher education.

4.5   Rock-like impermanence

If, amidst the ocean deeps of advanced studies and knowledge, we are to chart the isles where the blessed dwell, we have also to remember higher education's counterpart of Lanzerotta, Stirtsey and Santorini. For those of us whose interest in geophysics is sorely wanting, let me simply point out that what unites all three of these rocks is their highly noxious and volcanic activity. They come and go, change shape and explode with often legendary results. The virtual annihilation of Santorini, a small island to the North of Crete, eleven hundred years before Christ, gave rise to the legend of Atlantis. So it is with higher education studies. For if groups of scholars, like volcanic isles, come and go, it is not exaggerated to see changes in official policy as higher education's equivalent to seismic upheaval.

As the priorities of governments change so different perspectives and disciplines take on more weight in keeping with the issues and problems which the new political – or social – agenda for higher education reveals or seeks to rectify. The redefinition of old issues or the raising of new ones confers new weight upon a particular disciplinary perspective and very often, by the same mechanical process, diminishes the significance authorities attribute to those which, seemingly, have "been weighed in the balance and found wanting". Likewise, as the political reinterpretation of higher education, its mission and its goals takes place, so additional disciplines or perspectives are drawn into the field. Thus, for instance, the increase in the numbers of contributors to the general field whose background or Faculty of affiliation lie in business studies, in the organisation of the firm and the sociology of organisations, to cite but a few, make their entries on the stage of higher education with enhanced authority now that the latter has been recast as an entrepreneurial undertaking. Nor is the role of the "newly pertinent" field limited to reinterpreting the purpose and performance of higher education in the light of its own canons of scholarship. For every manifest function, a latent one is not far behind. Thus it is that the rise to prominence of a particular perspective is sometimes seen as a means for amplifying, giving intellectual substance to – and maybe even contributing to – changes, whether at institutional or systems level, which governments or supranational bodies see as desirable.

4.6   Institutional location: a formidable task

Plotting the institutional basis of higher education studies is then rendered singularly complicated not only because of the dualism of its basic purpose. Our task, to parody Marx, is not only to contemplate the world (the scholarly imperative), but also to change it (the practitioner viewpoint). Once we bear in mind this dual nature of higher education studies, it follows as inevitably as night follows day that the places – not to mention the personalities involved in scholarly inquiry – tend to be very different indeed from those wherein the denizens of practice reside and have their being. I am not saying that these are of necessity, inevitably and wholly separate worlds. On the contrary, there are examples aplenty of what is sometimes termed "the policy hybrid", those genial and mobile individuals who flourish across both the world of scholarship and the world of practice. But depending on whether we are conceited enough or sufficiently pragmatic to define the world of higher education studies in terms of research alone or in terms of research and practice, so we are faced with the intellectual equivalent of two very different cartographic projections, one being a minimum and the other a maximum representation of our world. When we add to this basic fuzziness the fact that the terrain of higher education appears to provide a fertile ground from which new intellectual perspectives emerge – some of which I have already mentioned as evidence of the buoyant state of our domain in the course of the present decade – it cannot be doubted that to trace its institutional location, quite apart from its tribal frontiers, is a formidable task indeed.

4.7   The dilemmas and discomforts of hastening maturity

It is at this point that we come across a number of other dilemmas and causes of great discomfort. And not a few of them spring not so much from our present condition as that condition which we would like ourselves to be, if possible, in the near as opposed to the distant future. To be cruel, such ambition involves the no less basic issue of our intellectual identity – not necessarily its professional counterpart which, as I have argued, is most certainly a concern to some of our number. In many respects, the quest to find out where in the higher education system the communities of higher education researchers and practitioners have an institutional implantation, may be seen as an attempt to provide in locational terms a coherence which from a "disciplinary" perspective neither has.

The question is, of course, should we have it? This has been a subterranean cause of ill-humour and conflict of interests for a good many years in CHER. Here, one should leave aside the ordinary ambitions of particular disciplines as they assert their claims to be the "Queen of social sciences all". The basis of the argument does not reside in the details but in the fundamental vision. These visions, and they can probably be reduced to two, turn around whether the study of higher education may be made to conform to what some would wish to see as a coherent "discipline" or whether, on the contrary, it should remain as a "domain", characterised by drawing from across a broad range of different intellectual traditions. As a problematic, it is far from being novel, involving as it does the eternal issues of intellectual Orthodoxy vs. Heterodoxy, of central coordination vs. individual cohabitation, of "regulation" vs. creative anarchy. These two visions pose other issues, which go well beyond the best way of "hastening maturity".

4.8 Conflicting visions

Not least amongst these issues is whether the eclecticism which characterises the various disciplinary components of our domain should be welded more closely together around a limited number of key paradigms or particular methodological approaches? Do we attain the status of a discipline by organising our field so that it come to resemble say, Public Administration or Sociology? Should it attempt to assume a core orthodoxy and methodology? Or do we put ourselves on the path towards what some see as this desirable state by trying to group together at institutional level, creating an organisational unity and a single administrative location for all those who, scattered across the whole gamut of the social, administrative, governmental and human sciences, contribute to the domain of higher education? This argument has certainly been aired. It has appeal for some. But others, content with a more relaxed, confederate entente, have dismissed it with contumely. Each to his – or her – own thing!

But there is an argument – and it has recently been aired amongst the sociologists of science and the students of science policy (Gibbons et al. 1994) – which says that the hitherto sacrosanct boundaries around disciplines are themselves undergoing fragmentation. According to this school of thought, the most important intellectual developments in fundamental research tend to take place less in the heartland of the disciplines. Rather, they are to be found on what one of our colleagues has recently termed "the developmental periphery" (Clark 1998).

Essentially, this argument says that innovative breakthroughs are more likely to occur at the interstitial points where different and established disciplines meet. Classic examples of this process in the sciences have been molecular biology, biophysics, bio-engineering or, for instance, medical computing. From this point of departure a whole spate of observations has followed, on the way research in the natural sciences is organised and, just as significant from our point of view, on the permanence of such arrangements. This is hugely important because, in our perceptions of our present state, we take for granted that the intellectual maturity of our domain ought to take us firmly along the path which leads towards a permanent and enduring process of coalescence and that coalescence ought to find its ultimate expression and success within the classic Departmental, School or Faculty structure.

Yet, the very point which lies at the centre of the thesis advanced by some students of the sociology of science is precisely that these self-same organisational forms do not tend to work in favour of interstitial break throughs. They are, so the proponents of what is becoming to be known as "Mode 2" science (Gibbons et al. 1994) point out, on the contrary, somewhat of a stumbling bloc.

The organisational pattern they suggest is most propitious to the development of trans- and interdisciplinary fields rather is to be found in task-oriented groupings, a species of task force or project group, a coalition in the exact meaning of that term; to wit, a coming together to fulfil a specified end. Once that is attained, the individuals concerned either revert to their former intellectual domiciliation or, if further work in the domain is to be undertaken, they then regroup, possibly with a slightly different line-up of skills, depending on the nature of the task to hand (Gibbons 1995).

Not surprisingly, such radicalism lends itself to all manner of criticism, not least of which that patterns of organisation that may be valid for the natural, exact and biological sciences do not always lend themselves to the social sciences and humanities; that the type, form and pace of intellectual production in the social sciences and humanities are indeed very different; and that arrangements such as these may go very far indeed in adding to the degree of precariousness which is itself one of the less noted, but in the long run no less deleterious, trends to beset the academic estate as a consequence of the mercantilisation of the university. Criticisms such as these are not to be dismissed lightly and most especially so given that, with certain notable exceptions, the overwhelming majority of those working, publishing and conducting research in the general domain of higher education tend to hail from the social sciences and the humanities.

4.9   A delightful paradox

However, whilst sharing many of the misgivings which our community may well feel about such developments, my point lies elsewhere. Principally, it lies in two aspects; the first is that the conviction of some that maturity in our domain should lead on to higher education studies formed into departmental and faculty structures may well be yesterday's vision. The second is the concomitant of this assertion. In our present state of organisation – or its noteworthy absence – we are perhaps nearer than we thought to that pattern of organisation which in the domain of the "hard" sciences appears to be the emerging and dominant form of research organisation.

If such an assertion is sustainable, then we find ourselves in a situation of extreme and perhaps even delightful paradox: by standing still whilst all others around us change, we have reached a point where, through no fault of our own, the very condition of creative "disorder" which some of our members bewail, is nearer by far to the "flexible" model which stands as the "cutting edge" in certain other fields of research. The cyclical vision applied to the history of the organisation of knowledge is not without certain advantages!

In putting this latter interpretation forward, I have little expectation that it will, in the long run, solve the issue of whether the studies of higher education ought to build up a series of "core fields", still less whether it should do so on the basis of certain formally recognised methodological principles or whether the problem should be solved by having recourse to a species of "cultural revolution" and "letting a thousand flowers – or journals, or perspectives – bloom". The latter is a healthy development in itself. And anyway, there is not much that could be done to call a halt to it, even if that were desirable – which most definitely it is not.

4.10 The exploration of alternatives, the avoidance of ignominy

What I am seeking to do, however, is to spare our community the ignominy of falling into the selfsame trap that has served to hobble the most essential debates in higher education policy these fifteen years past. This trap takes the form of the parrot-like squawk: "There is no alternative." Of course, there are alternatives. Their raising, their posing, their investigation and their testing are precisely what democracy, science, scholarship and teaching are about. And as fundamental issues, they cannot therefore fail to apply to our domain as well. The question is whether in debating them they provide us with greater insight into the nature and the task of our community; whether such a debate opens up new paths of development or permits us, temporarily, to close out old ones; in short, to assess the health, wellbeing and the type of work, whether theoretical or practical, those engaged in the study of higher education may – and should make – to the shaping of what is increasingly acknowledged as the institutional heart of the knowledge economy – namely, higher education itself.

If we conduct our debate simply with reference to the organisational forms – or for that matter, their institutional location – of yesteryear, however much of a desirable advance upon our present lot they might appear to us to be, we are by my book, deliberately and knowingly locking ourselves into our very own, self-imposed and latter-day version of an Orthodoxy; that is, excluding alternatives by rounding on the heretical. We are, in effect, saying that there is only one road to salvation, to standing and to excellence. There is only one route by which this may be achieved and organised. Clearly, this is not so. But, more devastating by far, if we fail to entertain alternative visions of the shape of things to come, we show ourselves unwilling to draw certain conclusions from our own work – which is ridiculous – or from the work of colleagues in close, if not convergent, fields – which is downright insulting. If those of us whose scholarly interests place us in the realm of seeking theoretical insights and understanding of the complex world of higher education, are not prepared to consider what the implications our research has for the way we go about our business, is there much chance that others will take us seriously when we suggest our findings have an important bearing on how they do theirs? Fellow physicians, let us heal ourselves.

There is good reason why this matter deserves our earnest attention and thought and never more so than now. Before going into why this is so and what its consequences are likely to be for the institutional siting of our domain, I want to make three conceptual distinctions in relation to the type of work involved in the study of higher education. Put succinctly, these are:

1. The advancement of knowledge through the development and testing of theory. Within this type of activity, naturally the imperative of elaborating new theories and explanations is the essential condition and prime task of work at this level. Were we to content ourselves simply with ascertaining the relevance or impertinence of theories already in place or mechanically and laboriously applying them incrementally across an infinity of sectors, levels, or institutional forms, we would indeed leave ourselves open to the charge – literally – of being unimaginative mechanicals. *Bis repetita non placent.* Enquiry at this level is predominantly driven internally either by the intellectual dynamic of the particular discipline or perspective dominant within a research centre or by the evolving scholarly interests of individuals within such a siting. Or, as a further possibility, it is generated as an offshoot of a long-term research programme undertaken by a research team. Some may call this "free" research inasmuch as the topic, theme, design and treatment are wholly set out, in first instance, by those who will conduct the investigation.

2. The development of institutional intelligence. There are two aspects to this particular type of work. The first is the development of intelligence about the institution which may range from the systemic level i.e. the university as an institution, down to individual base units. The second element is the development of intelligence for an institution which, equally may find support and backing from inter governmental bodies, through national cen-

tral administration down to the individual establishment. The basic feature of this type of work is not that it rules out the possibility of new theoretical insights and interpretations but that they are primarily subordinate to the task or to the mandate as negotiated and defined by the institution for which and by which the project has been commissioned. Choice of perspective, the type of theories to be tested are no longer wholly dependent on the free choice of a research centre or its members. Design and interpretation are subject to negotiation with the external party. Another name for this activity would be "commissioned research".

3. The "Servicing Function". The main line of distinction between work that falls into this category and the development of institutional intelligence lies in the fact that the conditions under which "servicing" is performed are almost wholly defined and set out by the external commissioning agency. Those engaged on such labour may indeed take the risk of using the exercise to test theory. But they do so at their risks and perils so long as such a specific activity has not been stipulated by the outside agency. The essential characteristic of work which corresponds to the "service function" lies in its purpose which is to gather and to collate information, usually of a highly factual and empirical nature, within a framework wholly determined from outside. The design of the study as too the interpretations and the purposes to which it shall be put, rest exclusively within the purlieu of those contracting it out. In effect and as its name implies, the "servicing function" is academia's form of "out sourcing". It is a particularly curtailed form of "contract research" in which the role of those fulfilling it, is largely confined to acting as the drawers of data and the hewers of statistics.

4.11 The use of blunt instruments

Clearly, these categories are not exclusive. Nor for that matter are they overly subtle or nuanced. In this exercise of institutional cartography, they have their uses *en attendant mieux*. The main use is heuristic in the sense that such a classification, in addition to allowing individual organised clusters of those working on higher education to be analysed in terms of the type of research they are undertaking at a given point in time, should be able to show us what could be done, were a more satisfactory instrument to be developed. The justification for such an instrument, though it does not have to be in this exact though somewhat blunt form, is not hard to find. To continue with the analogy of map-making, it provides us with a scale of activities which would permit us to characterise formal Centres, research units or institute-based clusters, to identify spatially those variations and commonalties expressed in terms of the type of work and the balance between the different types on which they are engaged. Agreed, many methodological details

would have to be worked out; for instance, are the individual activities –
knowledge advancement, institutional intelligence and the servicing function
– to be quantified in terms of individual projects, in terms of the numbers of
staff engaged on them as a percentage of all staff available in the unit, or in
terms of income generation?

These are rather important considerations since depending on how they
are operationalised, so our map will, not astoundingly, display a very different topography. Nor should we forget that implicit in this classification is a
certain value stance which, whilst probably shared by those active in research, is not necessarily supported to the same extent by practitioners:
namely, that advancement of theory carries greater weight than either institutional intelligence or servicing. In these wicked days, it is eminently reasonable to put more weight upon such "entrepreneurial" aspects as revenue
generation. Still, even if that should be so, it would be a significant finding
indeed, were our community to turn out to be driven by *amor pecuniae*
rather than *amor scientiae*.

4.12 Dire warnings

Before we become unduly enthusiastic about what can be accomplished
by this most primitive taxonomy, it as well to remind ourselves that on the
first time round, what ever is revealed has to be explained as well as described. Different national systems place very different boundaries – and
thus siting – around certain policy related elements in higher education. In
some, highly centralised systems of higher education, much of the work associated with the function of "institutional intelligence" tends not to be
farmed out to the university or to university-based research units. Rather, it
is jealously guarded as part of the national planning process or carried out
deep in the heart of the appropriate ministry (Neave 1997). One would expect therefore, that one feature of the work done by organised clusters in
such a setting would be either its concentration on the "servicing function"
or, at the other extreme, on the "advancement of knowledge". Conversely,
one might advance the notion that in those systems where "institutional intelligence" has long been a function of the higher education system, this activity would be reflected in a more balanced "task profile" of research units
specialised in the higher education domain.

What has to be borne in mind, and it is as well to remind ourselves, is
that by its nature, such an instrument will tend to emphasis what we hy-
pothesise are common traits. But, whilst it may well identify such commonalties across frontiers, it is singularly powerless to explain precisely why
these common traits are shared. Information unadorned by explanation tends
to be a truly tedious exercise unless, that is, it is seen as an explorative

probe, identifying on our globe of higher education studies only the grossest of features, the equivalent in mediaeval map-making to where swamps were to be found, where one might expect to come across hideous Basilisks and where there were unknown lands. In effect, anyone launching forth on such an undertaking would do well to look upon such instruments as "hypothesis generating", the explanation being provided by qualitative data and deep contextual knowledge, pursued, developed and applied in parallel.

4.13 La force du destin

With this yardstick to hand – or something resembling it – we are now in a position to turn to other issues which merit our attention. They deserve our keenest scrutiny because, whilst speculative in the sense that their consequences are by no means clear, it is nevertheless not misplaced to see them has having the potential to shape the spatial setting and task profile of higher education research in the near future. *Un nain averti en vaut deux.*

It is a banality to say that the amount of work available most assuredly influences where the study of higher education is undertaken. What type of work has been available? Of that, we have a good idea, just as we do about the current situation, though it is always good to know more. But what about the future? Will there be "work for the working man to do"? What is the likely nature of that work – the advancement of knowledge, institutional intelligence or servicing? On the basis of hopefully educated guesswork and in the light of recent trends, what may we say about where whatever work is to be had, might be located?

There are excellent reasons for being optimistic about the quantity of work that is likely to be available to the students of higher education, though whether one should be equally sanguine about the nature of what is to be done, depends of course, on how one views one's particular institutional niche in the ecology of higher education studies. First, let us simply note once again the influx of new perspectives into our domain during the past decade. This would not have happened were there not a demand for their expertise. Second, the rise of what has been called the "Evaluative State" has not only affected how universities are assessed and their performance and their "productivity" pinpointed. It has also nurtured – and given organised form to – this activity (Neave 1998). Indeed, a very good case could be made for saying that one result of the Evaluative State has been to draw – albeit perhaps temporarily – more people into an activity intimately associated with higher education studies than we are sometimes willing to recognise. If the truth were out, evaluation and assessment studies, supremely the realm of the research technician though they are, stand as an important exemplar of the expanding boundaries of our domain. By the same token, they are also an illustration of an important shift in its work profile through the reinforcement of the emphasis contained in "institutional intelligence" and "servicing". Drawing up the formulae for institutional evaluation and the monitoring of systems development are themselves good operationalisations of these two functions.

The rise of the Evaluative State is not the only development to have direct bearing on our collective fate and to be a challenge to our intelligence, technical or spiritual. There is also the parallel phenomenon, often couched in terms of the change in relationship between government and higher education from "state control" to "state supervision" (van Vught 1989; Neave & van Vught 1994) and its concomitant range of policies – diversification in sources of finance and of authority, enhanced responsibility for institutions to determine their particular knowledge profile, the notion of students as consumers and, last but not least, the rise of a "stakeholder society".

4.14 Intelligent risk-taking

All these initiatives have the makings of extreme volatility, and anticipate a degree of uncertainty which some amongst our more senior statesmen are now coming round to view as a permanent condition (Clark 1997), so much so that planning the future of an institute of higher education is beginning to be seen in terms of a "risk-taking" activity! But the capacity to take risks – or for that matter to avoid useless ones – rests without a shadow of a doubt on the flow of appropriate information, appropriate as to time, relevance, quality and precision. In short, it rests with awful weight upon "institutional intelligence" in the sense I have defined it and hopefully too in the sense of collective acumen. How far individual universities or for that matter, individual sectors or national systems of higher education are well geared towards devolving that function of research *qua* "institutional intelligence" away from central national administration and seating it in individual establishments is, for many of the major systems of Western Europe, the question of the hour.

The question which our community has to face is whether such a delegation of functions – or seen from our point of view, the challenge of providing such "intelligence" – will in truth be thrust upon us? Might it not fall within the purlieu of institutional administration? In short, will the quite massive growth in the need to know what exactly is going on – the basic and abiding issue in mass systems of higher education – be a task for the higher education research community or, on the contrary, will it serve to bolster the weight of the practitioner constituency? This is no idle point. For whilst it anticipates a situation within the research community which, potentially at least, is highly dynamic, it also raises once again the delicate question of the balance of power and standing between scholars and practitioners. Nor does the "press for intelligence", great though it is, necessarily mean that our fortunes are made. Is our scholarly community, even if defined *lato sensu*, sufficiently numerous to fulfil this task, assuming that it would be assigned it and assuming also our community would be willing to take it on?

This is not as straightforward as it seems. In the first place, lament it though we may, the ranks of those who have made a full-time career in the study of higher education – as opposed to its administration – are by no means plethoric. In the second place, it is a major assumption indeed to believe that our community would be prepared to live wholly on the basis of contract research, though one has equally to admit that this has become a way of life for some of the most enterprising of our colleagues. And finally, there is the most ticklish point of all. If the "press for intelligence" may cause rejoicing, the community of higher education studies is far from alone in the metaphorical rubbing of hands and the stretching out of itching palms. Information is today's most valuable form of capital. And whilst we might still cleave to the notion of scholarly repute and excellence as the prime coin in our realm, there are others for whom a claimed expertise in those fields we reckon our own, brings a very different form of reward.

4.15 Consultancy: a limicole world

One of the less noted developments on the fringes of our domain has been the steady encroachment over the past decade or so of consultancy bodies. Some are organised units in large international accountancy firms, specialised in giving expensive advice to the business sector and whose penetration into the university world is seen amongst other things, as an aid in nudging that institution towards "an enterprise culture". Others are individuals, recently retired from posts of varying eminence in higher education, who seek a supplement to their pensions. Yet a third group springs from the world of commerce and who, having taken early retirement often from multinationals, now seeks to put off life's tedium. Other variants exist: groups created by individual firms to bend institutional leadership to their way of thinking and finally, higher education's equivalent of the market research firm – cuttingly described by our French colleagues as *"boîtes d'études"*.

Many are the interpretations that may be laid upon this limicole world. It may be construed as an expression of the growing influence the private sector exerts upon the nation's higher education; as a derivative form of intermediary body; or as an inverse version of "stakeholder society", one which has a stake in the university as a source of revenue rather than claiming a stake as a result of having endowed it with spectacular largess. Call it what you will, it is a genus of not inconsiderable ambivalence. Where it does not claim knowledge of a technical nature, it trades upon personally uncertified experience. It has the practitioner constituency amongst its major clientèle. And, most assuredly, it dwells amongst the ranks of the profit-making. More to the point, however, it is also a competitor for certain types of knowledge "brokering" and most especially at the level of "intelligence" and "servicing".

4.16 Conclusion

The mass university both generates and consumes information. The need to know more about itself is, as many have argued, a prior condition successfully to meet those current priorities which society, or the interests that currently set contemporary values, place upon higher education. In principle, this situation holds out immense potential for the community which studies higher education. By the same token, however, it is also an opportunity fraught with tension. Such tensions do not stem entirely from competition for resources, though as I have pointed out, this is both present today and likely to be more feral in the future. They are also deeply set within the boundaries of our domain, whether we care to define it in terms of the disciplines and perspectives which figure therein or whether, as we are currently attempting to do, it is defined in terms of its institutional location. Even if we circumscribe our community to those within the higher education system, the fundamental duality between those engaged in research and those engaged in the "practical" aspects of administration, remains. Indeed, the locational dimension serves to bring it out even more sharply. Questions of boundary and "turf" extend to areas of work. Even if agreement were to be reached so that, for instance, research units and higher education based centres would enjoy an exclusive responsibility for "the advancement of knowledge", the task of providing "institutional intelligence" is likely to remain a function bitterly fought over, not least because, as we have noted earlier, it is here that those associated with newly emergent and specialist responsibilities in institutional administration seek to forge themselves a professional legitimacy. The same might be said of the "servicing" function as a zone of conflict, particularly if it carries hefty recompense with it.

But just as the problematic associated with the institutional location of higher education research has caused us to reconsider another aspect in the inherent dynamics of our domain, so it has also impelled us to take account of one constituency – the regiment of consultants – which whilst institutionally located outside higher education nevertheless, like the camel, has its nose firmly under the university tent flap. It is a matter of personal generosity whether this constituency is deemed to be of the world of higher education studies. One cannot contest, however, that it is in the general milieu and living well. It existence poses, once again, an essential question which is probably more an issue generic to higher education in a "service economy" than it is an issue wholly specific to our particular domain. That issue is whether reconsideration of the outer limits of our field is not called for over and above the criteria of discipline, field and location. I say this is a generic issue for the simple reason that the consultancy nexus may be seen as part of that broader phenomenon which some are pleased to identify with the "post modern" university, namely the blurring of operational and definitional boundaries around functions and fields of study once clearly demarcated (Scott, in press).

By mentioning the issue of demarcation, we return full circle to the question of how best to achieve the optimal organisation of our domain. The press to do so, just as the ways that might serve this end, have certainly taxed us over the years. They will continue to do so. The prospect of increasing competition from within – and no less from those interests that lie beyond – the currently acknowledged frontiers of our college , will serve as a powerful spur to this end. Our fate as an area of scholarly investigation certainly depends on the intelligence with which this challenge is handled. It depends also on the type of work by which we would wish our reputations to stand and to be judged. In this, as in the broader issue of how to hasten maturity, we should perhaps not be entirely forgetful of the infinite wisdom contained in the limerick by the American poet and publicist, Ogden Nash. It is called "On Growing Old."

> I have a bone to pick with Fate.
> "Come here and tell me, girlie,
> Have I merely matured late
> Or simply rotted – early?"

REFERENCES

Becher, A. (1992). 'Introduction', in Clark, B.R. and Neave, G. (eds.). *Encyclopedia of Higher Education*, 4 vols. Oxford: Pergamon Press. vol. 3, section 5, 'Disciplinary perspectives on higher education', pp. 1763 -1776.

Clark, B. R. (1995). *Places of Inquiry.* Berkeley/Los Angeles/London: University of California Press.

Clark, B. R. (1997). 'Common problems and adaptive responses in the universities of the world: organising for change', *Higher Education Policy*, 10 (3-4).

Clark , B. R. (1998). *Creating Entrepreneurial Universities: organisational pathways of transformation.* Oxford : Pergamon for IAU Press.

De Groof, J., Neave, G. and Svec, J. (1998). *Democracy and Governance in Higher Education.* Dordrecht : Kluwer International Law Series.

Gibbons, M. (1995). 'The University as an instrument for the development of science and basic research: the implications of Mode 2 Science', in Dill, D. D. and Sporn, B. [eds.] *Emerging Patterns of Social Demand and University Reform: through a glass darkly.* Oxford : Pergamon for IAU Press, pp. 90-104.

Gibbons, M., Limoges, C., Nowotny, H., Schwartzman, S., Scott, P. and Trow, M. (1994). *The New Production of Knowledge: the dynamics of Science and research in contemporary societies.* Newbury Park, CA: Sage.

Neave, G. (1997). 'Estar advertido es la mejor defensa. La Universidad como objeto de investigacion.' Paper presented to the Segundo Encuentro Nacional, Universidad de Buenos Aires (Argentine) November 26th-28th 1997.

Neave, G. (1998). 'The Evaluative State reconsidered', *European Journal of Education,* 33 (3).

Neave, G. and van Vught, F. (1994). *Higher Education and Government Relationships across Three Continents: the winds of change.* Oxford : Pergamon Press for the International Association of Universities.

Ruegg, W. (ed.) (1992). *History of the Universities in Europe, vol.1. The Mediaeval Period.* Cambridge: Cambridge University Press.

Scott, P. (2000). 'Higher Education Research in the light of a dialogue between policy-makers and practitioners' , in Sadlak, J. and Teichler, U. (eds.) *Higher Education Research: its relationship to policy and practice.* Oxford : Pergamon Books for IAU Press.

Teichler, U. (2000) 'The relationships between higher education research and higher education policy and practice: the researcher's perspective', in Sadlak, J. and Teichler, U. (eds.) *Higher Education Research: its relationship to policy and practice.* Oxford: Pergamon for IAU Press.

Van Vught, F. (1989). *Innovation in Higher Education.* London: Jessica Kingsley.

PART TWO

HIGHER EDUCATION RESEARCH: COUNTRIES AND CASES

Chapter 5

The Origins and Structures of Research on Higher Education in the United States

JAMES S. FAIRWEATHER
Center for the Study of Advanced Learning Systems, Michigan State University, MI, East Lansing, USA

For almost two decades the American higher education research community has been engaged in two debates: determining appropriate methodological (and philosophical) approaches to research and increasing the relevance of research to policy-makers of all types. The first conflict is symbolized by the ongoing debate between the likes of Lincoln and Guba (1985), who propose a qualitative research approach based on a relativistic philosophical position, and Phillips (1992), who rejects both the relativistic position and its accompanying singular devotion to qualitative research. The second debate is symbolized by Keller's (1985) criticism of the lack of relevance of higher education research to institutional, state, and federal policy-makers, and by Terenzini's (1996) more recent lament citing the lack of progress of higher education researchers in responding to Keller's criticisms.

Lost in these debates is an understanding of research themes, including how they are selected and the consequences of this selection process for policy. Also missing is an understanding of the mechanisms to fund research and the interrelationships between themes, funding mechanisms, and organizations that carry out the research. Finally, the portrayal of the "conflict" between different philosophical and methodological positions is frequently inaccurate, which makes it difficult to find a happy medium between themes, methodologies, and policy. The purpose of this paper is to address these issues by exploring the evolution of higher education research in the United States.

S. Schwarz and U. Teichler (eds.), The Institutional Basis of Higher Education Research, 77–85.
© 2000 *Kluwer Academic Publishers. Printed in the Netherlands.*

5.1 Evolution of higher education research in the United States

Higher education research in the United States did not evolve from a systematic effort to promote needed research by federal or state governments, state systems of higher education, individual institutions, disciplinary societies, or specific academic programs. Instead, research on higher education originally was carried out by a few individuals trained in various disciplines whose interest included colleges and universities. Authors such as Paul Dressel (1958) (trained in mathematics), David Riesman (1969) (sociology and law), and Lewis Mayhew (1969) (history) applied their disciplinary approaches to make pronouncements about the past and future directions of higher education. The topics they selected and the methodologies they employed reflected personal interest and training. As an example, in *The Academic Revolution* Jencks and Riesman (1969) used a sociological analysis of status to explain why small colleges and universities attempt to mimic their more prestigious counterparts.

Eventually the growth of American colleges and universities and the public investment in them required institutions to develop some type of systematic data collection. By 1987 the US had 3,389 accredited colleges and universities, 1,548 publicly funded (primarily by state subsidies supplemented by modest tuition revenues from students) and 1,841 funded privately (primarily by student tuition and endowment revenues) (Carnegie 1987). Federal and state governmental agencies started requiring colleges and universities to collect and deliver certain types of information, both to obtain continuing state subsidies (which applied to public institutions) and to become eligible for student financial aid (which applied to both public and private or independent institutions). Examples of required data included enrollment projections, number of faculty, financial status, and accreditation status. At the same time, the Carnegie Commission for the Advancement of Teaching and other non-profit organizations interested in higher education emerged to advance the dialogue about various policy themes. These external pressures led to the development of institutional research offices, which were then expanded by colleges and universities to perform various self-studies needed for accreditation and for institutional policy-making.[1]

The Office of Planning and Budgets (OPB) at Michigan State University is the modern version of an Office of Institutional Research. The OPB reports to the chief academic officer, the provost. OPB functions include budget planning and development, facilities planning and space management, institutional research, profile reports on faculty and student trends, and long range planning. The profile reports are prepared for state and federal governmental agencies. The other functions are primarily designed to assist in administrative decisions and planning.

During the 1960s, a few universities also created doctoral programs and research centers in higher education, the most prominent being those at Penn State University, the University of Michigan, and the University of California at Los Angeles. At Penn State University, for example, the Vice President for Academic Affairs (or Provost) created the Center for the Study of Higher Education (CSHE), an independent research center for higher education studies, in 1969 to supplement its graduate programs in higher education. The CSHE research agenda focused originally on institutional research and on state policy issues. Over time, Penn State developed its own internal research capacity, the Office of Planning, Budget and Assessment, which freed the CSHE to focus on national research issues. CSHE staff held (and still hold today) both faculty and research associate rank with the tenure-track faculty appointments being administered by the College of Education. The Higher Education Program in the College of Education works with CSHE to offer masters and doctoral programs in higher education.

In addition to training the large number of administrators required to manage and lead the growth industry of higher education in the 1960s, these doctoral programs also prepared a group of individuals to carry out and expand research on higher education. Originally the research carried out by doctoral students in many of these academic programs focused on local issues, such as those related to institutional research and institutional histories. Over time, these academic programs, which have proliferated to their present number of about 150, succeeded in creating and legitimizing a separate research culture, embodied by the Association for the Study of Higher Education. This research culture responds to traditional academic norms that emphasize individual research productivity and accomplishment (Fairweather 1996). In this climate, professionally-trained higher education researchers, whether faculty members, members of independent research organizations, or institutional researchers, achieve visibility through publishing, obtaining externally-funded grants, giving invited presentations, and so forth. For many of these professionals, especially those with some involvement in academe, this evolution has reinforced the pursuit of individual research agendas with less attention paid to broader policy concerns.

In the United States, we are left today with at least four distinct research traditions in higher education, each with different institutional and spiritual affiliations:
- Offices of Institutional Research
- Academic Programs and Research Centers in Higher Education
- Non-profit Policy Research Organizations
- State and Federal Government Agencies.

Within the academic setting, we have offices of institutional research (e.g., the Office of Planning and Budgets at Michigan State University) and academic programs or academic research centers in higher education (e.g., the Center for the Study of Higher Education at Penn State University). The former responds to institutional needs for information, whereas the latter focuses on preparing future researchers (and administrators) for independent careers (often as faculty members). Both groups have their own professional affiliation, the former with the Association for Institutional Research (AIR) and the latter with both the Association for the Study of Higher Education and the American Educational Research Association-Division J.

Because of their focus either on local institutional issues or on issues of interest to the individual researcher, neither institutional research nor research-based academic programs in higher education are particularly useful to help federal or state government policy-makers address difficult policy issues. To fill this gap, organizations such as Stanford Research Institute (now SRI International), RAND Corporation, the American Institutes of Research, the National Center for Higher Education Management Systems (NCHEMS), and the National Institute for Public Policy and Higher Education created research units to carry out major federal and state government research initiatives. These organizations focus less on promoting the reputations of individual researchers and more on enhancing the credibility of the research organization. As one example, SRI International is a non-profit research institute employing about 3,000 professionals. Encompassing fields as diverse as computer engineering and policy research in education, SRI focuses its research on solving client problems, including those of state and federal education officials. As another example, the National Center for Higher Education Management Systems focuses on management consulting to help colleges and universities as well as state government agencies to design effective solutions to their problems. Both SRI and NCHEMS address problems and incorporate research techniques not typically found in higher education academic programs.

Finally, many federal and state governmental offices also created their own research staff to gather information crucial to informing legislative actions. The Pennsylvania Office of Legislative Research, for example, was created by the Pennsylvania legislature to carry out analyses relevant to state policy considerations. Similarly, the California Department of Education maintains a large staff of researchers and analysts to address questions posed by the state government.

5.2 Funding mechanisms and selection of research themes

Perhaps the best way to understand the "system" of higher education research in the United States is to examine the various mechanisms for funding research:

- Institutional Support
- Open-ended Grant Programs
- Targeted Grant Programs
- Collaborative Agreements
- Contracts.

Individual faculty members often pursue research without any external funding. Instead their subsidy consists of small grants from their own universities or some form of release time (or no subsidy at all). This type of research follows the traditional model found in the liberal arts, where research is primarily a function of individual interest and the typical method of data collection is archival, that is, from library resources.

One type of funded research follows the same appeal to individual investigators although the focus is not limited to academic faculty. Open-ended grants announcements, small or large, are used by various non-profit foundations as well as state and federal agencies to foster research. Other than specifying that the research involve higher education, for example, open-ended grants announcements rely on the individual researcher (or sometimes a small research team) to propose a topic of interest. Several grant programs from the Spencer Foundation, a non-profit organization that funds research, follow this approach. Because of the focus on individual ideas and on the credentials of the applicants, academic faculty (and a few well-known individuals working in non-profit organizations) have the advantage in these grant programs.

Other types of grant programs, usually (but not always) authorized by federal government agencies, are more targeted. These programs may specify a set of topics of interest to the agency and ask proposers to come up with a particular research problem and approach. This funding mechanism is more in line with policy issues of interest, although the funding agency typically maintains a rather loose relationship with the researcher or research team relying instead on field-generated ideas to address the general policy issue. Depending on the size of the proposed work, non-profit research centers can effectively compete with college and university faculty for these types of awards.

In contrast to grant programs, funding agencies use collaborative agreements and contracts to address immediate policy concerns. Collaborative agreements specify a joint working relationship between a funding agency (governmental or non-profit) and a researcher or research team. The topic area typically is specified but the research project or projects are worked out jointly between the parties. The National Center for Postsecondary Improvement (NCPI), funded by the US Department of Education for five years to explore a variety of agreed upon topics, is an example of this type of funding relationship. Managed by Stanford University in conjunction with the University of Pennsylvania and the University of Michigan, the NCPI covers six research areas developed in conjunction with staff from the US Department of Education: organizational improvement, the transition from school to work, postsecondary markets, faculty development, student learning and assessment, and productivity and accountability.

Funding agencies prefer to use contracts when they want the strictest control over problem specification and the approach to conducting the research. A request for proposal for research contracts often defines the policy problem, specifies the work needed to address the problem, and leaves it to various competitors to propose the best way of carrying out the research. Sometimes contracts are used by federal agencies to supplement their own work force rather than to carry out policy research *per se*. For example, the National Center for Education Statistics, a part of the US Department of Education, hires an outside contractor to carry out its mandate to gather periodic data on college and university faculty because it does not have sufficient staff to complete the work on its own. For both contracts and collaborative agreements, the larger the project and the more specific the time constraints, the more competitive are larger (often non-academic) research groups.

For-profit companies also fund research projects. Although industry traditionally has had limited involvement in educational research, increased interest in the Internet, WEB-based instruction, and improved professional education such as in engineering (National Research Council 1985) may well lead to increased involvement by industry in educational research. If funded by non-profit corporate-based foundations, the research mechanism resembles traditional grant programs. Otherwise, the research may be proprietary, focused on providing information for the funding corporation. As an example, IBM funded several research projects to determine the academic quality of doctoral programs in computer science with an end goal of improving the personnel recruiting policies of IBM rather than enhancing general knowledge about how to measure the quality of academic programs (Fairweather 1983).

5.3   Dissemination of research results

Each type of funding mechanism and each type of participant – whether an individual faculty member or a non-profit research organization – relies on different avenues for disseminating research results. These avenues range from in-house reports for private corporations and state and federal governmental agencies, to research reports distributed to libraries and a select set of recipients, to data tapes and videotapes and software, to presentations and speeches, to refereed articles and books. Occasionally the researcher or research group may be asked to testify to a legislature (state or federal government) or to present the results to agency staff. The combination of a loosely-coupled research community using diverse dissemination approaches, an ever-increasing number of journals, increased internationalization of research, and a growing "hidden" literature consisting of technical reports and memoranda makes it difficult for higher education research in the United States to achieve a collective, large-scale effect.

5.4   Cumulative result

In aggregate, this decentralized, disparate approach to funding and conducting research has the advantage of being fairly responsive to new research topics (and potentially to emerging policy initiatives). It spreads research to a substantial number of organizations and individuals, thereby maintaining or even increasing the size of the research community in higher education and enabling researchers to establish successful careers. This diversity in funding and in dissemination has the disadvantage of making it difficult to achieve systemic effects, to foster a shared information base, and to form meaningful linkages between policy-makers, funding agencies, and the full array of organizations carrying out higher education research.

5.5   Research training and practice: the need for a new approach

Understanding the research training in higher education (and related) doctoral education is equally fundamental to understanding the American higher education research enterprise. As doctoral programs in higher education increasingly mimic those in the social sciences, students are trained in specific research methods and taught to adapt their research problems to those methods. Whether applying survey techniques, traditional case studies, ethnographies, or econometrics, the focus of research training is on the method – sometimes only one method – more often than on application and interpretation.

The current philosophical disagreements within the higher education research community do not help. The quantitative-qualitative debate is not the only one at play. Qualitative researchers are often at odds with each other, one tradition following a model to identify generalizable findings (Miles and Huberman 1994) and the other denying that generalizability is possible (Lincoln and Guba 1985).

None of these developments leads to a coherent research approach, one based on identifying problems for study and then selecting an appropriate methodology. Nor does mimicking the traditional social sciences help us evolve analytical strategies more in line with solving important problems in higher education. In particular, traditional analytical strategies do not incorporate a systems perspective (Senge *et al.* 1990), which limits the potential policy utility of the research.

As an example of the limitations of traditional analytical strategies in higher education, consider Bowen and Sosa's (1989) attempt to project faculty shortages in the late 1980s. Applying sophisticated supply-and-demand econometric models based on enrollment trends and faculty age distributions, Bowen and Sosa anticipated large shortages of faculty in specific disciplines. Their projections fell far short because the supply-demand model did not incorporate or anticipate strategies that institutions might follow to fill personnel needs. Rather than replacing full-time faculty who retire, college and university leaders have replaced full-time retiring faculty with a collection of part-time faculty or simply have increased class sizes to accommodate more students. The lesson here is: However well a research method is applied, if it is a bad fit with the problem being studied or does not lead us to understand the implications of the research for future administrative and policy actions, then the approach is inadequate.

An alternative approach being considered at the Center for the Study of Advanced Learning Systems (ALS) at Michigan State University is to replace traditional courses in research methods with interdisciplinary policy-oriented research courses. These new courses will combine research design and analytical techniques with specific policy issues rather than keeping them separate. ALS faculty also will develop research apprenticeships to enable students to experience research in real settings. This model, or another like it, is necessary to restore the relevance of research to the practice of higher education.

NOTES

1   Accreditation is the process whereby academic institutions and selected programs achieve at least a minimally acceptable level of performance. Institutional self-study data are combined with information gathered by external experts during site visits to determine ac-

creditation status, which is reviewed every five years by different regional accreditation bodies and by professional societies.

REFERENCES

Bowen, W., and Sosa, J. (1989). *Prospects for Faculty in the Arts and Sciences: A study of factors affecting demand and supply, 1987 to 2012*. Princeton, N.J.: Princeton University Press.

Carnegie Foundation for the Advancement of Teaching (1987). *A Classification of Institutions of Higher Education*. Princeton, N.J.: Carnegie Foundation for the Advancement of Teaching.

Dressel, P. (1958). *Evaluation in the Basic College at Michigan State University*. New York: Harper.

Fairweather, J. (1983). *Ratings of Selected Programs in Engineering, Computer Science, and Business*. Menlo Park, CA.: SRI International.

Fairweather, J. (1996). *Faculty Work and Public Trust: Restoring the value of teaching and public service in American academic life*. Boston: Allyn and Bacon.

Jencks, C. and Riesman, D. (1969). *The Academic Revolution*. Garden City, N.J.: Doubleday.

Keller, G. (1985). 'Trees without fruit: the problem with research about higher education', *Change* 17: 7-10.

Lincoln, Y. and Guba, E. (1985). *Naturalistic Inquiry*. Beverly Hills.: Sage.

Mayhew, L. (1969). *Colleges Today and Tomorrow*. San Francisco: Jossey-Bass.

Miles, M. and Huberman, M. (1994). *Qualitative Data Analysis*. 2nd ed. London: Sage.

National Research Council (1985). *Engineering Education and Practice in the United States: Foundations of our techno-economic future*. Washington, D.C.: National Academy Press.

Phillips, D. (1992). *The Social Scientist's Bestiary: A guide to fabled threats to, and defenses of naturalistic social science*. New York: Pergamon.

Senge, P. et al. (1990). *The Fifth Discipline: The art and practice of the learning organization*. New York: Doubleday.

Chapter 6

Higher Education Research in the UK: A Short Overview and a Case Study

JOHN BRENNAN
Centre for Higher Education Research and Information, The Open University, London, United Kingdom

6.1 Introduction

This paper is in two parts. The first is a short overview of the institutional basis for higher education research in the UK. This is attempted schematically rather than descriptively. Details of individual research centres and programmes are not provided. Rather, the policy, funding and interest-group characteristics of the national and institutional contexts for higher education research are described and the problems and prospects which these pose for researchers are discussed. The case study of the second part of the paper examines the problems and prospects of one higher education research centre. It poses the question of whether hybrid forms of organisation are necessary in order to meet the distinctive features of higher education research.

6.2 A short overview

Within the UK, the institutional basis for research into higher education is fragmented. The few specialist "centres" which exist rarely employ more than a handful of researchers who typically are employed on contracts as short as the increasingly short-term projects on which they work. Permanent staff belonging to such centres usually have a "proper job" in university teaching or management with higher education research as a sideline. Opportunities for funded research studentships are few and far between.

However, the limitations of the institutional base do not seem to have prevented the development of an active higher education research commu-

S. Schwarz and U. Teichler (eds.), The Institutional Basis of Higher Education Research, 87–97.

nity within the UK. Several specialist journals exist, books are regularly published on higher education themes, the Society for Research into Higher Education has a membership in excess of 800, several hundreds of whom regularly attend its annual conference. Where do all the people who are contributing to these activities come from?

Part of the answer lies in one of the consequences of the increasing centralisation of management in British universities. In many universities, this has led to the creation of internal units concerned with institutional arrangements for such things as staff development, planning, institutional research and quality assurance. Primarily institutional support units, the staff employed by them have a mainly institutional loyalty rather than a subject affiliation. Backgrounds may be administrative or academic but the latter are not necessarily in any of the social science disciplines generally associated with higher education research. The possession of relevant postgraduate qualifications or training in research is rare. But the nature of the jobs in these institutional units disposes people towards an interest in higher education developments generally. It is an interest that tends to be practical rather than scientific, grounded in experience and current higher education politics rather than research and the academic literature in the field.

This wider higher education community may be interested in research into higher education although few of its members will be doing any research themselves. Who does the research? To answer this question, we must also ask who pays for the research. For research which extends beyond the boundaries of an individual institution, the answer is primarily government departments and the higher education funding agencies. This research tends to be of three sorts: (1) action and development oriented, concerned with influencing practice within institutions (e.g. by making courses more geared to the needs of employment); (2) part of the national policy formation process, informing national commissions, agencies and government departments (e.g. on access and participation policies); (3) evaluation studies, which may be concerned with the impact and value for money of activities carried out under (1) and (2).

These various kinds of studies are carried out by a very wide range of people, including management consultants. The results of these studies - reports to funding bodies, practical developments in institutions – may not be reported in journals or books or otherwise communicated to a wider research community. In many cases, the authors will not consider themselves part of, nor even be aware of the existence of, such a community. If they are aware of it, they may have little personal incentive to contribute to it. And in some cases, funders claim their ownership of the project results and prefer to control dissemination themselves rather than to cede it to the networks of journals and commercial publishers.

Alongside these policy-directed research activities is a much smaller volume of work funded by research councils and foundations. Although these kinds of studies are invariably carried out by experienced researchers, take account of the academic literature in the field and publish their results in the academic journals, there is an increasing tendency for the priorities of the councils and the foundations also to be influenced by contemporary policy agendas. For example, the Economic and Social Research Council has supported special research programmes on "the learning society" and "teaching and learning", both areas which are in vogue in British policy debates at the present time.

To complete the picture are the research and publications of the several scholars working in the higher education research field in the UK. Unencumbered by the pressures of managing large research centres, of the needs to secure funding for sizeable numbers of young researchers, of the problems of directing upwards of a dozen different research projects at any one time, they can be remarkably productive in their own writing and research.

Thus, the British higher education research community can be characterised as having primarily practical interests, few full-time trained researchers, limited funding opportunities for research which lies outside of short-term applied policy concerns, and is spread across higher education as a whole rather than being concentrated in a few specialist centres.

Nevertheless, a small number of specialist centres do exist. They can be found linked to or as part of education or social science departments in several universities. Occasionally they are free-standing. In the former case, the centres may employ few staff of their own but draw on the research interests of tenured academics in the host departments in a form of voluntary collaboration on projects and publications. The focus of centres of this kind tends to reflect the interests of its members. For the second, free-standing kind of centre, the focus is likely to derive from the need to survive, to secure funding from the limited opportunities which exist. To illustrate the dilemmas facing research centres of this kind in the UK, the rest of this paper will focus on one such centre, the author's own. In doing so, no claim to typicality is being made and there are some very specific historical factors at play in this particular case. Nevertheless, the problems and prospects of this centre derive from the broader environment for higher education research in the UK and, therefore, may be of general interest.

6.3 A case study

The short history of QSC[1] is a story of the uses of constructive ambiguity.[2] It is also a story of the effects of a change in organisational home on the work of a small group of higher education researchers. Part of the ambiguity of the story is whether the researchers are researchers at all and, if they are, how and when they became so. The story raises general issues about the funding and management of research into higher education and about the appropriateness of existing functional and organisational boundaries within higher education.

QSC was created in 1992 as part of the UK Open University. Its full name was the Quality Support Centre. It was located in central London in a building which housed several higher education organisations. It was some 50 miles away from the University's main campus. QSC was not part of the University's academic structure. It had a location of convenience as part of the Vice Chancellor's office. It was intended to be a self-financing unit of the University. Beyond that, its brief was unclear.

6.4   The current picture

In September 1998, QSC is still a self-financing unit and still formally part of the Vice Chancellor's office of the Open University. It remains based in central London but it has recently changed its name to the Centre for Higher Education Research and Information. It has eight staff and two main areas of research activity: higher education and work, quality assurance. It undertakes externally commissioned projects in those fields, its main funders being UK government and national higher education agencies, the European Union and other international bodies with interests in higher education. More than half of its current projects are outside the UK or have a strong international element. All projects have a policy or applied orientation, reflecting the interests of the funders.

As well as research projects, QSC engages in related activities such as conferences, publications and consultancies. These activities bring a number of benefits: promotional, networking, information-gathering. But above all they aim to cross-subsidise the research activities which are rarely able to recoup their full costs from their funders. The absence of core funding renders these non-research activities essential to QSC's financial viability. The funding base also makes it difficult for QSC's staff to engage in interest-led individual research and scholarship. Publications are mainly limited to project-based papers and reports.

Another feature of QSC's current activities is that they are mainly collaborative with other centres or organisations. This partly reflects the international nature of so much of the Centre's work but it also reflects the difficulties of building up core staffing when most of the Centre's income is short-term and insecure. For the same reason, QSC makes much use of part-time consultants to work on activities alongside its own staff.

6.5 Pre-history

QSC had an organisational existence prior to that provided by the Open University in 1992. The original staff of QSC had worked together in the Council for National Academic Awards (CNAA), a national accreditation and quality assurance body which served the large non-university sector of polytechnics and colleges in British higher education from 1964 to 1992. When the polytechnics achieved university status in 1992, the CNAA was wound up although some of its activities, functions and staff were taken over by other organisations.[3]

From the mid-1980s onwards, the CNAA had begun to place more emphasis on the support services which it provided for the polytechnics and colleges. As these institutions became more confident and experienced, the CNAA reduced its controls and complemented them by the provision of information and development services to help enable the institutions to take greater responsibility for their own quality and standards. By 1992, these services had been grouped organisationally within the CNAA under the generic heading of "quality support".

A number of features of the "quality support" services of CNAA should be mentioned. First, they were mainly funded out of CNAA's core income which came from student fees. Second, they were justified in terms of their "usefulness" to the polytechnics and colleges. Third, their organisation reflected the committee structure and "academic ownership" of the CNAA: committees comprising academics (members) from UK universities, polytechnics and colleges made the decisions and these were carried out by the CNAA's staff (officers). Fourth, most of the research projects ("development projects") funded by the CNAA were carried out, not by its own staff, but by groups of academics based in higher education institutions.

These characteristics of its mode of operation reflected the political circumstances in which the CNAA operated. There were sensitivities in the CNAA's relations with both government and the higher education institutions with which it worked. For the latter, the continued existence of the CNAA was an affront to their claims for autonomy and equality with the universities, their growing experience and maturity as institutions. At the same time, some of the specific activities of the CNAA were perceived by many in the institutions to be quite useful. Many of these were "quality support" activities.

For the staff working in "quality support" in the CNAA, the organisational context was one of political constraint. Sensitivities surrounding the role of the CNAA and its relations with institutions meant that all activities needed to be legitimised through Committee endorsement and support by senior management. Much time was spent in justification, in writing and rewriting objectives, in attempting to demonstrate "usefulness" and "appropriateness". Although several of the CNAA quality support staff had academic and research backgrounds, their prime role was administrative. Much of the work of the staff involved the coordination of a wide range of research and related activities supported by the CNAA across UK higher education.

6.6 Change of ownership

In the autumn of 1992, a small sub-group of the CNAA "quality support" staff began their employment by the Open University. The general brief was to "carry on the good work" of the CNAA in providing information and development services to UK higher education. But the status and authority of a national agency had gone as had the CNAA committees. Most fundamental of all, the CNAA funding had gone. QSC was expected to be self-financing. The political constraints of the CNAA had been replaced by economic constraints.

Initially, the newly established QSC placed its emphasis on continuing to provide the kinds of services which the CNAA had offered, but now on a full-cost basis. Some activities and services continued to be financially viable, e.g. conferences and certain kinds of publications; others were too costly or were being taken up by new national agencies, notably the Higher Education Quality Council. Funding support was sought for project work. Contacts were developed among the key players in the newly-unified higher education system and in Europe.

Freed from CNAA politics, QSC sought to develop a neutral position within the still heavily politicised world of British higher education. Its work could no longer be legitimised by reference to a powerful national agency. Legitimacy depended on the credibility of QSC staff and activities. The Open University had its own agenda and interests and these could not be shared too openly by QSC if it was to achieve a reputation for objectivity and neutrality. The Open University connection was deliberately downplayed. Many of QSC's clients were unaware that it was part of the University. It was frequently mixed up with the new Higher Education Quality Council.

Existing outside the Open University's academic structure, the core staff of QSC were not accorded the status of researchers within their University. They were employed as administrators which gave no rights to study leave. Yet there were ambiguities. The staff spent much of their time engaged in research, they obtained research grants, and they published. Research staff were employed on temporary contracts. Visiting professors were appointed. The University's expectations of QSC were hardly explicit: "pay your bills and don't discredit the University" might best describe them.

During the six years of its existence, the balance of QSC's work has shifted steadily from the old CNAA mix of publications, conferences and research to a much firmer focus on the latter. Nearly £2 million of external research funding has been obtained over the last two years. There has been encouragement from other parts of the University to develop the features of a more traditional kind of university research centre. And yet QSC continues to remain a peculiar sort of hybrid, both within its own University's structures and within the higher education research community.

Before considering some of the implications of this hybrid status, it is worth summarising the main differences between the CNAA and Open University incarnations of QSC.

Figure 1: The Effects of changing ownership on QSC

CNAA 'agency' ownership	Open University ownership
1. Strong steerage of QSC's work by parent body	1. Weak steerage of QSC's work work by parent body
2. Work legitimised through authority of parent body and its committees	2. Work legitimised through expertise and credibility of QSC staff
3. Most work internally funded	3. Most work externally funded
4. Work closely integrated with the other activities of the parent body	4. Few direct connections with the other activities of the parent body
5. Staff employed as "administrators" within clear bureaucratic framework	5. Some staff employed as "administrators", some as researchers within a loose academic framework
6. Major constraints political	6. Major constraints economic

6.7 A hybrid

As has frequently been remarked[4] (e.g. Teichler 1998), higher education research centres face a number of difficulties not generally encountered by research centres in other fields. Central to these is the confusion of researcher and practitioner knowledge and roles. For the higher education researcher, there is the difficulty of achieving objectivity and of demonstrating it. By being part of the object of study, the researcher has to attempt to put aside a myriad set of perceptions and prejudices based on the interests and experiences of someone working in higher education. The fact that colleagues within academia also have interests and experiences which might be in conflict with the results and conclusions of higher education research creates acceptance problems for research results which do not exist in other fields. In short, the higher education researcher faces an objectivity problem in carrying out his or her work and a credibility problem in how that work is received elsewhere within the academy.

In some ways, QSC's independence from the rest of the Open University's academic structure is an aid to its objectivity and neutrality and to its capacity to act 'entrepreneurially'.[5] However, its reliance on external funding creates the danger of uncritical acceptance of the policy and value frameworks of the funder, a potential bias which closer disciplinary affiliation within the University might go some way towards mediating. The risk, however, is that closer integration with the rest of the University would produce a different set of biases.

Closer integration would certainly bring with it conflicts of culture. The individualism of academic culture sits uneasily – perhaps impossibly – with the disciplines imposed by self-financing funding arrangements. Activities which are seen as essential pre-requisites of academic freedom – to pursue independent inquiry through fundamental research – are hardly possible within the constraints of contract deadlines and the continuing search for new projects.[6]

In any case, as the work of Gibbons and others (1994) suggests, the days of the classic university-based research centre might well be numbered. As more and more knowledge is generated through interdisciplinary problem-solving outside of the walls of the universities, as access to knowledge is opened up through new technologies, as the relationship between disciplinary knowledge forms and experiential problem-based forms becomes more complex, traditional assumptions about the conditions necessary for the generation of new knowledge break down. In these new circumstances, QSC's peripheral organisational location, its transcendence of academic and administrative cultures, and its mixed portfolio of information and consultancy services alongside research might prove to be virtues rather than faults.

The problems which QSC faces are likely to be shared to a greater or lesser extent by other higher education research centres. The answers to those problems will vary according to context but there is likely to be increasing benefit to be gained from the exchange of information and experience between centres on questions of organisation, management and funding as well as on academic and research matters. In this spirit of collegial information exchange, the following set of problems and issues are likely to be faced by QSC for some time to come:

1. how to secure core funding (for what purposes and on what terms);
2. how to build for the long-term whilst reliant on short-term funding;
3. how to square individual interests of staff with the collective interests of the Centre and both with market requirements and the interests of clients;

4. how to ensure that clients get what they want (good reports produced on time) and to also maintain a critical perspective in QSC's work;
5. the implications of combining research with related activities of consultancies, conferences, etc.; the need for hybrid staff or a division of labour;
6. how to balance knowledge and expertise based on rigorous academic research with knowledge and expertise based on experience and practice; implications for staffing: do we need more PhDs or more experienced academic administrators;
7. how to ensure that our work contributes to cumulative higher education research which builds on earlier work (when such considerations appear to be of little importance to funders).

No doubt there are many other problems around the corner. In seeking answers to them, there might be greater safety in being part of the academic structure of our University, supported by and integrated both academically and financially within one of the faculties. The hybrid existence of QSC is uncomfortable at times. And yet within it, rather than within more conventional research settings, may lie rather more of the answers to the kinds of problems which we, and perhaps some other higher education research centres, are likely to continue to face. Ambiguity may continue to have its uses.

6.8 Conclusion

The QSC case is not claimed to be typical of the organisation of research into higher education in the UK. But QSC's problems and dilemmas do reflect a wider context for higher education research shared by many who work in the field. Briefly this context can be summed up as follows. Academics do their scientific work in disciplinary cultures which possess their own rules, conventions and values. Academics also inhabit an everyday higher education world but their engagement with this world is more about vested interests, politics, administration and advancement than it is about science. The academic who attempts to apply his or her science to this everyday world is likely to receive little thanks or support (or funding). As Howard Becker aptly wrote some years ago:

"Interpreting the events of daily life in a university department or research institute as sociological phenomena is not palatable to people who run such institutions or to those who live by them and profit from them; for, like all institutions, universities and institutes have sacred myths and beliefs that their members do not want subjected to the sceptical sociological view" (Becker 1994).

But the sceptics have a point. Why should they believe that the higher education researcher has set aside his or her interests and is speaking as a researcher rather than as an engaged participant in the object of their study? Should the higher education researcher be able to claim a privileged status in debates about higher education policy? Is it inevitable that higher education research must be subservient to the agendas of current power and policy rather than be capable of offering critique or counter-perspectives on these agendas?

The institutional basis for higher education research shapes the nature of that research to a considerable extent. Firm disciplinary locations are likely to provide one sort of research agenda. The location of research in institutional management or development locations is likely to provide another sort of agenda. National agencies provide yet another.

Where does it all come together? It may be that the international groupings of higher education researchers are especially valuable in providing a context for the conduct and critique of research which can be relatively immune from the politics and interests of institutional and national policy contexts. Not as a retreat from the real world of experience, interests and practical problem-solving, but as a place where this world can be confronted more dispassionately and more democratically, where assumptions can be challenged and the unthinkable thought.

NOTES

1   With the adoption of its new name of Centre for Higher Education Research and Information, QSC has recently become known as CHERI.
2   The concept of constructive ambiguity as applied to higher education has been developed by Maurice Kogan (1996).
3   A history of the CNAA has been written by Harold Silver (1990).
4   E.g. Teichler 1998.
5   In Burton Clark's terms QSC is on the "development periphery" of its University (Clark 1998).
6   An Open University colleague aptly commented that ideas which would be turned into journal articles in the rest of the University were turned into money within QSC.

REFERENCES

Becker, H. (1994). Sociology: The case of C. Wright Mills, in R. C. Rist (ed.). *The Democratic Imagination: Dialogues on the work of Irving Louis Harowitz.* New York/NJ: Transaction Publishers, pp. 180-81.

Clark, B. R. (1998). *Creating Entrepreneurial Universities: Organisational Pathways of Transformation.* Oxford: Pergamon.

Gibbons, M., Limoges, C., Nowtny, H., Schwartzman, S., Scott, P. and Trow, M. (1994). *The New Production of Knowledge: The Dynamics of Science and Research in Contemporary Societies.* London: Sage.

Kogan, M. (1996). *Relationships between higher education and the state: overview of the issues*. Presented to the QSC/CEPPP Seminar, London.

Silver, H. (1990). *A Higher Education: The Council for National Academic Awards and British Higher Education, 1964-89*. London: Falmer.

Teicher, U. (1998). *Themes and Institutional Basis of Research on Higher Education*. Presented to the International Symposium, Kassel.

Chapter 7

Research on Tertiary Education in Australia

GRANT HARMAN
Centre for Higher Education Management and Policy, University of New England, Armidale, Australia

7.1 Introduction

While research on tertiary education in Australia is still a relatively new activity, over the past three decades it has expanded significantly and today there are an impressive number of researchers with interests in higher education and vocational education and training (VET). A substantial body of literature has been built up (Anderson and Eaton 1982a and 1982b; Beswick 1987; Hayden and Parry 1997) and each year the quantum of research publications and reports continues to increase. Leading researchers have established effective networks with scholars and associations in other countries and, as Hayden and Parry (1997) have noted with regard to higher education, current research effort shows remarkable dynamism. Two key factors have facilitated recent expansion of activity – substantial expenditure by government agencies on research studies and the staffing of academic development units in higher education by personnel with academic rank and appointments.

On the other hand, there is some measure of disappointment about the extent of achievements in relation to the expertise available, about the continuing gaps in the knowledge base and about missed opportunities. As in many countries, research effort is fragmented and few research centres have what researchers regard as a critical mass. There are unfortunate divides between the community of scholars working on higher education teaching and learning topics and those working on higher education policy, while both communities are largely isolated from the research community whose members carry out work on the VET sector. While considerable funding is available, much of it is for government-sponsored projects where time-scales

S. Schwarz and U. Teichler (eds.), The Institutional Basis of Higher Education Research, 99–115.
© 2000 *Kluwer Academic Publishers. Printed in the Netherlands.*

are limited and topics are set by policymakers. Although there is a national research centre for the VET sector, there is still no parallel centre for higher education research. In numerous ways, research findings make useful contributions to policy and practice, but many researchers actively seek better linkages with national, state and institutional policymakers, and better mechanisms for dissemination of results.

This paper uses the current Australian (Commonwealth) Government definition of tertiary education as including "the new national apprenticeship system, nationally recognised industry training, TAFE (i.e. Technical and Further Education), private training providers and public and private universities" (Kemp 1998, p. 7). The higher education sector consists of 36 public universities that together in 1997 had a total enrolment of 659,000 students, while the extensive VET sector enrols some 1.75 million students in TAFE institutes and with community-based and private providers. In addition, there are two small private universities, a number of small private colleges that offer higher education degree courses and an extensive provision for adult and community education. Unfortunately, this range of post-school provision has been treated by both federal and state governments in a segmented fashion, with the university sector being funded and coordinated on a different basis to the VET sector. Government financial support for higher education comes almost exclusively from the Commonwealth Government and, while most public universities are state or territory institutions, they are essentially controlled by the Commonwealth Government through the Department of Education, Training and Youth Affairs (DETYA). In contrast, government funding for the VET sector comes mainly from state and territory sources, with some Commonwealth contributions. National VET sector policy is set by the Australian National Training Authority (ANTA). TAFE institutes are operated by state and territory governments.

7.2 Research communities and associations

The main research effort comes from three separate communities of researchers: a community concerned with academic practice in higher education; a community concerned with higher education policy; and a community concerned with VET sector research. While there is some overlap between these communities and some fluidity with regard to boundaries, to a large extent the three communities operate independently of one another, each addressing its own research agenda, interacting with different client groups, operating from different institutional bases and with funds from different sources, and largely having its own associations and professional networks.

Members of the research community concerned with academic practice in higher education are mainly located within academic development units within universities, although some members come from education faculties or from university departments in disciplines such as psychology and sociology. Their primary concern is with such topics as student learning and assessment, evaluation of teaching, and innovative approaches to curriculum design, learning and delivery to off-campus students. While the efforts of this group are mainly directed to informing practice within academic departments, some of their work is of interest to institutional and national policy makers on topics such as approaches to the evaluation of teaching and strategies for institutional teaching improvement. Members of the research community concerned with higher education policy are drawn from more diverse institutional settings, but are mainly located within university faculties of education, university social science departments (especially economics, sociology and management), planning units within university administrations, special university based research centres, and government agencies. However, the community also includes some staff in academic development units and professional staff in major consulting firms, as well as former academics and senior administrators who now work as consultants. Compared to the academic practice research community, there is greater fluidity in membership, particularly in the case of researchers who have ongoing interests in other topic areas in education or other disciplines. Some researchers, such as a few leading figures in university economics departments, are attracted to work on higher education policy topics from time to time, mainly in response to particular requests from national policy-makers or from government enquiries. Members of the higher education research policy community address a range of issues, including student participation and financial support, institutional structures and governance, finance and resource allocation, the management of research and assessment of research outputs, performance indicators and the conditions of academic employment. Their research efforts are directed to both scholarship and informing policy making and management at both institutional and national levels.

Less documentation is available about the third community made up of researchers concerned with work on the VET sector and on related topics, such as workplace training and apprenticeship programs. In various discussions of research in tertiary education, in fact, many researchers located in higher education institutions neglect to include this community at all. Again the membership is diverse and includes researchers in the government-supported National Centre for Vocational Education Research (NCVER), in state and territory TAFE departments and agencies, in TAFE institutes and in a small number of specialised university departments and centres. In addition, a number of individual researchers in university faculties of education pursue research on particular VET topics. For a number of years the main focus of work has been on topics including the evaluation of TAFE and various training programs, adult learning, and student participation and student characteristics. Recently, however, with the establishment of the Monash University-ACER (Australian Council for Educational Research) Centre for the Economics of Education and Training, important work is now being pursued on topics such as the costs of and student satisfaction with workplace and TAFE accredited training from an economics of education perspective.

It is difficult to estimate the size of these three different communities. Hayden (1998, p. 2) estimates that there are some 30 to 50 Australian academics and consultants who contribute regularly to the higher education policy literature. This includes a core group of more senior scholars recognised internationally for their work and whose primary objective is to develop knowledge and understanding about the processes and outcomes of higher education, a group of scholars who contribute from time to time and a third group made up of consultants, many of whom are retired university academics or former university or government agency administrators whose technical knowledge equips them well for undertaking commissioned projects.

The community concerned with academic practice is larger in size and probably numbers more than hundred researchers. Most of these workers are located in academic development units but, as already noted, others work in education faculties and psychology departments and in a number of cases follow the same topic areas for both higher education and in relation to primary and secondary schools.

A variety of academic and professional associations play important roles in supporting researchers from these three communities, particularly in organising conferences and seminars, establishing networks and interest groups, and providing outlets for publication and communication. These associations include the more general academic and education professional bodies, such as the Australian Association for Research in Education and the Australian College of Education, and the more specialised tertiary education associations, especially the Higher Education Research and Development Association of Australasia (HERDSA), the Association of Tertiary Education Managers (ATEM), the relatively newly established Australian Association for Institutional Research (AAIR) and Australian Vocational Education and Training Research Association (AVETRA).

HERDSA was established in the early 1970s and is the main organisation for specialist higher education researchers, although it tends to be dominated by members of the academic practice research community. Of the current Executive Committee, twelve are from academic development units in Australian and New Zealand universities, while the other two are from regular academic departments. HERDSA's formal aims are to encourage and promote quality teaching and learning in higher education; provide forums for the exchange of information on higher education; and develop and publish material for higher education teachers. It now has branches in Queensland, the Australian Capital Territory, Victoria, South Australia, Western Australia, and New Zealand as well as Hong Kong. Since 1982, it has produced the refereed journal, *Higher Education Research and Development*, which now is published by Carfax Publishing Ltd of the UK on behalf of the Association. In 1994, HERDSA had about 1,000 members (Hayden and Parry 1997, p. 169).

ATEM was founded in 1976 as the Australasian Institute of Tertiary Education Administrators to foster the professional development of tertiary education managers. It now has over 2,000 members, drawn from all areas of administration in institutions and bodies associated with tertiary education, although its membership also includes a number of higher education policy researchers and researchers interested in the VET sector. Except for the President who is a senior officer of the New South Wales TAFE system, all current Executive Committee members are administrators in Australian and New Zealand universities. Since the late 1970s, ATEM has produced the *Journal of Higher Education Policy and Management* which currently is published on behalf of the Association by Carfax Publishing Ltd. While researchers amongst its membership look mainly to other associations and networks for academic and professional interaction, ATEM provides a convenient meeting place between researchers and administrators.

Modelled on the successful American and European Associations of Institutional Research, AAIR was established about ten years ago. It runs regular conferences and publishes a journal. Its membership is drawn mainly from university and VET sector researchers and managers concerned with institutional research.

AVETRA was established in 1997 and already has a paid up membership of well over 200 persons. It is a body of VET-based and university-based researchers whose work depends on funding, direct or indirect, from ANTA. However, its leaders see the association as being independent of the interests or VET policymakers and VET research funding bodies, even though senior officers of government agencies concerned with VET are within its membership. Of its current Executive Committee of ten members, four are university-based researchers, while most of the others come from TAFE institutes or government agencies concerned with the VET sector.

Two recent developments have been the formation of an Australian Network of Higher Education Management and Policy Researchers and efforts to form a new collaborative research group centred on the University of Canberra. With funding from a grant from the Special Initiatives Program of the Australian Research Council (ARC), the Network of Higher Education Management and Policy Researchers aims to increase collaboration and cooperative development of research capacity through the sharing of scholarly expertise, encouraging joint projects and mutual intellectual support, attracting distinguished international visitors, facilitating joint applications for project funding and helping bridge the gap between the higher education policy research community and policymakers (Australian Network 1997). Currently it has about 60 members. The proposed new research group aims to establish a network to "undertake data and quality analysis for governments, institutions and non-government organisations of current policies and practices as well as inform on possible impacts of future directions in post-compulsory education and training" (National Policy Research Network 1998, p. 1).

7.3 Institutional and funding support

Institutional settings and funding sources have a significant influence on the establishment of research groups as well as on their research agendas; on the scope, type and sophistication of the work attempted; and on publication and other communication of results. Different institutional settings and funding sources will be identified and comments will be offered with respect to some consequences.

It should be noted, however, that other important contextual influences on research directions have been the rapid rate of change in the tertiary education system and the types of new problems and issues that this has produced, the new policy directions which have emerged from government initiative, and the impact on the local research communities of new international directions in research. The rapid pace of growth and organisational redirection in the higher education system following the Dawkins' reforms, for example, drew attention to such research topics as evaluation of amalgamation efforts and the consequences of abolition of the binary line, while recent attempts to introduce a more market oriented system has led to efforts to monitor closely the results of changes in the Higher Education Contribution Scheme system and assess the impact of charging fees for postgraduate coursework programs.

The main institutional settings are universities and TAFE institutes; independent national research institutes; and government agencies and consulting firms. Each will be discussed separately.

7.4 Universities and TAFE institutes

In universities and TAFE institutes the main settings are academic development units, education faculties and other academic departments, special research centres, and units attached to University administrations, especially those concerned with planning and evaluation activities.

Academic development units were established in most Australian universities in the 1970s and 1980s; by 1994, a total 24 of the 36 public universities had such units (Hayden and Parry 1997). These units are special support groups usually located outside the regular academic structure and with a mission to support University purposes especially in relation to teaching and learning. They differ considerably in their titles; some are called teaching and learning units, while others emphasise professional development, staff development, or academic methods. While all these various centres have a commitment to improving teaching and learning and working with academic staff, many have a mix of additional responsibilities in areas such as student evaluation of teaching, professional development of general staff, institutional research, media services, and advisory services to academic departments on curriculum development and assessment. Some offer credit courses leading to a Graduate Certificate or Diploma, or even a Masters degree. Some are free standing, reporting directly to senior management, while others are part of larger professional development or academic services departments. Some have links to or are part of education faculties or other faculties. Most units have from three to ten academic and professional staff plus support staff, but some of the most successful units have had at times up to a total of 40 or more staff, many on short term contracts for particular projects. More recently larger TAFE institutes have set up academic development units on a similar model.

The research efforts of the early academic development units at the University of New South Wales and the University of Melbourne in the 1960s set the pattern for the development of units across the higher education sector. They were concerned mainly with student failure rates and aspects of student services, and then expanded their interests to projects related to improving the quality of teaching (Johnston 1982). Most significantly, the founding units successfully persuaded their institutions that units should be staffed by academics and that their directors should hold the rank of professor or associate professor. While the main research focus today of academic development units is on teaching and learning, curriculum and assessment, many also work on topics related to student access and participation, and student social and educational backgrounds. A fairly typical research agenda is that of the Centre for Educational Development and Academic Methods at the Australian National University which in recent years has focussed on theoretical and practical aspects of teaching, learning and professional practice, with individual projects on flexible structures for post graduate supervision, peer review of teaching, student learning, and information technology support of teaching and learning. Staff of academic development units have contributed extensively to the research literature. A survey of first authors in the international journal, *Higher Education*, for the period 1985 to 1992 indicates that almost one half of the Australian contributions came from academic development units (Hayden and Parry 1997, p. 166), while an earlier study indicated that 32 per cent of papers published in *Higher Education Research and Development* from its foundation until 1989 came from these units (Moses 1989, p. 98). While academic development units provide a strong base for much research effort, there are sometimes tensions for researchers between the time demands of research projects and university support responsibilities.

The second group are academics within education faculties and other academic departments. These include individual staff with interests in tertiary education research and staff located in specialist academic departments or groups within education faculties, such as the School of Administration and Training at the University of New England which offers graduate programs in tertiary education administration, and groups specialising in work on the VET sector within the education faculties at the University of Technology, Sydney and Griffith University. This group is more diverse than those in academic development units and overall their comparative importance has probably waned over the past decade. But at the same time, they make important contributions to the literature.

Special research centres within universities constitute another important group. Examples are the Monash University-ACER Centre for the Economics of Education and Training, the Centre for Higher Education Management and Policy at the University of New England, the Centre for Learning and Work Research at Griffith University, and the Research Centre for Vocational Education and Training at the University of Technology, Sydney. The Monash-ACER Centre is a relatively new cross faculty and cross-institutional centre, involving collaboration between the ACER, Monash University's Faculty of Education and Department of Management, and the Faculty of Education at the University of Melbourne.

While Australian universities generally have not developed institutional research offices on a similar scale to those in major North American universities, useful research and policy analysis is carried out within various administrative support units, such as those concerned with planning, statistics and evaluation, in a number of universities and TAFE institutes. However, much of the work is mainly related to institutional policy-making and monitoring needs and in the past the results were seldom reported publicly.

7.5 Independent national research institutes

Two independent national research centres work in the tertiary education area. The first is ACER, which is Australia's leading independent educational research centre. Located in Melbourne, it was founded in 1930 with a grant from the Carnegie Foundation of New York. Being organised as a private, not-for-profit company, it prides itself on being able to bring an independent perspective to research, although it does receive core funding from Commonwealth and state governments. It has a total staff of over 120, of whom about 50 hold full-time academic/professional research positions. Its main research focus traditionally has been on the school sector, but in recent years it has conducted major longitudinal studies of Australian youth and the transition from school to work, and studies of education and training and costs and funding within the VET sector.

The second independent centre is the NCVER, whose head office is in Adelaide. Established in the late 1970s as a result of a joint Commonwealth-State initiative following recommendations made by the Williams Committee, its main focus is research and evaluation of national significance in the VET sector. Apart from carrying out studies, it collects and disseminates official TAFE and VET statistics, offers consulting services, runs national conferences, allocates grants to researchers, produces an extensive list of publications and operates an information clearinghouse. NCVER stresses its close links with industry; significantly, of its current board, all members except for one representing Commonwealth and state ministers are drawn from industry.

Over a period of some 30 years, various efforts have been made to establish a national centre with Commonwealth Government funding for research in higher education, but despite various recommendations from government committees of enquiry, ministers and others, and support from government officials, such as centre still has not yet eventuated. To some degree, the Education Research Unit within the Research School of Social Sciences at the Australian National University (ANU) operated as a national policy research centre for about a decade from the late 1960s, but it was closed in the late 1970s during a period of substantial reductions in funding to universities. Apart from research on basic processes in higher education from different social science disciplinary perspectives, this unit carried out a number of major projects for government agencies. About the same time as the Educational Research Unit at ANU was closed, the Williams Committee which investigated post-school education and training saw the need for a University institute to provide a focus for the work of individual researchers and groups, and to extend work on higher education processes and policies within the context of the whole system. It specifically recommended that such an institute should be concerned with "… an extension of systems research which probes the role and performance of Governments, Government Commissions and Boards, universities, colleges of advanced education and TAFE institutions and appraises proposals for their reform" (Education, Training and Employment 1979, p. 815).

As already noted, the current NCVER was set up as a National TAFE Research and Development Centre but the Committee's recommendation for a university institute was not taken up.

A similar need for a national research centre was recognised in Bourke's (1986) report on *Quality Measures in Universities,* while soon after the Commonwealth Tertiary Education Commission (Hudson Committee) (1986) commented with approval on Bourke's suggestion, recommending that a special research centre should be funded at an appropriate institution for a period of five years (Review of Efficiency 1986, pp. 264-265). With the demise of the Commonwealth Tertiary Education Commission soon after, this recommendation too was not acted upon.

More recently, in his Ministerial paper entitled, *Higher Education: Quality and Diversity in the 1990s,* Peter Baldwin announced that the Government intended to establish a policy research centre or foundation to encourage more serious analysis of policy options (Quality and Diversity 1991, p. 33), but a change of Minister interrupted this development. A couple of years later, as Minister for Employment, Education and Training, Kim Beazley approved funding for a joint University of Canberra – Australian National University higher education research centre. Funds were allocated for construction of a building, but operational funding did not follow as planned because of a change of ministers following a Cabinet reshuffle.

A number of higher education researchers and University Vice Chancellors have been strongly supportive of establishment of a national higher education research centre, especially one with an emphasis on policy research and with a degree of independence from government. But there has been some difference of views about how such a centre should be established and funded. One possible model that may receive wide support is for a multi-institutional centre modelled on the very successful Cooperative Research Centres model used for industry related applied research.

7.6 Government agencies and consulting firms

Some research on both the higher education and VET sectors is carried out by government agencies at Commonwealth and state levels and by individual consultants and large consulting firms. Some projects attempted are sophisticated in nature, but many tend to be largely data collection work.

Often the results are not made widely available or, if published, they seldom lead to contributions to the scholarly literature.

7.7 Funding

The most important single source of funding for both policy related and academic practice research in universities is salary support provided for academic and professional staff who are able to spend part of their work hours on research activities. This arrangement applies not only to academic staff in academic departments, but in many cases to staff in academic development units and to a limited degree to staff involved in institutional research. There are often tensions, however, about the amount of time that such staff can spend on research activities and about the conflicting demands of teaching and service functions as opposed to research.

There are little published data on the extent of university funding for research on tertiary education. Hayden and Parry (1997 p. 170) estimated that at least 100 Australian and New Zealand academic development unit staff work at least two days per week on research on higher education topics. Assuming an average salary cost per staff member of about AUD$50,000 pa this would amount to about AUD$2 million p.a. However, Hayden and Parry went on to suggest that if all academic staff in Australian and New Zealand universities engaged in research on higher education were to be included the total salary costs could amount to as much as AUD$10 million p.a. In making any estimates, it is important to include both salary and salary related costs as in many universities salary related costs amount to 30 per cent. However, if we were to accept these estimates, it would be necessary to include at least another AUD$1 million p.a. for university staff engaged in research on the VET sector.

Government departments and agencies are another important source of funding. For research on higher education, the most important departmental sources in recent years have been DETYA, the National Board for Employment, Education and Training (NBEET) and two of NBEET's related councils, the Higher Education Research Council and the ARC. In the case of research on the VET sector, the main sources of funding are ANTA and state and territory departments and agencies with responsibility for the VET sector or for adult education. While some departments and agencies carry out in-house research and analysis, in many cases their main roles with respect to research is in sponsoring and funding projects and publishing the results. The most common approach of Commonwealth agencies concerned with higher education research is to negotiate contracts with universities for individual scholars or groups of researchers to undertake studies in areas of specific interest. Sometimes universities compete for contracts for advertised projects, but in other cases individual researchers are approached directly to undertake particular projects, or universities are able to propose projects which their staff will undertake. Funds provided seldom cover the full costs of projects, but the work enables researchers to undertake large scale studies and generally the resulting reports are published and researchers are also able to use the data for their own academic purposes. In recent years, an increasing number of major contracts have gone to private consultants and major consulting firms. Such contracts are often for highly specialised work (such as the 1995 and 1997 national audits of research publications which went to a major accounting firm and contracts for the design of a computerised grant application system went to an information technology firm). With respect to the VET sector, until late October 1996 ANTA allocated project grants and funding to research centres through its Research Advisory Council. For the 1994 calendar year, the Research Advisory Council allocated a total of AUD$1.5 million and for 1995 a total of AUD$2.25 million. Since 1996, ANTA research funds for projects have been distributed through NCVER but ANTA still manages centres directly.

The extent of the funding provided through contracts and other means by Commonwealth agencies is significant. In 1993, a total of AUD$1.2 million was provided through the Evaluations and Investigations Program for projects to inform decision-making and to help develop the higher education system's capacity to evaluate and assess performance. About half of this was used to support reviews of selected discipline areas and the remainder to commission projects. Additional amounts were available from the National Priority (Reserve) Fund to support projects of national significance including research projects, while NBEET had an Innovations Grant Program which funded investigations related to its role in advising the government about employment, education and training. In 1993, only a small proportion of the AUD$33.7 million in the National Priority (Reserve) Fund was spent on research, but all the NBEET Innovations Grant Program was spent for this purpose.

As a result of this level of expenditure on studies, DETYA and other Commonwealth agencies have been able each year to publish large numbers of separate reports and other publications. In the six months up to 1 July 1998, eleven separate substantial reports had been published by DETYA (covering a range of topics including demand for tertiary education, university autonomy in twelve countries, the management of higher education, research in the creative arts, and law graduates' career destinations), while throughout 1997 a total of 22 research reports had been published.

Other sources of external funds are the various grant and fellowship programs of the ARC and the programs of Committee for University Teaching and Staff Development. Established in 1988, from the base of the more limited Australian Research Grants Scheme, the ARC now has a total annual budget exceeding AUD$400 million with the brief of supporting basic research across a wide range of disciplines, but excluding medical research and agricultural research for which there are separate agencies. The main ARC programs relevant to tertiary education research are the Large and Small Grant Schemes, the Strategic Partnership with Industry-Research and Training Scheme (SPIRT) which provides grants and PhD scholarships for collaborative projects with industry, and the Special Research Centres and Key Centres for Teaching and Research programs. The Small Grants Program is administered internally by each university on behalf of the ARC, and this provides easier access to funding for many tertiary education researchers than for other ARC programs that are even more highly competitive. No Special Research Centres or Key Centres have yet been awarded for research in tertiary education, while only about one application in five succeeds with the ARC Large Grants Scheme. Still, a small number of tertiary education research groups have been highly successful with ARC and other competitive grant programs. Since 1993, for example, the Centre for the Study of Higher Education at the University of Melbourne has attracted about AUD$1.3 million in external funds (with about AUD$250,000 in ARC Large Grants and about AUD$280,000 from DETYA and NBEET) while researchers in the Centre for Higher Education Management and Policy Research at the University of New England attracted AUD$791,000 over the four year period, 1992-1995 (with AUD$403,000 coming from the ARC).

Built on the work of the former Committee for the Advancement of University Teaching and the former Commonwealth Staff Development Fund, the Committee for University Teaching and Staff Development (CUTSD) was established in 1996 with the brief to identify and promote good teaching, learning and staff development practices, and to encourage and foster innovation. It has been provided with a budget of AUD$20 million over three years and is proving to be an important source of funding for research on academic practice, as well as for R&D projects related to improving practice.

7.8 Training of researchers

Opportunities for postgraduate study in tertiary education are now available at a number of Australian universities. A growing number of academic development units offer graduate programs, mainly at Graduate Certificate and Graduate Diploma levels, as part of their staff development efforts, while masters degrees specialising in higher education or VET sector studies have been offered for many years by education faculties in a small number of universities, such as the University of Melbourne, the University of New England, the University of Technology, Sydney and Griffith University.

Since the Australian PhD degree is generally based solely on research rather than on research and coursework, it can be undertaken on tertiary education topics in many Australian universities, depending on the availability of supervision. However, the main concentration of PhD effort in recent years has been in a limited number of universities that have special strength in research in the area. Over the past decade, in these universities there has been a steady output of PhD graduates, but most of them have undertaken the PhD degree for purposes other than to pursue a career in full-time research. Of the 18 PhD graduates in tertiary education at the University of New England since 1985, currently only one is working as a full-time researcher in tertiary education research, although three others work as consultants with periods of full-time research. Of the remainder, six are employed as academics and five as senior university administrators.

The two main problems that limit further expansion of PhD enrolments are the lack of full-time research career opportunities and the lack of scholarships to enable students to undertake study full-time. While the ARC offers an extensive program of Australian Postgraduate Awards, these are highly competitive and their stipend level is more appropriate for young honours graduates than mid-career professionals or academics wishing to upgrade their qualifications. An important additional contribution to research and research training in the area of tertiary education research that the Commonwealth Government might make would be to fund annually a small number of PhD scholarships with appropriate living allowances, together with post-doctoral awards to enable relatively recent PhD graduates to gain overseas experience.

7.9 The future

While substantial progress has been made and significant research findings and research expertise have been built up, there are reasons for concern about the future, especially as government policy at both Commonwealth and State levels tends to be moving to further reductions of public expenditure and to increased competition and opportunities for private providers. Universities, especially, face particularly tight budgetary conditions, and University postgraduate courses apart from research degrees are moving to be offered only on a full-cost fee basis. Under the current Government, the amount of discretionary funding available to DETYA and other agencies has been somewhat reduced. On the other hand, the emphasis being given to quality assurance and improving teaching is likely to largely protect funding for academic development units both in universities and TAFE institutes, while the encouragement of private providers and associated concerns about quality will necessitate governments doing more in commissioning evaluations and supporting external monitoring of quality. This, in turn, may provide strong arguments for DETYA and other agencies to maintain a reasonable level of funding for commissioned studies.

At least in the short term, it seems highly likely that considerable funding will continue to be available for the ARC's competitive grant schemes and for contract research and evaluations sponsored by government agencies. Establishment of a national centre for higher education research remains a possibility, but this will require an enthusiastic Minister as sponsor and probably a high degree of consensus among universities about the type of centre that should be established and how it should be funded. With appropriate funding and independence, a national research centre could clearly play an important role in undertaking major projects, tackling neglected topics, coordinating effort, and providing visiting appointments.

Overall the funding of numerous studies by government agencies has worked well and has made an important contribution in building up research capacity and the information base. Moreover, these arrangements have brought many researchers into close relationships with government officials who, by and large, have come to increasingly value the contribution of research to policy development. Admittedly, there are some limitations with these arrangements, particularly the short time frames for commissioned projects and their concern with short-term issues rather than matters of longer term concern. According to Hayden, in many cases project reports "... make little difference to the mainstream of policy-related literature, as can be seen from the fact that there is not a high rate of follow-up publications from these reports in refereed journals. There is minimal use of conceptual frameworks that could provide a link with more enduring themes in the literature, and the resulting reports are sometimes highly descriptive and concerned with particular issues and events. Yet narrowly conceived reports provide the main link between policy researchers and policy makers, even though they do not normally tap the full potential of policy researchers to integrate knowledge from related fields, to address long-term themes and to challenge accepted viewpoints. At the same time, the research agenda for policy research is strongly influenced by the commissioning of narrowly focussed reports because these projects represent an important source of external funding for research" (Hayden, 1998, p. 10).

Three particular needs for the future are the establishment of one or a small number of centres with greater critical mass in staffing, more effective collaboration and interchange between the three separate research communities identified in this paper, and some additional special funding to allow more to be done in terms of reviewing and synthesising research findings. In most research groups and research centres, the number of professional researchers, as distinct from research assistants, is relatively small and often too small to allow for multi-disciplinary work on major projects. It is particularly difficult in the current environment for most academic development units, research centres and research groups in education faculties and academic departments to build up their numbers of research staff, especially more experienced staff, since even if project funding is available this is generally inadequate to enable tenured or longer term appointments to be made. An adequately funded national centre clearly could make a major difference to higher education research. While increased collaboration between researchers and research communities is developing, a major need is for increased effort to synthesise and integrate the research knowledge that has been built up. Many of the studies that have been completed in recent years, especially those commissioned by government agencies, lack conceptual sophistication and are not well integrated into the body of literature. A decade ago Beswick commented that "the general picture remains one of short-term mission-oriented studies with staff being inclined to hurry on from one service obligation to another without those opportunities for the growth of understanding in depth that must form a part of a secure long-term development" (Beswick 1987, p. 208). This remains largely the situation today.

REFERENCES

Anderson, D. S. and Eaton, E. (1982a). 'Australian higher education research and society. Part I: Post-war reconstruction and expansion 1940-1965', *Higher Education Research and Development*, 1, 5-32.

Anderson, D. S. and Eaton, E. (1982b). 'Australian higher education research and society. Part II: Equality of opportunity and accountability 1966-1982', *Higher Education Research and Development*, 1, 89-128.

Australian Network of Higher Education Management and Policy Researchers: Directory, 1997-98 (1998). Armidale: Centre for Higher Education Management and Policy, University of New England.

Beswick, D. (1987). 'Trends in Higher Education', in Keeves, J.P. (ed.). *Australian Education: Review of Recent Research*. Sydney: Allen and Unwin for the Academy of Social Sciences of Australia, pp. 205-238.

Bourke, P. (1986). *Quality Measures in Universities*. Canberra: Commonwealth Tertiary Education Commission.

Commonwealth Tertiary Education Commission (Hudson Committee) (1986). *Review of Efficiency and Effectiveness in Higher Education*. Canberra: Australian Government Publishing Service.

Education, Training and Employment: Report of the Committee of Inquiry into Education and Training (Williams Committee) (1979). Canberra: Australian Government Publishing Service.

Hayden, M. (1998). 'Higher Education Policy Research in Australia', unpublished paper.

Hayden, M. and Parry, S. (1997). 'Research on Higher Education in Australia and New Zealand', in Sadlak, J. and Altbach, P. G. (eds.). *Higher Education Research at the Turn of the New Century: Structures, Issues and Trends*, Paris: UNESCO Publishing and New York and London: Garland Publishing, pp.163-188.

Higher Education: Quality and Diversity in the 1990's: Policy Statement by the Hon. Peter Baldwin, MP, Minister for Higher Education and Employment Services (1991). Canberra: Australian Government Publishing Service.

Johnston, R. (1982). *Evaluative Studies Program: Academic development units in Australian universities and colleges of advanced education*. Canberra: Commonwealth Tertiary Education Commission.

Kemp, D. (1998). Address to the OECD Thematic Review Seminar on the First Years of Tertiary Education, Sydney, 21 April.

Moses, I. (1989). 'Higher Education Research and Development in Retrospect', in Harman, G. (ed.). *Australian Research Journals: What They Do and How Well They Do It*. Armidale: Australian Association for Research in Education.

National Policy Research Network on Post-Compulsory Education and Training (1998). Belconnen: University of Canberra.

Chapter 8

The Institutional Basis of Higher Education Research in Latin America with Special Emphasis on the Role Played by International and Regional Organizations

CARMEN GARCIA GUADILLA
Research Professor, CENDES/Universidad Central de Venezuela, Venezuela

8.1 Introduction

Higher Education Systems in Latin America represent a heterogeneous universe. The diversity in terms of the size of the national higher education systems reveals highly unmatched situations among the countries: *Mega systems* (over one million students): Argentina, Brazil, and Mexico; *Large systems* (between one million and a half a million): Colombia, Peru, and Venezuela; *Medium systems* (between 500,000 and 150,000): Bolivia, Cuba, Chile, and Ecuador; *Small systems* (less than 150,000): Costa Rica, El Salvador, Guatemala, Honduras, Nicaragua, Panama, Paraguay, The Dominican Republic, Uruguay.

The total higher education (HE) enrolment in the region is almost 7.500.000, and the total HE institutions approx. 5.500. The total private sector represents 38 percent, where some countries, e.g. Chile, Brazil and Colombia show an enrolment rate higher than 50 percent in the private sector, and countries such as Bolivia, Panama, Uruguay and Cuba, less than 10 percent. The average enrolment rate is approximately 18 percent, but it conceals many differences among the countries, as one country, Argentina, has reached the enrolment rate of the *universal access model,* with 39 percent; 12 countries the *mass model* (between 15 and 35%): Bolivia, Colombia, Costa Rica, Cuba, Chile, Ecuador, El Salvador, Panama, Peru, The Dominican Republic, Uruguay and Venezuela; and seven countries still have the *elite model* (less than 15%): Brazil, Paraguay, Mexico, Nicaragua, Honduras, Guatemala, El Salvador.

S. Schwarz and U. Teichler (eds.), The Institutional Basis of Higher Education Research, 117–135.
© 2000 *Kluwer Academic Publishers. Printed in the Netherlands.*

In Latin America, Higher Education Research (HER) and its institutional bases are also heterogeneous. These issues have been analysed from different perspectives in other studies, three of which were published in English (García Guadilla, 1992; 1997; 1999).

The aim of this paper is to complement these studies by highlighting the importance of the international and regional organizations in the development and institutionalization of HER in Latin America. The approach here is close to the conceptual framework described by El-Khawas at the Tokyo Round Table in 1997 and at the International Symposium in Kassel in 1998 (El-Khawas 1998; 1999). She presents three spheres to study the communication patterns and problems that affect HER: Research, Policy and Practice. They are: a) Researchers who occupy academic positions in universities; b) Policy officials who have direct responsibility for policy either at the state or at the national level; and c) Practitioners who occupy administrative positions in universities.

As we shall see in this paper, the situation in Latin America tends to be more complex, *as the presence of international and regional bodies in HER is linked to each of the distinct spheres in a particular way, depending on the mandates of each institution.*

According to El-Khawas, different relationships between the spheres may be found in issues related to the functioning or effectiveness of higher education. They may be close or distant. Two may work in close collaboration, with the third being more distant. Concerning the United States, she points out that "There is a great deal of continuity research activity in the US and, typically, a substantial degree of policy change as well, but the relationships among these spheres are quite limited. The dominant pattern is one of considerable distance and disconnection" (El-Khawas 1998, p.3). As in other regions, the situation seems to be somewhat different, as this same author explains: "for example, Teichler has noted that there are quite close ties between research and policy for most European settings" (Teichler 1996 cited in El-Khawas 1998, p.2).

Generally speaking, Latin America is closer to the United States than to Europe, i.e. the distance between the spheres is quite evident. But in the few countries where the institutionalization of HER is more developed, there is a closer relation between the three spheres, including the international and regional organizations. But, as this paper shows, Latin America has its own identity and specific traits.

8.2   National research, policy and practice spaces

8.2.1   HER in the academic world: HE postgraduate studies and HE study centres (research sphere)

HER in Latin America emerged in the 1970s when certain countries introduced postgraduate studies. Most of these were in education, from which higher education research was developed. Countries such as Venezuela, Brazil and Mexico created them in earlier decades,[1] others, such as Bolivia and Argentina, developed them in the 1990s. Most are ascribed to Faculties of Education. Only some are more interdisciplinary, e.g. Management and Administration Postgraduate Studies which are not ascribed to any school in particular but concern university administrators. There are some programmes of this kind in Latin America, but little research has been undertaken on them.[2] Postgraduate HE programmes that are oriented towards research are emerging at doctoral level.[3]

Higher Education Centres were created in certain universities. Between 1980 and 1995, over 3,500 documents on higher education were recorded in the region. Mexico, Brazil, Venezuela, Chile, Colombia, Argentina, Costa Rica and Cuba have the greatest number.[4]

Generally speaking, university research did not relate to policy-makers and practitioners before the early 1990s (García Guadilla 1999), when both began to feel a greater need for information and knowledge about the institutions for which they had to take decisions because the changes required by these institutions were of a different nature from the traditional ones.

One can say that the countries with greater HER institutionalization are those with University Study Centres (Mexico) or those which have recently created such centres as a consequence of new demands (Brazil).[5]

In Mexico, some of the research centres or units were created over two decades ago. The largest is the Centre for University Studies (CESU), National Autonomous University of Mexico (UNAM), which was founded in 1976. It has a body of 66 researchers[6] and a specialized library with 45,700 volumes and 1,160 journal titles, as well as a Higher Education Journal Index (IRESIE) with a database of 46,100 records that can be consulted by topic, author, or article. Much of this material is accessible on the Web (http://www.unam.mx/cesu). The Centre also has a Publishing Department, where most of its production is published, including translations of foreign authors.

Another Unit is the University Research Unit of the Metropolitan Autonomous University, Azcapotzalco Unit, created in 1987. One of the activities of this group during the nineties has been the study of the academic profession, where 23 researchers of different academic institutions participated.

The conclusions were taken into account in the Govermment's Professors Amelioration Programme (PROMEP). Some of those researchers also participated in the International Carnegie Foundation Project about the Academic Profession.

The Department of Education Research (DIE) of the Centre of Advanced Studies (CINVESTAV) at the National Technical Institute (Instituto Politécnico Nacional) has a group of highly qualified researchers who took part in the 1990s in a Ford Foundation comparative study on the reforms in five countries of the region.[7] The Autonomous University of Aguascalientes has an Education Department that focuses on HE. It created the Interinstitutional Programme in HER (PIIES) to give financial support to HER projects.

In Brazil, the Higher Education Research Nucleus (NUPES), University of Sao Paulo, was created in 1988 with specialists from different fields. It publishes a) Work Document Series: 16: b) Postgraduate Studies: 70: c) Preliminary Analysis Series: 9: d) Seminar Series: 2.

Other Centres include: the University Study Group (GEU), Federal University of Rio Grande do Sul; Study Programme and Education and Society Documentation (PROEDES), Federal University of Rio de Janeiro; Higher Education Study and Research Group (UNIMEP), University of Sao Paulo; and NESUB, Brazilian University.

RAIES (Institutional Evaluation Network of Higher Education) was created in 1996. It publishes *Evaluation*, which focuses on university reform, and more especially on evaluation. In 1998, it created the Interdisciplinary Centre for Higher Education Development (CIPEDES), which is intended as a virtual centre to establish a network of researchers from Brazil and abroad (http://www.ilea.ufrgs.br/cipedes/index/html). It has its own section in *Evaluation.*

Another important initiative in Brazil was the creation of a database on higher education in Brazil (UNIVERSITAS), which contains over 5,000 summarized and classified documents dating back to 1968. The material is available on CD ROM. The project was launched by Brazilian universities which are part of the Higher Education Work Group (ANPED) (Morosini et al. 1999).

Cuba has had a Study Centre for Higher Education (CEPES) for over two decades. It is located at the University of La Havana. It has 30 specialists and resembles the centres that were created earlier in the Socialist countries of Europe.

Researchers in other universities of the region are working in the field of higher education, but they belong to the social sciences and/or education research units. This is the case of certain researchers at the University of Costa

Rica, the University of Buenos Aires, Argentina, the Central University of Venezuela, the National University of Colombia, and the National University of Chile.

In Argentina, a group was constituted recently by researchers who are creating production, interchange and dissemination spaces between different universities of the country. Eight Higher Education Postgraduate courses were launched in the 1990s. In 1995, one hundred researchers from all over the country attended the first meeting on Higher Education Research organized by the University of Buenos Aires at which the first Higher Education Researcher Board was founded. Brazil and Mexico also have such Boards.

Journals on higher education published *from within the academic space* include: *Pensamiento Universitario* (University of Buenos Aires, Argentina); *Evaluacion* (Institutional Evaluation Network of Higher Education, Brazil); *Perfiles Educativos, Revista Mexicana de Investigación Educativa, Revista Latinoamericana de Estudios Educativos*;[8] *Revista Cubana de Educación Superior (*Havana University, Cuba).[9]

Several countries have associations of researchers in education. Most have HE commissions. They play a crucial role in promoting research through their annual and biannual National Congresses. The most important are the National Association of Research and Postgraduate Programs in Education (ANPEd) in Brazil and the Mexican Council of Education Research (COMIE). But there are also National Education Councils in other countries, such as Venezuela.

In Mexico, a University Researchers Network (RISEU) was created recently to discuss higher education issues via Internet. It was rapidly extended to other Latin American countries and Spain. It transmits information, but also organizes debates.

8.2.2 Academic administrators (practitioners sphere)

Practitioners are often unaware of researchers' work, especially when these are in schools of education. The same occurs with higher education postgraduate studies offered in schools of education.

Practitioners tend to have their own associations which also undertake HE studies for their own purposes. Certain associations, most of which were created in the 1970s, were modernized in the 1990s. The National Association of Universities and Higher Education Institutes of Mexico (ANUIES), founded in 1950, is one of the few institutions which continues to be active in the field of higher education policies related to decision-making. It also has up-to-date statistics and publishes the *Higher Education Journal* that has maintained its periodicity. This is not always the case with other journals. It also organizes training programmes and plays an important role in helping researchers, politicians and practitioners to exchange their experiences.

The Colombian Association of Universities (ASCUN) includes public and private universities. Others, such as the Federation of Private Mexican Higher Education Institutions (FIMPES), only include private institutions. These associations also undertake HE studies which meet their own needs.

Some National Associations publish journals on HE, though not as regularly as ANUIES. They include: *Cuadernos ASCUN* in Colombia; *Revista Calidad en la Educación Superior*, published by the HE Council in Chile; *Analysis*, published by the National University Council in Venezuela; *Review CRUB,* published by the Brazilian University Council.

It is difficult to say whether most of the coordination boards belong to the policy or practitioners sphere, since they are financed by the government, but are autonomous. This is the case of the National Higher Education Council in Chile, the National University Council in Venezuela, and ANUIES in Mexico. In some countries where the private sector prevails, as in Colombia, the National Council of Higher Education was created by academics.

8.2.3 Governmental planning, research and statistics bodies (policy officials sphere)

In the 1960s and 1970s, with the increase in the number of higher education institutions, most Latin American governments established National Higher Education Bodies, as well as government offices which coordinate higher education policy planning, research and statistical information. Over the years, many of these have become bureaucratic and have little resources. This not only prevents them from making plans or carrying out research, but also from having updated statistics. Some of these bodies, such as the Colombian Institute for Higher Education Development (ICFES), are doing efforts to being modernized.

There are also countries where governments have had to create different spaces. This was the case of Bolivia at the beginning of the 1990s when the Social Politic Analysis Unit of the Ministry of Planning and Coordination implemented the government's action to reform higher education. In 1994, the Unit for the Development of Higher Education was created at the Ministry of Human Development. But these initiatives are usually short-lived.

Some countries have created National Boards of Evaluation and Accreditation. In certain cases, they are associated with the Computer Information Systems. They include the National Evaluation and Accreditation Council in Argentina (CONEAU); the National Council Evaluation (CONAEVA) and National Centre for Evaluation (CENEVAL) in Mexico; and the National Council for Evaluation in Colombia, which is part of the National

Council of Higher Education. In Chile, the National Higher Education Council is an autonomous public body under the responsibility of the Ministry of Education which is responsible for the accreditation policy of the country. In Brazil, the National Evaluation Committee is integrated, with the Ministry of Education support, by associations of different university sectors.

Specific government programmes for the modernization of HE include the Modernization for Higher Education Program (FOMES), Mexico, and the Improving Quality of HE Program (FOMEC) in Argentina.

Some governmental bodies also publish journals, e.g. the Bulletin of the University, published by University Policy Secretariat of the Ministry of Education, Argentina.

8.2.4 "Ad hoc" work groups

In some cases, special National Commissions are nominated to work as task forces for a given period of time. They carry out studies from the perspective of their mission, sometimes in collaboration with the best researchers of the country.

8.2.5 Private research centres

There are no national private centres whose specific mission is to carry out higher education studies. The few that do are social sciences study centres, where these studies are one of several projects. Two have undertaken important research in this area. They are the State and Society Study Centre (CEDES) in Argentina and the Analysis for Development Group (GRADE) in Perú, the Center of Social Sciences Research (CIESU) in Uruguay; and Carlos Chagas Foundation in Brazil.

8.3 The main international and regional bodies involved in HER

8.3.1 CRESALC (IESALC) / UNESCO[10]

The UNESCO Regional Centre for Higher Education in Latin America and the Caribbean (CRESALC/UNESCO) deserves special mention. It originated from a recommendation of the Conference of Ministers of Education and of Ministers of Science and Technology of Latin America and the Caribbean to *support higher education research activities in the region.*[11] It was created in 1979 and was mostly involved in research during the first period of its existence. It was a pioneer, since it was the first to undertake comparative research in the region[12] and it has carried out National Studies on the higher education systems of all the countries of Latin America and the Caribbean.[13]

96 percent of the Centre's publications were published between 1980 and 1989 (García Guadilla 1994). Its Information and Documentation Centre holds a large collection of international higher education periodicals and books in this field from all the regions of the world. During the first decade of its existence, the Centre published the *Analytical Abstract Bulletin*. Since the 1990s, it publishes *Revista Educación Superior y Sociedad* which targets researchers, policy officials and practitioners.

In the 1990s, the Centre became the discussion platform for the reforms to be brought to the higher education centres of the region. It organised two regional meetings – one at the beginning and the other at the end of the 1990s – which over 700 people attended.[14] A series of volumes based on the papers presented at these meetings was produced.[15] During this period, research was left to the UNESCO Chairs. One carried out a comparative study of the higher education systems of the region.[16]

The Centre has now become an Institute. Programmes that support research include: a) Priority in developing a regional higher education information and documentation system with the most advanced telematic techniques. b) Developing an articulation function with the main Research Centres and/or Groups in the region.[17] c) Through the UNESCO Chairs priority will be given to training researchers by means of postgraduate programmes. The UNESCO Chairs will also support research aimed at strengthening decision-making by providing a follow-up to the academic evaluation and management programmes that are being implemented in the region.[18]

8.3.2 World Bank

The World Bank's action in the region in the 1990s is at government policy level. Funds to reform higher education were used to support government action through specific projects. The Bank has allocated funds for the following: a) Science and technology projects in Brazil and Mexico on two occasions. b) Reforms of Higher Education in Chile and Argentina. Other countries involved in discussions to obtain funds to reform their higher education system are Bolivia, Brazil, Colombia, Uruguay and Venezuela.

These projects led to a series of studies that are important to understand the higher education system. Some were carried out by the experts of the Bank head office, sometimes with recognised researchers of the region.[19] Others were carried out by the head office experts or hired international consultants on reform-related topics. They focus on financing.[20]

The Work Bank studies – especially the national reports – usually remain confidential and are only distributed to the governments. Now, the World Bank has decided to make all studies available to the public in the form of Bank publications.[21]

8.3.3 Inter-American Development Bank (IDB)

The World Bank supported HE reforms projects in the 1990s, but this was not the case with the IDB. This Bank was very present in the 1960s, but it was not until the end of the 1990s that it began to take part in higher education-related projects.[22]

In the 1960s – a period of hegemony of the so-called "development" economic model –, one of the IDB directors (Felipe Herrera) gave much support to Latin American universities (human resources training and science and technology research). Hence, according to the present director, Enrique Iglesias, there was a time when the IDB was considered to be the Bank of Universities. "The Bank has collaborated with over one hundred universities, many of which are the large Latin American universities; over time, it has allotted over seven hundred million dollars directly and an additional one thousand millions through contributions in the science and technology area" (Iglesias 1996, p. 1 in Malo and Morley 1996).

In 1996, the IDB and the Union of Latin America Universities (UDUAL) organized a Seminar of Rectors from the main public universities of the region to discuss the first draft of what was to be the IDB Document for the region in matters of higher education. But some rectors decided to elaborate a document that criticized it.[23] The IDB Report, *Higher Education in Latin America and the Caribbean*, was published the following year (1997). It took into account some of the observations of the rectors.

In the light of the position adopted by the Bank, some countries approached it for support for higher education reforms. This was the case of Venezuela, which signed an agreement in 1998 to develop the first phase of a major project which includes studies in areas that guide the higher education system. They are carried out by local researchers and are coordinated by an administrative counterpart representing the Government.

8.3.4 Other international bodies involved in research or training cooperation programmes

The International Development Research Centre (IDRC), Canada, and the Ford Foundation, United States, have financed comparative studies in the region. In the 1980s, the IDRC financed the most important comparative research on postgraduate studies in Latin America. It was coordinated by

CRESALC/UNESCO. The Ford Foundation financed one of the most important comparative studies carried out in the 1990s which analysed such aspects as financing, legislation and reforms in Argentina, Brazil, Chile, Colombia and Mexico with the participation of local researchers.[24]

The Carnegie Foundation supported a comparative international research on the Academic Profession in the 1990s in which Mexico, Chile and Brazil participated.[25]

The World University Service, with headquarters in Santiago de Chile, has undertaken studies on human rights, academic freedom and problems of inequality in higher education.

ALFA (Latin American Academic Teaching) and CEFIR (Training Centre for Regional Integration) are two programmes which are supported by the European Union. Both are more oriented towards postgraduate education than towards research.

8.3.5 Other regional and sub-regional bodies

Other regional and sub-regional bodies that support practitioners' activities are:

UDUAL (Union of Latin American Universities, Mexico): Founded fifty year ago (in 1949), this institution, with 165 member institutions of all Latin American countries, is one of the oldest universities organization in the region. It action has been associated with university encounters on relevant topics such as academic integration and autonomy. It promotes annual rewards for research projects; and publishes the results of those researches and topics of their interest. It also publishes several periodical publications such as: *Bulletin UDUAL* and *University Review*

Inter-American Organization for Higher Education (IOHE): This organization, with headquarters in Canada, was created in 1980 and promotes interuniversity cooperation. One of its most important programmes is the Management and University Leadership Institute (IGLU) that develops training activities for higher education institution leaders who are members of the organization. It collaborates with five regional centres in organizing Seminars and Workshops for Practitioners and publishes *University Management.*

CINDA (Inter American Development Centre, Santiago de Chile): CINDA is a non-governmental body which receives external funds.[26] At present, it is developing horizontal academic cooperation activities. In twenty years, this Centre has published over 50 books, more especially in the areas of university management and evaluation.

FLACSO (Latin American Social Sciences Faculty): The Chile Office played a fundamental role in higher education research in the region when José Joaquín Brunner worked there. But it is no longer very active in this field. The Argentina Office is more oriented towards other levels of education. But it publishes an important journal (*Propuesta Educativa*) which sometimes includes studies on HE.

CLACSO (Latin American Social Sciences Commission): Through the Education Commission and the Science and Technology Commission, this Centre has played an important role in the exchange of ideas and reflection between recognized researchers of the region. The reflections launched in the 1970s and 1980s led to publications.[27] But it has not been very active in higher education activities in recent years.

Other sub-regional institutions that promote exchange, training programmes and other activities are: CSUCA (Centre American University Council, San José, Costa Rica); UNAMAZ (Amazonian Universities Association, Belen do Para, Brazil); AUGM (Universities and Institutes Association of the Montevideo Group, Montevideo, Uruguay); UNICA (Universities Association and Research Institutes of the Caribbean, San Juan de Puerto Rico); ARCAN (Universities for the MERCOSUR, Montevideo, Uruguay); Andrés Bello Pact (SECAB) has done research on university and productive sector relationship in the Andean countries; the Multinational Programme of HE of the Organization of American States (OEA), the Latin America Economic Commission (CEPAL). Mexico is the only Latin America country, which belongs to the OCDE that has done diagnostic studies on HE in the fist period of its ascription.

8.4 Disciplinary perspectives and their relationship with research, policy, and practice

HER in Latin America has been performed from very different fields of knowledge, associated to distinct spheres. Taking into account the disciplinary classification of the Encyclopaedia of Higher Education edited by Neave and Clark (1992), a brief account of the Latin American situation will be done.

The perspective *Comparative Education* has been associated to the International Bodies work, specially UNESCO, CEPAL (Latin America Economic Commission), and World Bank; and also to International Founding Organisations, such as Ford Foundation, IDRC, and The Carnegie Foundation. This perspective – as has been indicated in this work – has had an important presence in the last two decades.

The *Economy* perspective has been associated especially to the works realised and/or financed by the Word Bank. The *Policy Analysis* perspective has had a relevant weight in the "evaluation" policy. Research in that dimension has been the responsibility of the governmental sphere in countries where the government has had an important leadership in those reforms.

That has been the case in Argentina, Mexico and Chile. In countries where the university has had an important role in the institutional evaluation process as in Brazil, this dimension has been responsible of the research sphere, with the exception of the Postgraduated Programs.

The *Organisational Theory* perspective has been linked to practitioners and researchers, most of the times associated with the work of Burton Clark. The research sphere has developed the *Science Studies*. Authors associated to the research sphere, especially in Mexico, within the Center for University Studies have developed the History perspective. The different spheres have developed *Higher Education Studies*. The *Macro-Sociology and Micro-Sociology* approaches have been the responsibility of the research sphere. *Woman's Studies* have been developed mostly by international organisations such as UNESCO and the World University Service. In the *Literature and HE Studies*, there is the novel *Tarzan and the naked philosopher,* a satire of Colombian academics and intellectual traditions. In general terms it can be said there has been research in all the disciplines, however, the studies that have had more visibility have been related to economics and public policy, financed by international organizations, as can be seen in the Navarro's article of 1998.

8.5   The need for actions that ensure greater HER continuity and articulation in order to construct more sustainable institutional bases

The dynamics of higher education research have not been completely worthless in Latin America. But, except for two or three countries, many of these efforts have failed to strengthen higher education institutionalization as a field of study. This may be because of the multiplicity of spaces from which studies are produced and a lack of connection between them. For example, the country reports by the project-financing banks are for exclusive use by policy officials. Much research carried out by consultants or the planning offices of higher education institutions remain confidential. But even when studies undertaken by researchers associated with university postgraduate programmes are disseminated in academic publications, they are little used by practitioners and policy officials, either because these are unaware of their existence, or because the pertinence of the research is limited. Sometimes governments request help from an international body to carry out studies that already exist, or local researchers are unaware of research undertaken by international bodies, in which case the same studies may be repeated.

The regional and sub-regional bodies can be in an intermediate position because they are more equally linked to the three spheres.

In short, *convergence* spaces between the different spheres in which re-search and/or studies are produced are few and far between. In this paper, we saw that Brazil and especially Mexico have the highest degree of HER in-stitutionalization and that the relations between the different spheres of re-search, policy and practice are closer than in other countries. But, as Wilsen de Vries pointed out in his comments on this paper, the articulation is due to the existence of an informal network of researchers which emerged in the 1990s around the modernization reforms. This group is made up of a new type of researcher who is a combination of researcher and consultant. But this group is integrated by individuals, not by centres as is the case of CHEPS in the Netherlands.

What could one recommend for Latin American countries that do not have an HER institutional basis? This question requires different answers according to the context of each country. One could consider the creation of at least one University HER Centre in each country – even a small one that is not ascribed to any discipline in particular to ensure its transdisciplinarity. This would secure the continuity and convergence to develop more solid in-stitutional bases for this field of study in Latin America. But the Centre must respond to research, policy and practice needs, with the help of international and regional cooperation, with special emphasis on the development of dy-namic networks.

The question then is how to strengthen the Centres that already exist and to develop new ones, which could guarantee: a) *continuity*, which is funda-mental in this field of study which involves different actors who carry out studies and research without necessarily belonging to the field of higher edu-cation, and b) *convergence*, i.e. articulation between the different spheres, including international and regional organizations and other local activities in this field which are not included in the three spheres of research, policy and practice.

The continuity and space convergence guaranteed by the Study Centres could help to overcome the transient aspect that characterizes much of the research that has been carried out, filed and forgotten after having served to solve a specific problem and of many of those who undertake studies or re-search as consultants of practitioners or policy officials and for whom higher education is only one of their many areas of expertise.

This does not mean that higher education research cannot be undertaken from each of the different spheres. On the contrary, we believe this to be fundamental, both because of its applied and multi-dimensional character and because alliances are needed between knowledge producers and users on account of the new forms of knowledge production (Gibbons et al 1994). The issue is how to guarantee a space that is capable of providing: a) conti-nuity in knowledge construction and accumulation; and b) convergence of the different spheres (research, policy and practice) and international and regional bodies, as well as other local initiatives that do not belong to these three spheres, but are part of higher education research.

We agree with the authors who believe that one of the most important mandates of higher education research is to investigate and understand higher education in order to improve it. It is imperative to have spaces that guarantee the articulation of the efforts and the availability of relevant knowledge. Knowledge that is capable of classifying and ranking information when it is transmitted in such a way that it is not of much use to the practitioners or policy officials because of its miscontextualisation of the specific problems of Latin American societies. But the Centres must ensure greater possibilities of integration and articulation with the research carried out in distinct spheres in the different countries of the region. This is important to enable them to form their own view on the foundations on which the higher education institutions of this region are based.

International bodies could contribute to the creation of these Centres in the countries in which they do not exist, especially those which lack resources.[28] Existing Centres and Postgraduate HE programmes which only respond to the research sphere will have to be developed. International bodies could also help to consolidate the institutional basis of HER by financing comparative research projects and developing networks in the production, debates and dissemination of knowledge.

Some conceptual inquiries from a Latin American perspective

Several issues remain open for further analysis:

- Although the spheres categories are useful to understand the relationships among policy officials, practitioners and researchers, however it seems that for some group of countries the international organisations could constitute a sphere by their own. Moreover, the role play for international organisations does not only apply to non-advance countries, but also to other categories of countries, as can be the case with the OCDE for the industrialised countries.

- Centres of HE Studies could be important not only as continuity spaces but also as reference point where the different spheres could intersect. But even though some formal structures need to exist for the development of institutional bases in HER, it is important to emphasis the relevant role of networks, and informal coordination and relationships of researchers, as they could enhance the relationships among the different spheres.

---

to be continued

- A look toward HE as a field of study in the international arena indicates this field has been commanded by the Anglo-Saxon academic culture. A brief analysis of the references used in the chapters of the Section V: Disciplinary Perspectives on Higher Education, of the Encyclopaedia of Higher Education, edited by Clark and Neave, 1992, all of the 1020 references are in English, except: 13 in German, 3 in French; 3 in Russian; 1 in Italian. Concerning the origin of the authors no one of them are from Latin America, and probably the same could be said for other regions different to the Unites States or some countries of the Western Europe. This poses the question of the field as if it is responding to a world wide reality.
- How new communication technologies are going to influence the communication to open the field of HER in a broader global perspective, but at the same time having to respond to local traits?
- The last question has to be with the pertinence of the HE as a field of study in the so-called learning or knowledge society. More and more, continuing higher education will go further that the formal system, as other learning spaces will spread out in society. In this new context, how should the HER field be envisaged?

ACKNOWLEDGEMENTS

I would like to thank Luis Yarzabal, IESALC/UNESCO, and Jamil Salmi, World Bank, for granting me an interview. I would also like to thank Wietsen De Vries, Angel Días Barriga, Manuel Gil Antón, and Roberto Rodríguez in Mexico, Marilia Morosini, José Días Sobrinho and Helio Trindade in Brazil, Pedro Krosch in Argentina, Gustavo Rodríguez in Bolivia and Elaine El-Khawas in USA, for their valued comments on this article.

NOTES

1 Mexico has some 180 postgraduate education programmes, some of which are on higher education.
2 For example, the University Management Master at the Los Andes University, Colombia, and University Management at Guadalajara University.
3 One in Institutional Evaluation at Campinas University, Brazil and the other in International Higher Education at the Autonomous University of Morelo State, Mexico
4 These documents include research and reports, as well as other types of publications. Many fail to reach research status.
5 According to Morosini's comments on the first draft of this paper, the Centres, Groups or Units of Research in Brazil developed recently because of the convergence of several aspects, especially those linked to the government education policy which encourages research activities through the New Education Law of 1996.
6 The number of researchers at this Centre increased when it absorbed CISE (Education Research Centre) that used to function separately at the same university.
7 The results of the comparative study were compiled by Rolin Kent under the title *The Critical Themes of Latin America Higher Education.,* FLACSO & Editorial Fondo de Cultura Económica, México, 1996.
8 They also serve to disseminate research. Another journal, *Future University,* has been discontinued for financial reasons.
9 There are other journals on HE, e.g. that of ANUIES, CRESALC, IOHE, CSE, ASCUN. They are cited in the section where these institutions are mentioned.
10 The Regional Centre for Higher Education in Latin America and the Caribbean (CRESALC) became IESALC at the 29th General Conference of UNESCO in 1997.
11 The objectives established at the time of its creation were: a) To contribute to the strengthening of cooperation among the Member States in the field of higher education; b) To contribute to improving mutual knowledge about the higher education systems of the Region ; c) To assist the Member States of the region in their efforts to develop or improve their HE and research systems and in reform processes; d) To promote greater mobility of professionals who form the higher education systems in order to make better use of the human and educational resources of the region; e) To contribute to the exchange of information and experiences with the institutions and regional centres of other parts of the world.
12 The most important was a comparative study of postgraduate courses in Brazil, Mexico, Colombia and Venezuela. It was financed by the International Development Research Centre (IDRC) of Canada and published in five volumes, four on the national cases, and one comparative volume.
13 They resembled those published in Europe by CEPES/UNESCO.
14 During the preparatory phase of the Havana meeting, held in November 1996, "over 4000 people associated with higher education and governmental management were mobilised, with 36 meetings at a national and sub-regional scale" (CRESALC/UNESCO, 1998, p.3).
15 The papers of the 1991 meeting were published in five volumes in Spanish and two in English: Reflections on the New Roles of Higher Education at a World Level: The case of Latin America and the Caribbean, Future and Desirable Scenarios. The papers of the 1996 meeting were published in two volumes in Spanish: HE in the XXI century. Latin America and the Caribbean Vision.
16 It was published by CRESALC/UNESCO (*Situation and Main Transformations in HE in Latin America*). 35 researchers participated in the national study cases. The study was co-ordinated by Carmen García Guadilla.

17 For example, CIPEDES and NUPES in Brazil; CESU and DIE in Mexico; CEPES in Cuba; CENDES in Venezuela.

18 Interview with Luis Yarzabal, Director of IESALC, December 26th 1998 for this paper.

19 José Joaquín Brunner, from Chile, and Simón Schwartzmann, from Brazil, participated in studies that were part of World Bank Projects in different countries.

20 One should note the following: Ernesto Schiefelbein, Equity Aspects of Higher Education in Latin America, 1985; Donald R. Winkler, Higher Education in Latin America, 1987; Sam Carlson, Private Funding of HE in Latin America and the Caribbean, 1992 ; Douglas Albrecht & Adrian Ziderman, Funding Mechanisms for HE, 1992; Wolff and Albrecht, HE Reforms in Chile, Brazil, and Venezuela, 1992 ; Jamil Salmi, Mexico, HE. Financing Project, 1997; and Strategy for HE Development in L.A. 1998.

21 Telephone interview with Jamil Salmi, January 8th, 1999, for this paper.

22 It should be noted that this Bank has always participated in science and technology projects in some countries of the region, e.g. Chile and Venezuela.

23 The document signed by the rectors of the principal public universities and published under the title *Proposal for the BID policy towards HE Institutions in Latin America, with particular emphasis on the Universities* states that "We wish to emphasize that many of the most prestigious higher education institutions of Latin America are embarked on profound reform projects (...) It is precisely these projects and these decisions that are placed in danger with some of the proposals and approaches of the Bank's document". The text offers suggestions in an attempt to make the proposals of the IDB and those of the rectors coincide.

24 See 7.

25 Published in Philip Altbach, *The International Academic Profession*, The Carnegie Foundation, 1997, as well as in other Mexican publications.

26 The IDB has financed a programme on "The Strengthening of the Capacity in the Management and Administration of Projects and Science and Technology Programmes in Latin America."

27 For example, the following books compiled by: a) German Rama (1982) *University, Social Clases and Power,* CLACSO/Edit. Ateneo, Caracas; b) Vanilda Paiva (1994) *Dilemmas of Latin America Higher Education*, CLACSO/Edit. Papairus, Sao Paulo.

28 In the 1950s, UNESCO, with the help of other international financing bodies, provided support to the creation of the National Boards of Science and Technology, which played an important role in the institutionalisation of S&T research in the countries of the region

REFERENCES

Altbach, P. and Sadlak, J. (1997). *Higher Education Research at the Turn of the New Century. Structures, Issues, and Trends.* Paris and New York, London: UNESCO Publishing and Garland Publishing.

Clark, Burton and Neave, Guy (1992) *The Encyclopaedia of Higher Education*, London: Pergamon Press.

Díaz Barriga (1998). *Informe de Actividades 1997-98* (Report of Activities 1997-98). Mexico City: CESU-UNAM.

CRESALC/UNESCO (1998). *Plan de Acción para la Transformación de la Educación Superior en América Latina y el Caribe (*Action Plan for Higher Education Transformation in Latin América and the Carribbean*).* Caracas:CRESALC/UNESCO.

El-Khawas, E. (1998). Research, Policy and Practice: Understanding the Linkage Mechanisms. Presented to the Round-Table on *The Relationship among Research, Policy and Practice in Higher Education,* Tokyo.

El-Khawas, E. (1999). Higher Education Research, Policy and Practice: Patterns of Communication and Miscommunication. Presented to the International Symposium *The Institutional Basis of Higher Education Research – Experiences and Perspectives,* Kassel.

García Guadilla, C. (1994). *Informe de Evaluación y Propuestas para el CRESALC* (Report of CRESALC Evaluation and Propositions), Work Paper. Caracas.

García Guadilla, C. (1992). Looking at the future from a retrospective view: The case of research on higher education in Latin America, in CRESALC/UNESCO, *New Contexts & Perspectives, Vol. 1.* Caracas.

García Guadilla, C. (1997). Research on higher education in Latin America and the Caribbean, in Altbach and Sadlak (1997), op. cit.

García Guadilla, C. (1999). Latin America: The research on higher education in a transformation context, in Teichler (2000), op.cit.

Gibbons, M. et al. (1994). *The New Production of Knowledge.* London: Sage Publications.

IESALC/UNESCO (1998). *Propuesta de Plan Estratégico para el desarrollo del IESALC (Strategic Plan for IESALC).* Caracas.

IDB (Interamerican Development Bank) (1997). *Higher Education in Latin America and the Caribbean.* Washington: Strategy Paper.

IDB (Interamerican Development Bank) (1998). IDB Projects, Vol. V, Issue 8. Washington.

Krotch, P., Nosiglia, M.C. and Pisani, O. (Coord.) *La Universidad como Objeto de Investigación (The University as Research Subject).* Buenos Aires: University of Buenos Aires.

Malo, S. and Morley, S. (1996). *La Educación Superior en América Latina. Testimonios de un seminario de rectores (Higher Education in Latin America: Testimonies of a Rectors Seminar).* Washington, Mexico City: BID/UDUAL.

Morosini, M. C. (1998). *Desafíos da construçao/consolidaçao de uma rede académica de la Educación Superior* (Challenges about the Construction and Consolidation of an Academic Network), Working Paper. Porto Alegre.

Morosini, M.C. et al. (1999). *UNIVERSITAS. A Produçao científica sobre educaçao superior en Brasil, 1968-1995 (The Scientific Production on Brazilian Higher Education).* Porto Alegre: GT Política de Educaçao Superior/ANPED.

Navarro, J. C. (1998) '*Una agenda de investigación en educación superior para América Latina: explorando las consecuencias de diversas perspectivas disciplinarias (An Agenda for Higher Education Research in Latin America: Exploring the Consequences of Diverse Disciplinary Perspectives)',* Sociológica, 36.

Rodríguez, R. (ed.) (1998). *La Integración Latinoamericana y las Universidades (Universities and Latin American Integration).* Mexico: Colección UDUAL.

Silvio, J. (1995). 'La investigación sobre educación superior en América Latina y el Caribe: un estudio introductorio (Higher Education Research in Latin America and the Caribbean: an Introductory Study)', *Educación Superior y Sociedad,* 6, (1).

Teichler, U. (1996). 'Comparative Higher Education: Potentials and Limits', *Higher Education,* 32, (4).

Teichler, U. *Higher Education Research and its Relationships to Policy and Practice* (2000).

World Bank (1994) *Higher Education: Lessons of Experience.* Washington: World Bank.

SOME LATIN AMERICAN HE WEB SITES:

Argentina
CONEAU (Evaluation and Accreditation National Council): http://www.coneau.ar
SPU (University Policy Secretariat): http://spu.edu.ar/principal.htm

Brazil
NUPES (Research Centre for Higher Education, Sao Paulo, Brazil):http://www.usp.br
CIPEDES (Interdisciplinary Centre for the Development of Higher Education, Brasil) :
http://www.ilea.ufrgs.br/cipedes/index/html
CRUB (Council of University Brazilian Rectors): http://www.crub.org.br

Chile
CSE (Council of Higher Education, Chile): http://www.cse.cl

Colombia
MDU (Master in University Leadership): http://www.uniandes.edu.co
ICFES (Colombian Institute for the Development of Higher Education):
http://www/icfes.gov.co
ASCUN (Association of Colombian Universities): http://www.interred.net.co/ascun

Mexico
CESU/UNAM (Centre for the Studies of the University, Mexico): http://www.unam.mx/cesu
COMIE (Mexican Council of Education Research): http://www.unam.mx/comie
ANUIES (National Association of Universities en Institutions of Higher Education):
http://www.anuies.mx

Regionals
CSUCA (Centre América University Council): http://www.csuca.ac.cr
AUGM (University Association of Montevideo Group): http://rau.edu.uy/universidad/gmdeo
UDUAL (Latin América Universities Union): http://www.unam.mx.udual
UNAMAZ (Amazonian Universities Association) http://www.amazon.com.br.unamaz

Chapter 9

Higher Education Research: Reflections on Argentina and Latin America

PEDRO KROTSCH
School of Social Sciences, University of Buenos Aires, Argentina

9.1 Introduction

In this paper, I shall analyse the present status of higher education research in Argentina within the broader context of Latin America and describe the major dynamics that give rise to a specific field of research in a country that, unlike the rest of the continent, did not reform its higher education system in the 1960s. Until then, the Argentinian university could be considered to be the region's most mature in terms of academic and scientific tradition. It had been built on the basis of the French and German models which was consolidated in the late 19th century. While the higher education systems in Latin America were rapidly expanding and being modernised according to the American model, the Argentinian system grew quantitatively but remained subject to the prevailing political authoritarianism. Despite this growth, neither its academic structure nor the orientation of its courses were modernized. It therefore evolved at a different pace from the rest of the region.

Argentina has now adopted the public policies that prevail in Latin America and that were designed along guidelines set by the World Bank. This homogenisation is only hindered by the great autonomy of the local university, the strong resistance put up by old academic structures, and the actors who oppose government measures.

In this paper, I shall analyse the debate on higher education research in general and the difficulties it faces in becoming a relatively autonomous field. Then, I shall describe its status in the rest of Latin America so as to put into context the Argentinian case and the lag observed. I shall also refer to

S. Schwarz and U. Teichler (eds.), The Institutional Basis of Higher Education Research, 137–155.
© 2000 *Kluwer Academic Publishers. Printed in the Netherlands.*

new forms of cooperation developed in the southern region of the continent in order to open up a path for the development of higher education research, assuming that this requires certain basic institutional prerequisites. Finally, I shall describe the situation in Argentina and propose ways of developing a strategy that aims to promote the constitution of a more structured field of study. I shall assume that, unless the present fragmentation is superseded by a unified field of study, one cannot hope for a significant contribution of this field to the development of the Argentinian and Latin American university.

9.2 Research on the university: a review of the on-going debate

The history of research on the university runs along erratic paths, cutting across different disciplines and spheres. First, reflection on higher education has tended to remain subsumed within the broader thinking on education as a whole, when it is not completely absent as an object of study. Yet the need to account for this level of education was given some importance by the philosophical thought of the 18th and 19th centuries, as well as by Ortega y Gasset's more recent reflections. They exercised a strong influence on this field both in Argentina and the rest of Latin America during the 1930s through what may be called the philosophical-political tradition where the university acquired meaning as the locus of knowledge of the nation-states that emerged with Modernism.

Reflections on the university can also be traced to the social sciences. Durkheim played an important role here, although it has not always been given due recognition, by conducting these studies from a modern perspective, breaking with the previous philosophical-political tradition. The significance of *The History of Pedagogic Ideas in France* (1869), which is based on his teaching experience and was not published until 1932, lies in Durkheim's will to found a positive and empirical study of society and in his introducing a theoretical approach that, through functionalism, has come to be hegemonic as regards analyses of the university and higher education. His work clearly shows the importance of the Medieval university in the constitution of modern educational systems. It is also an example of historical sociology: the strong morphogenetic component of existing structures is analysed, but society's role in the formation and reproduction of this social institution is also considered.

I have evoked this tradition because it can be found in the writings of Burton Clark. His book *The Higher Education Systems: Academic Organization in a Cross-National Perspective* (1983) exercises a great theoretical influence in Latin America. This does not mean that other works have not had an impact. In the 1970s, many books by scholars writing from different

Marxist perspectives also exercised a strong influence. However, these and work carried out in regional social and economic research centres were occasional and isolated and were inscribed in the educational disciplinary tradition, when it existed. The notion of an autonomous sphere for higher education research prevailed in centres such as CRESALC-UNESCO (Centro Regional para la Educación Superior en America Latina y el Caribe). But it seems incredible that Pierre Bourdieu's *Homo Academicus* (1989) should have had such little resonance in the region, when he was, and still is, a reference whenever the subject of education was dealt with there. Although his theory of reproduction had an influence, this and other works which analyse the role played by the cultural capital and the university in economic and social reproduction have not had the same impact.[1]

The legitimacy of higher education research is only just beginning to be an object of reflection. Different authors have attempted to place this issue at the centre of the debate, while contributing to the promotion of organisational forms (institutions, publications, meetings, and associations of researchers) that professionalise this new field of study.

In his approach to the subject, Ulrich Teichler (1996) recognises the restraints that the multiple disciplinary perspectives and analytical objects can impose upon scholars' exchanges. Hence, he points to some of the difficulties faced by higher education research: (a) it is driven by the social relevance of its core theme; (b) it requires great knowledge of the field; (c) it cuts across disciplines. This multidisciplinarity implies the existence of an area that exerts some dominance over the rest. According to Teichler, the dominating area in the United States used to be law. Now, it is education. He also stresses that researchers – both academics and practitioners – contribute to the multiplicity of this field, since: (a) their work is closely linked to problem-solving; (b) there is no clear-cut distinction between researchers and practitioners; (c) there is a systematic lack of integration as regards research, given its complexity and the relevance of local knowledge; (d) there is a strong thematic content. Although this is true and the attempt to find communicating channels and areas of unity should be considered legitimate, we should agree with several authors (Thorstendahl 1996; Gibbons 1995; Neave 1994; Alexander and Davies 1993) that the disciplinary bodies that were born of and developed with the advent of Modernism are becoming progressively weaker, that criteria of efficiency and impact have acquired greater importance than the traditional dynamics centred on disciplines' internal problems, and that application contexts have become extremely important. In some respects, the situation faced by higher education research is not very different from that in other spheres of knowledge, whether it be the "hard" or "soft" sciences. Gibbons distinguishes the Mode 2^2 of producing knowledge.

This situation is fostered by the new vocationalism which focuses on business and which is studied by G. Neave (1994) or by the university which is shaped by business and politics and which is analysed by Alexander and Davies (1993). It is obvious that the production of knowledge is not divorced from its application or thematic orientation: various disciplines emerged as practical knowledge and were later legitimised as disciplines, as the modern university introduced them in its logic and legitimacy. But again one must acknowledge that here too we are undergoing a crisis as a result of the de-centralisation of the spheres of knowledge production and of the blurring of the organisational borders of the modern university.

To conclude, and acknowledging the obstacles that the unification of higher education research entails, Teichler evokes the need to draw a map that makes it possible to cut across disciplinary subjects and perspectives so that mechanisms of information and visibility can be established. He also stresses the need to encompass disciplinary borders in order to enrich the different approaches: maybe, this practical task would be the soundest if the field is to be consolidated.

In *Perspectives on Higher Education*, Burton Clark (1984) underlines the importance of disciplinary outlooks and the need for their development to enlighten higher education as a whole and continues his search for perspectives that could provide points of convergence and which focus on history and organisational theory and include political economy, the institution, culture, and the republic of science. I personally share his hope in the disciplines' capacity to enlighten the whole field, even though their outlook may only be partial. I also believe that they play a relevant, though indirect, role in organisations' decision-making.

Yet other authors adopt positions that do not stress the importance of disciplinary studies. Altbach (1996), for example, posits the existence of a tension between applied and disciplinary knowledge, between research and decision-making. He also adds an element that should be central in the reflection on higher education: the influence of politics on the use of information. He seems to consider that the bridge between both research modes has to be built by producing more "hard data" and finds it of key importance to account for the issues at the centre of the on-going debate from multiple methodological and ideological perspectives.

There are radical positions about what should be done in connection with higher education research. Terenzini (1996) believes that it has been taken over by disciplinary interests and that "we have forgotten our roots", roots which would focus on problem-solving. He seems to overestimate the power of disciplines when he states that: "We have underestimated the power of the disciplines to control and focus scholarly attention. The conception of higher education as a discipline requires the rigorous application of research designs and analytical methods that are widely accepted in the discipline. The concern with theory and fidelity to a set of methods (whether quantitative or qualitative), in turn, leads to an examination of narrow, more precisely defined topics and questions. It also promotes a tighter, more specialised language. The cumulative effect of these tendencies is the placement of one's work within an established discourse among a community of like-minded scholars with training and interests similar to one's own. Such specialisation and narrowness, however, also reduces or eliminates access to that work by practitioners and policymakers who may be able to apply it to the solution of educational problems. I say again: as a profession, we have forgotten our roots."

Like many others in Latin America, Terenzini calls for a closer link between research and the problems faced by universities. But I do not believe that this issue can be solved on the basis of a unifying perspective or by thinking in terms of dichotomies or by suppressing methodologies or analyses. I do not share his perception of the threat posed by disciplinary isolation, least of all in relation to our region, where higher education research is only just emerging and most scholars are focusing on pressing problems and needs. I think the responses we could give would not be satisfactory in the face of present problems if we had not been preceded by people who have spoken of rates of change, of forms of organisation, of the distribution of power, of the world of symbols and the isolation of the disciplinary tribes, and of the history of higher education.

On the contrary, I believe that disciplines have a great potential to offer higher education research in Latin America. It is the disciplines and their heuristic power that make it possible to analyse – however unilaterally – the object of study, creating multidisciplinary insights, outlooks, and meanings that will then need to be unified and integrated. Moreover, I think that the viability of developing higher education research in the region will depend on our capacity to mobilise traditions and disciplinary bodies, as well as their mutual disputes, summoning them to produce knowledge that will add to the set of assumptions with which the subject of higher education is now addressed. This will have to be taken into account when designing a research agenda in Latin America.

9.3   Latin America: is there a field of production and dissemination of knowledge on higher education?

In Latin America, the debate on what to do with the different types of research has been conducted within the broader field of educational research. José Joaquín Brunner (1990) has done a great deal to make higher education research in Latin America progress. He has also made the thoughts of Burton Clark known and supported the measures to rationalise the university that are widely being implemented in the region. He is against the image of the traditional "critical intellectual" and suggests, instead, the adoption of the image of Reich's (1993) "symbolic analyst" and of his mode of producing knowledge and taking decisions. In Brunner's view – which corresponds to Gibbons' Mode 2 –, knowledge is a localised product, which is constructed in the application context. This invalidates the traditional notion of knowledge production as discipline-founded. He also announces the demise of the technocrat and of the cognitive and epistemological assumptions on which his social intervention rested. Knowledge and action thus become by-products of a negotiation conducted in many areas of application. But it should be stressed that a perspective which focuses on negotiation and the respect of the social powers taking part in it can be conservative in nature, as Lindblom (1980) recognised. This becomes even more conflictual in societies where the distribution of power is as inequitable as in Latin America.

In Mexico, this issue has led to a debate on the importance of the different modes and spheres of production of educational knowledge. As a result, an educational research agenda on diversity has been formulated. Weiss (1994) summarises it as follows: (a) sustained research, conducted autonomously in universities and research and development centres, and not funded on the basis of predetermined agendas (both as regards subject matter and methodology) but within the framework of global programmes; (b) specific studies, such as diagnoses, assessments, or projections to generate short-term information, as required by governments or agencies. These studies should be conducted by external sources; (c) design of a prototype of information and analysis systems, sectorial systems, institutional management and organisation, curricula, teacher training programmes, teaching aids, with a greater involvement of research teams. Weiss basically wishes to validate and advocate non-interested production of knowledge. He believes that it has proved to be both capable of approaching new aspects of educational reality and of informing governmental educational policies. But this debate has been pervaded by the issue of the influence exerted by where the discourse is produced (either the disciplinary basis of the system or the State).

After this brief outline of what has been done in the field of higher education research – an issue that is related both to the kind of research that should be undertaken and to the area in which it should be conducted –, I wish to stress once again that I do not share reductionist views and that I believe this subject should be approached from the analytical perspective of *field*, as posited by Bourdieu. The question we should ask is whether there exists a field of higher education research. It also seems necessary to see whether such a field can be constituted in a unified way.

If a field is a space that is structured with positions (the properties of which can be analysed independently from their holders) and is a place where a struggle for hegemony is conducted and where admission criteria are constructed, one can raise certain questions: how can one structure a field that implies both a certain degree of control or domination and fairly formalised borders and admission criteria in a sphere which is full of tensions in different disciplinary fields, which each have their own criteria of prestige and analytical objects with their corresponding modes of research (basic or applied); how far is it legitimate to refer to higher education research as a field which is unified on the basis of rules and modes of consecration? Do the researchers in this field share and compete in the same game, or are we facing a situation that can be compared to the no-rule football field, present in Baldridge's metaphor (1986) of *"organised anarchy"*?

Generally speaking, and following Tenti's (1988) claim in connection with the broader field of educational research, I believe that there is neither in the region nor in Argentina a unified field of production and dissemination of knowledge on higher education, i.e. the existence of rules that structure the conflict and competition between objective positions linked to the different modes of producing knowledge on higher education. This situation differs from other fields, such as history, chemistry, philosophy, etc., where a structured system or tension configuration exists. In more consolidated fields, admission criteria, modes of production of knowledge, and symbolic rewards are more consistent and objective than in the more unstructured field of higher education research. Hence, there is much improvisation, a great number of researchers and amateurs entering and leaving the field, and a lack of debate on modes of research. From a sociological point of view, a unified field is a social construct which largely depends on the existence of institutions devoted to the production (institutes, centres, programmes) and dissemination of knowledge (journals, magazines, events, etc.) This social construct is progressing unevenly in the region: in Mexico, it is more developed than in the other countries of the region. In Argentina, it is only at the initial stage.

9.4 A panorama of higher education research in Latin America

In Latin America, higher education research is only just beginning to draw its borders. This could be due to the professionalist nature of the university and to the "benevolent policy" as regards accountability and financing which prevailed until the 1980s. This, in turn, has to do with the application of the "principle of trust", linked to legitimacy, which prevailed in the region until the 1980s and in Argentina until the 1990s. As Trow (1996) points out, the breach of the traditional trust was the necessary condition for the introduction of evaluation, but also for the emergence of higher education research.

There are implicit disputes over research conducted at different centres and by different actors that imply another dispute over the control of the production of knowledge. At the same time, the conceptual frameworks and the disciplinary origin of the researchers of the traditional field of educational research are slowly disappearing. Today, it is possible to speak of the existence of specialists, researchers, and scholars in higher education. This field is no more than ten years old. No doubt, its future will depend on the importance that the institutions and actors taking part in it give to its development.

There have also been other restraints. Although in Latin America mass higher education and the proliferation of its institutions can be traced back to the 1960s, a traditional notion of the university as the nation's central institution continues to exist. It posed, and still poses, an obstacle to thinking the university as an organisation. In this context, reflection on the university has taken the form of strongly idealist philosophical-political thinking, which is not consistent with the present development and complexity of the system.

In this matrix, knowledge produced in Argentina and in Latin America as a whole has been normative and ideological in content. In broad terms, the disciplinary base on which the production of this knowledge was founded was Law. It lasted until the end of the 1950s and coincided with the *élite university* and with the existence of few central universities. The subsequent institutional proliferation and the problems caused by mass higher education were to create the structures for the present development of higher education research. Obviously, this is a general assertion.

The following are some of the factors which, in my opinion, have exerted a direct influence on the social receptivity to higher education research since the 1980s: (a) the emergence of a private sector; (b) the growing number of public and private universities competing for students, teachers, and prestige; (c) public policies concerning the operation of the university system, as well as the production of information on this system; (d) evaluation policies and accountability requirements; (e) policies implemented by international organisations and foreign foundations that fund research in the public or private sector; (f) the emergence of post-graduate studies on university management and teaching. They can make research progress, provided there are agents who are more interested in building an autonomous field of study than in pursuing a given policy through research.

Mass higher education began in 1950. It was accompanied by differentiation according to function specialisation. It is still in progress. Thus, the *élite university* has disappeared, but not the traditional modes of thinking about the institution. Between 1950 and 1960 the number of universities almost doubled: from 75 to 139. By 1990, there were some 500 universities and six million students. The growth in the number of teachers was similar. By 1990, the schooling rate for Latin America was 17 percent. In Argentina, it was approximately 27 percent. There are now some 850,000 students enrolled in 85 public and private universities. The share of the private sector is approximately 25 percent.

The rise in the number of teachers, students and educational institutions has brought greater diversity in terms of levels and sectors and new interests to a system that had been primarily public and relatively homogeneous: professionalist in character and with a prominence of traditional studies. The prevailing profile of training has been shaped by new and emerging professions in the service area. Less research is undertaken in the different fields than in the developed regions, or even in emerging areas such as Southeast Asia.

What distinguishes Argentina from the rest of Latin America is the fact that it has preserved a basically European university construct. It remained isolated from the trends that prevailed in the region between 1966 and 1984. It is only now that the American model is beginning to be adopted. The Argentine University has been both modern and prematurely old as a consequence of the political context in which it developed.

The institutional capacity for the production of knowledge on the university at the system level (whether it be in terms of programmes, centres, or institutes) was limited in Latin America. To this should be added the fragmentation of activities: there has been no interaction, understood as competitiveness in terms of orientation, prestige, and resources. As has already been stated, Mexico has undertaken the greatest number of studies within the sphere of the university, followed by Brazil and Chile. But its contribution will probably decrease because of its incorporation in NAFTA (North American Free Trade Association). Mexico has several higher education research centres: the Centro de Estudios sobre la Universidad (CESU) at the Universidad Nacional Autónoma de México; a consolidated research programme at the Universidad Metropolitana (UAM); and an important centre within the Department of Educational Research (CINESTAV) at the Instituto Politécnico Nacional. In the private sector, the Universidad Iberoamericana has a higher education research centre. In addition, ANUIES conducts research on the subject and produces information on the system. Some of these programmes are international in scope and are funded by American foundations. There are also specialised academic journals.

Brazil, despite the dynamism and extension of its university system, does not have such an institutionalised and complete system as regards the production and dissemination of knowledge or such institutional diversity. The Núcleo de Pesquisas sobre Educación Superior (NUPES) at the Universidad de São Paulo is the country's most important centre in the field. There are also teams who carry out research programmes in universities such as the State University, Minas Gerais, the Federal University, Río Grande do Sul, and the University of Río de Janeiro. But it seems surprising that, before the publication last year by the Universidad de Campinas of *Avaliaçao*, a journal on university performance evaluation, there was no journal on higher education.

Chile has many higher education research centres. They were mainly constituted during the military dictatorship. They include: the Centro de Estudios Nacionales de Desarrollo (CINDA) that advises universities on reforms and innovations; the Corporación de Promoción Universitaria (CPU); and FLACSO (Facultad Latinoamericana de Ciencias Sociales). In Venezuela, CENDES (Universidad Central de Venezuela) is carrying out an important research programme at the Latin American level. Also, the Venezuela Institute of Scientific Research, and Columbus are conducting research in Science and Technology, with the help of the university. In Colombia, there are research teams at the Universidad Nacional de Colombia and the Universidad del Valle who are working on teaching and research. There are also other research groups in smaller countries of the region.

At the Latin American level, CRESALC-UNESCO (Centro Regional para la Educación Superior en América Latina y el Caribe) and UDUAL (Unión de Universidades de América Latina) have been of key importance in producing, disseminating, and advancing research, publications, and in organising meetings in Latin America and the Caribbean. The Latin American University Group for Education Reform and Enhancement (GULERPE) has also played an important role in developing higher education research in Latin America.[3] The development of these institutional bases mainly took place in the 1970s. Argentina, however, remained isolated. This isolation – due to the successive military dictatorships between 1966 and 1983 – cut off the universities from regional coordination agencies and postponed reflection on higher education.

In the last twenty years, the region has constituted spheres and resources in connection with higher education research that will no doubt expand. But it cannot be expected that the present fragmentation will be overcome soon. In order to change the present trends, the professionalist pattern that has characterised the Latin American university should shift to a more basic or applied research-focused model. But the present modernising policies are geared to the introduction of a new professionalism and a more effective organisational framework, especially as regards budgets.

9.5 Research and publications

Between 1980 and 1995, the research team led by García Guadilla (1996) recorded 3,315 research documents on this subject, i.e. approximately 220 per year. It cannot be established whether they have increased in number since 1995. There are few publications on this subject (no more than 20) and few books and articles that have been translated. Again, Mexico takes the lead here. Most publications are merely informative and do not always include research reports. Their international circulation and institutionalisation are relatively limited.

In broad terms, it can be stated that a field of higher education research does not exist at present in Latin America, since there are no explicit disputes over its symbolic or actual control or unified criteria that specify who or what belongs to this field. Research institutions are too varied (system coordinating agencies, ministry offices, research centres, programmes, etc.) and, although they mainly belong to the public university sphere, they remain isolated. At the same time, researchers come from different disciplines (mostly social sciences). In Argentina and Brazil, the field of education is hegemonic as regards research, although there is a shift towards the constitution of an autonomous field.

At present, the problem of a fragmentary sphere of production is largely a consequence of fragmentary university systems and academic fields. The lack of consolidation of academic communities, the weakness of research activities, and the strong political bias of university discussion in Latin America hinder the development of this field. In this respect, the emergence of new forms and models of interuniversity cooperation can help to create the necessary conditions to develop research in this field in the southern region of the continent.

9.6 The birth of interuniversity cooperation. The Montevideo Group Association of universities and higher education research

Formal interuniversity exchanges and calls for cooperation have a long history in Latin America. But it is only from 1990, with the creation of MERCOSUR (economic integration agreement signed by Brazil, Argentina, Uruguay, and Paraguay), that university cooperation has occupied a prominent position. The novelty of the present situation lies in the fact that cooperation now implies a degree of integration and complementarity that goes beyond agreements signed by the university authorities. It is now driven by forces which originated in integrating movements, which are an expression of the social and economic reality, and the protection afforded by a relatively closed state configuration in relation to universities is beginning to wane.

The case of the Montevideo Group is interesting because it was launched by the institutions through the exercise of their autonomy. The distinctiveness of this horizontal cooperation is due to the incremental character of the incorporation of new universities and the fact that the protagonists of the exchanges are no longer the upper levels of institutional government, but the disciplines themselves. This search for substance in the exchange process is a novel experience in the region. In this respect, it could be said that this constitutes a gradual progress towards greater interdependence and integration, compared to the traditional modes of formal cooperation.[4]

This process of building a configuration of tensions and potentialities in terms of human, scientific, and material resources should guarantee the introduction of innovation and change: cooperation should have an impact on each of the participating units as regards the dimensions of their internal life. Only then shall we be able to claim that an "innovative system" has been set in motion. The possibility of putting an end to fragmentation provides fertile ground for the development of higher education research on a new basis in the southern region of the continent.

The contacts between systems, the development of more comparative perspectives on system operation and the need to coordinate future development are beginning to work as a dynamic element of higher education research. No doubt, this effect will be stronger in the future. I believe that association, in particular with the Brazilian academic community, may be one of the most fruitful strategies for modernising and de-provincialising higher education in Argentina. Greater cooperation between these countries can already be observed in the field of higher education research. It has not yet crystallised in joint programmes but mainly in comparative studies, joint publications, and greater participation of the researchers in the meetings held in both countries.

9.7 Argentina: a late though rapid development of research on higher education

Here, I shall analyse the Argentinian situation in connection with higher education research. I shall also refer to the emergence of post-graduate studies where research on higher education is conducted. I believe that these activities can become a basis on which to build research centres and programmes in many universities – particularly, public ones – in this country. Higher education research in Argentina goes back to 1988, if we consider it in terms of work conducted within the framework of research programmes or by research teams (in public or private centres or at universities) who consult internationally recognised bibliographies and identify themselves as members of a specific sphere of knowledge production.

It was only in1985 that academic works on higher education which can be included in social science research began to be published in Argentina. In 1988, the first Specialisation Course in University Teaching was created at the Universidad Nacional de la Patagonia. It included specific bibliographies, particularly American ones. By the end of that decade, when evaluation, accountability, and reform policies were incorporated in the on-going debate, a programme on higher education research was established at the Centro de Estudios sobre el Estado y la Universidad. It is funded by the Ford Foundation and is linked to similar centres in Latin America. But despite the results obtained in terms of production, it has not had a demonstration impact on universities, which seem to follow a different path in the constitution of higher education research. Later, research groups were created at the Facultad de Ciencias Sociales (Universidad de Buenos Aires), at the Facultad de Humanidades (Universidad de La Plata), and at the Universidad del Litoral, as well as in other Argentinian universities. They all have a strong disciplinary character (social sciences), independently of their localisation and orientation. Their transformation into multidisciplinary centres or institutes will depend on their capacity to mature and develop.

As from the 1990s, reform was placed at the centre of Argentinian university policy, culminating in the 1995 Law on Higher Education and in different policy measures to introduce competitiveness and to reform the academic structures of the university. At the state level, policy-oriented research began to be conducted and systematic information on higher education to be produced. Thus, a bureaucratic centre is beginning to take shape in addition to the National Committee on Assessment and Accreditation that produces information on the university without necessarily developing academic research.

In 1993, a group of researchers founded *Pensamiento Universitario*[5], which is devoted to higher education research. It aimed to break the traditional discourse on the university by analysing disciplinary developments in other regions of the world, whilst fostering the production of local knowledge. The founding hypothesis was that academic communities are unique propagators and generators of a demonstration impact. But although disciplines enrich the field through their specific views and methods, they can also reinforce isolation. It is therefore necessary to build bridges between the different research modes that characterise the disciplines and positions in the field.

In 1995, the Facultad de Ciencias Sociales, Universidad de Buenos Aires, organised the First National Meeting on *The University as Research Subject*. The idea of visibility, the lack of political bias, and the fact that academics were being convened to discuss a new topic broke with the traditional "concept of the university", i.e. a university that is capable of constructing social and natural truths but is unable to become the object of its own study. At the same time, it was possible to generate competitiveness amongst potential researchers and institutions and to exert a demonstration effect on the system as a whole. Although the principle of academic autonomy could not be sustained because of the interference of political interests, the historical relevance guaranteed its impact on the system. More than two hundred papers were sent and a far greater number of participants took part – as was the case with the second meeting. Institutional research and activities linked to the fields of education and pedagogy were the main themes.

In 1997, a new phenomenon arose that had as its sole precedent teacher training activities. But these activities must now be clearly defined as postgraduate studies in higher education research. Postgraduate courses leading to diplomas and MAs in university management and teaching emerged simultaneously in the framework of the "boom of postgraduate studies" that began in Argentina in 1993. Some ten programmes, 300 junior researchers in different disciplines, and teachers specialising in this subject will no doubt play a crucial role in the constitution of this field. It should be remembered that university activities tend to produce a legitimating effect as regards the setting up of new fields of study. The programmes now have to face the problem of their continuity and enhancement, especially as regards their links with research programmes. In some cases, these training activities can be considered as the seeds for future research centres that may drastically modify the scope of higher education research in Argentina.[6]

Although many of these activities will probably not become established programmes, or will fail to be sustained in time, an interuniversity cooperation programme in the fields of teaching, research, and publications and the creation of networks of researchers and institutions may lead to an infrastructure that will support programmes and link research programmes at the basis of the system. But this will greatly depend on the actors' awareness of the potential for the establishment of a new field of study that is strategically important for the reshaping of the Argentinian University. One obstacle that will be more difficult to overcome is the academic and institutional fragmentation that characterises the Argentinian University. I have briefly described the emergence of this new field in Argentina, a field that is plagued by the same tensions as its counterparts in other parts of the world.

9.8 Conclusion

Some elements enable one to speak of a rapid and growing institutionalisation of higher education research: (a) the emergence of researchers and centres devoted to research and the training of researchers; (b) the consolidation of theoretical and empirical positions; (c) greater specificity as regards researchers and specialised knowledge; (d) diversification of the field through the creation of research centres at the disciplinary and institutional level in the framework of programmes conducted at research centres and faculties, by the government, etc.; (e) the remarkable expansion of postgraduate training/research activities; (f) the emergence of a disguised dispute over the symbolic and material control of the field, dispute that, although still held within the political arena, seems to be gradually shifting to an autonomous sphere; (g) greater participation of researchers in regional and international meetings. But we must be wary when talking about the existence of a field when there are no rules of the game that give prestige to the different modes of conducting research, or regulate access to and membership in the field. Ultimately, it can be said that a field exists when there is a hegemonic paradigm and frontiers that establish social interaction.

As happens with every configuration of actors and positions, this field constitutes a configuration where the balance of power is unstable. In Argentina, tensions are diffuse in higher education research and distances are created by the isolation of the different positions and actors. In this regard, various cleavages can be observed which nourish, but also jeopardise the potential development of the field: (a) the interface of government and university knowledge production spheres is filled with political tension which prevents the creation of channels of communication; (b) within the university itself, there are no exchanges between researchers who carry out institutional research, between those in disciplines such as education sciences or history, and between those working on interdisciplinary topics such as the labour market, government, etc.; (c) policy-oriented programmes outside the university are more linked to governmental policy than to the university; (d) activities related to training in university teaching and management have no interconnection and adopt different positions towards government policies. As a result, the quantitative growth in this field was based on isolated and fragmented activities. The present task is to find ways of building bridges between different positions, so that disputes can be formalised and discussions be launched.

In the central countries, there are more institutions that coordinate and regulate interaction; also, supranational pressure in Europe creates adequate conditions for the development of inter-regional associations. But this is neither the case in the different Latin American countries nor in the region as a whole, where institutionalisation of higher education research is only just beginning and relationships between countries are less subject to unified processes of regionalisation.

The recent progress of higher education research in Argentina has been remarkable, although there has been no explicit policy to promote it. If the actors involved become aware of the bearing this research may have on the transformation of the Argentinian University, the existing potential may develop into intellectual production.

I believe that the consolidation of higher education research depends on the development of the teaching and research training activities that have recently emerged. These should be improved by relating them more closely to research. But it is essential to seize this opportunity to create permanent research centres in different universities of the country.

I believe that the centres which are at the basis of the system and are oriented towards disciplinary or focused research can benefit from a long term development of higher education research. In this respect, it will no doubt be more crucial to discuss strategies to develop studies of different kinds and character and their mutual connections, than to theorise about the existence of a field along the lines of the disciplinary communities inherited from modernism. Both these communities and the institutions that house them are undergoing deep but not yet recognisable transformations.

NOTES

1 Burton Clark provided a theoretical framework for the constitution of this field of study, basically through American funding institutions, such as the Ford Foundation. Despite Pierre Bourdieu's assertions about Clark's analytical perspective explicatory power, it has led to a discipline-founded analysis in the comparative organizational tradition that has made it possible to break with the prevailing philosophical-political tradition through the

incorporation of the issue of power in the system and the institution. Although Clark's perspective does not postulate a theory of the relation between the field of social domination and higher education, it helps to conduct analyses that had not existed in the region before. In this regard, he has instituted an empirical object that accepts approaches from other disciplines, such as history, economy, sociology, political science, which had been previously working on the subject, but from their own disciplinary fields and not as potential members of a new multidisciplinary sphere.

2   Gibbons points that the Mode 2 of production of knowledge is characterized by the fact that knowledge is produced within contexts of application. At the same time, this Mode is transdisciplinary in that there is no previous theoretical framework, which is instead developed as practice proceeds; thus, knowledge does not necessarily accumulate as disciplinary knowledge. Also, this Mode implies a de-centralization of production processes, as well as a shift towards forms of evaluation and quality control that are more social and less disciplinary in nature.

3   Most of this information was taken from Carmen García Guadilla (1997).

4   In August 1991, the Acta de Intención Fundacional was signed by eight public universities (five in Argentina, and one in Uruguay, Brazil, and Paraguay, respectively). In December of that year, another Brazilian university joined and an institutional profile began to be outlined on the basis of academic cooperation in the following disciplines: molecular biology, natural product pharmacology, applied mathematics, education for integration, rural development, microelectronics, and chemistry. By 1992, meetings were organized for each discipline. The AUGM statutes were signed in 1993. In 1993, academic committees on interdisciplinary areas (environment, health, integration policies) were set up. The following activities and programmes can be mentioned: annual research and extension meetings for junior researchers, teacher and researcher exchanges through the academic mobilization programme. In 1994, the deans of the participating universities suggested implementing a Scale Program to create funds to support the AUGM activities, which would be added to those provided by each university. In this context, responsibility for each academic area was assigned to a different university. Finally, other Brazilian universities were incorporated, closing a first stage since, as from 1995, incorporations have been temporarily restricted. AUGM is made up of the following universities: Universidad de Buenos Aires, Universidad Nacional de Entre Ríos, Universidad Nacional del Litoral, Universidad Nacional de Rosario, Universidad Federal do Río Grande do Sul, Universidad Federal do Santa Catarina, Universidad federal do Paraná, Universidad de San Carlos, Universidad de la República, and Universidad Nacional de Asunción.

Disciplines in which cooperation and exchanges are organized include: molecular biology, applied mathematics, chemistry, natural product pharmacology, microelectronics, education for integration, academic networks, regional development, university strategic planning and management, applied meteorology and remote sensing, environment, water, human and animal health, and political science.

5   Another journal, *Universidad Hoy*, was published almost at the same time. They were followed by many others that disseminate information at state level and made it possible for researchers and administrators to gain greater and better access to information. However, all these journals will have to consolidate their basis.

6   Although there have been similar experiences, they were not as structured as the ones we mention next. As can be seen, 1997 witnesses the development of this type of second university degree courses.

Postgraduate Studies (MA) in University Education, Facultad de Humanidades, Universidad Nacional del Comahue, 1997.

Postgraduate Diploma in University Policies and Management, Unigestión, Universidad Nacional del Litoral, 1997.

Postgraduate Studies (MA) in University Management, Rectorado, Universidad Nacional de Catamarca, 1997.

Postgraduate Studies (MA) in University Management, Facultad de Economía, Universidad Nacional de Mar del Plata, 1998.

Specialization Course in University Teaching, Facultad de Humanidades, Universidad Nacional de Mar del Plata, 1998.

Postgraduate Studies (MA) in Higher Teaching, Facultad de Humanidades, Universidad Nacional de Tucumán, 1998.

Postgraduate Studies (MA) in University Management, Universidad Nacional de Santiago del Estero, 1998

REFERENCES

Alexander J. and Davis C. (1993). 'Teoría democrática e incorporación politica de la educación superior', in Tenti F. (ed.), *Universidad y Empresa*. Buenos Aires: Editorial Miño y Dávila S.R.L..

Altbach, P. G. (1996). The review and the field of higher education, *The Review of Higher Education,* 20 (1), p. 2.

Baldridge, V. et al. (1986). 'Alternative models of governance in higher education', in M.W. Peterson (ed.) *ASHE Reader on Organization and Governance in Higher Education*. Massachusetts: Ginn Press.

Bourdieu, P. (1989). *Homo Academicus*. Stanford: Stanford University Press.

Brunner, J. J. (1990). *La Educación Superior en América Latina*. Santiago de Chile: Flacso-Fondo de Cultura Económica.

Clark, B. R. (1983). *The Higher Education System: Academic Organization in Cross-National Perspective*. Berkeley and Los Angeles: University of California Press

Clark, B. R. (1984). *Perspectives on Higher Education*. Berkeley and Los Angeles: University of California Press.

García Guadilla, C. (1996). *Conocimiento, Educación Superior y Sociedad en América Latina*. Caracas: Cendes-Nueva Sociedad.

Durkheim, E. (1969). *L'évolution pedagogique en France*. Paris: Presses Universitaires de France.

Gibbons, M. (1995). 'The university as an instrument for the development of science and basic research: The implications of Mode 2 Science', in D. D. Dill and B. Sporn (eds.) *Emerging Patterns of Social Demand and University Reform: Through a Glass Darkly*. Oxford: Pergamon/IAU Press.

Lindblom, C. E. (1980). *The Policy Making Process*. New Jersey: Prentice Hall.

Neave, G. (1994). Significación actual del Vocacionalismo, *Pensamiento Universitario* (2), p. 42.

Reich, R. (1993). *El Trabajo de las Naciones*. Buenos Aires: Javier Vergara Edit.

Teichler, U. (1996). 'Comparative higher education: potentials and limits', *Higher Education: the international journal of higher education and educational planning*, 32 (4), p. 431.

Tenti, E. (1988). 'El Proceso de Investigación en Educación – El Campo de la Investigación Educativa en la Argentina', in *Curso de Metodología de la Investigación en Ciencias Sociales*. Rosario: CONICET/Universidad Nacional de Rosario.

Terenzini, P. (1996). Rediscovering roots: Public policy and higher education research, *The Review of Higher Education,* 20 (1), pp. 5-7.

Torstendahl, R. (1996). La transformación de la educación profesional en el siglo XIX, in *La universidad europea y americana desde 1800.* Barcelona: Edit. Pomares-Corregido

Trow, M. (1996). 'Trust, markets and accountability in higher education: Comparative perspective', *Higher Education Policy*, 9 (4), p. 309.

Weiss, E. (1994). Investigación educativa en América Latina: presente y futuro, *Universidad Futura* (16), p. 20.

Chapter 10

Creating a Community of Scholars and Institutionalizing Higher Education Research in Israel

SARAH GURI-ROSENBLIT
The Open University of Israel, Israel

10.1 Introduction

Research on higher education in Israel is carried out by only a small number of scholars from different institutions. None of the Israeli universities operates a research centre or offers an academic program on higher education. In the last decade, the system has been faced with growing pressures to enhance the diversity of academic styles and traditions and to expand its boundaries. The rapid growth of the non-university sector, a developing private sector and the 'import' of many extensions of foreign universities have shaken the relatively conservative and stable foundations of the system. The present and future agendas of universities and colleges are frequently debated in the Knesset (Israeli Parliament), in the media and within academia. The need to create a community of scholars and to institutionalize higher education research has been felt and expressed by many actors involved in higher education policy, administration, research and private enterprise.

Most of the data on higher education is published by the Central Bureau of Statistics and the Council for Higher Education. Occasionally, reports and articles on various issues are published in scholarly journals in Israel, in international publications (in fields such as sociology, public policy, economics, education, etc.) and in newspapers. Some recent articles and reports contested data published by the Council for Higher Education, stressing that part of the information and its interpretations were policy driven and arguing that some important indicators and factors were left out. Even such a simple and innocent indicator as the percentage of 18-year-olds enrolled in higher education does not appear in the official statistical data and can be debated.

S. Schwarz and U. Teichler (eds.), The Institutional Basis of Higher Education Research, 157–165.
© 2000 *Kluwer Academic Publishers. Printed in the Netherlands.*

For example, in the report on higher education which was published by Adva Center in 1997, the percentage of the relevant age cohort (high school graduates) in higher education stands at a mere 15 percent (Svirsky and Svirsky 1997), as compared to nearly 30 percent of the 21-24-year-old group in the publication of the Council for Higher Education (Herskovic 1997). The fact that most students enter university after their military service and that Israel is continuously absorbing immigrants complicate the standard calculations of the relevant age cohort in higher education, since, in other countries, most students enrol immediately after completing high school. But there is no justification for a 15 percent gap between various reports relating to the same age cohorts in Israel.

In this paper I shall focus on the *raison d'être* of the Rethinking Higher Education Program (RHEP). RHEP was launched in 1995 as a partial response to the need to create an interdisciplinary and interinstitutional project on higher education that would attract scholars from different fields and enhance higher education research in Israeli academia. The final section presents the main trends to institutionalize higher education research beyond this specific program.

10.2 The rethinking higher education program (RHEP): its underlying principles

RHEP was launched as a collaborative venture by the Van Leer Jerusalem Institute, the Israel Academy of Sciences and Humanities, and the Council for Higher Education. The three institutions joined forces in 1995 to establish a special program to promote a scholarly and fruitful discourse on higher education between academics, administrators and policy makers and help to create a research infrastructure on higher education within universities. The following underlying assumptions shaped the creation and operation of RHEP:

10.2.1 An interinstitutional program on 'neutral grounds'

The fact that none of the Israeli universities were well equipped to establish a centre or program of studies on higher education led to the creation of an interinstitutional program which appealed to scholars from various higher education institutions. The national and international prestige of the Van Leer Jerusalem Institute made it an ideal 'neutral' gathering place for a scholarly community. It carries out many scholarly and social-oriented projects which are important for Israeli society at large. Hence, it was chosen as a perfect place to encourage collaboration within the academic world in Israel and between Israeli scholars and the international community. Furthermore, the buildings of the Israel Academy of Sciences and Humanities and the Council for Higher Education are located on the same campus. This facilitates regular collaboration between the three bodies.

10.2.2   An international comparative orientation

From the outset, RHEP adopted an international comparative orientation. The first step that was taken by the founding parties was to nominate an International Advisory Committee composed of eminent scholars. It is chaired by Sheldon Rothblatt (University of California at Berkeley). The six other members that joined the Committee in 1995 were: Martin Trow (USA); Guy Neave (France); Frans van Vught (The Netherlands); Ulrich Teichler (Germany); Thorsten Nybom (Sweden); and José Luis García-Garrido (Spain). Lee Shulman (Stanford University and President of the Carnegie Foundation for the Advancement of Teaching) joined RHEP's International Advisory Committee in February 1997.

The members met at the Van Leer Jerusalem Institute in May 1995 and helped to shape the nature and potential activities of the newborn RHEP in collaboration with Israeli scholars and members of the Council for Higher Education, the Planning and Budgeting Committee and the Israel Academy of Sciences and Humanities. Rothblatt, in his summary report of this meeting, highlighted the importance of linking Israel to the international networks: "The Israeli voice has been conspicuously absent from higher education networks, if not other networks, but we see this omission as being swiftly rectified. (...) We noticed the existence of a highly competent cadre of Israeli talent which could easily establish and manage a higher education program. That talent could be supplemented by visitors from other countries. Indeed this has now become the pattern for all national programs as international cooperation grows and each national system evinces more complexity and expense" (Rothblatt 1995). He also observed that "The members of the International Advisory Committee have expressed the unanimous opinion that the Jerusalem meetings were amongst the most memorable they have attended. One member in particular has several times stated that our mutual conversations reached the level of intellectual stimulation and intensity that he had not experienced in international symposia since the early 1980s" (ibid).

The successful international gathering paved the way for RHEP to start as a program with a reputable international backing and convinced some skeptical policy makers to assist in co-sponsoring the program on a regular basis. This highlights the potential importance of older higher education centres and eminent scholars in this field in assisting new born programs to gain legibility and respectability in countries where higher education was not historically considered a subject that deserved systematic and analytical scholarly research.

In three years, the international orientation of RHEP has taken on various forms: invitation of scholars for short seminars and symposia; participation in international bodies and consortia; the creation of a special fund for experts on higher education to spend short sabbaticals at Israeli universities, which was approved by the Council for Higher Education. A meeting in Malta on *Higher Education in the Mediterranean* in November 1996 led to a collaborative venture between the editor of the *Mediterranean Journal of Education Studies* and RHEP to publish a special issue on 'Higher Education in the Mediterranean' (Guri-Rosenblit and Sultana, 1999). Other international projects on the agenda of the program's participants include: the impact of blending various academic cultures in Israeli higher education; the integration of the new information technologies in traditional universities; accreditation models; interrelations between university and non-university sectors in various national settings.

10.2.3   Interdisciplinary nature

Higher education as a field of study is interdisciplinary by its very nature. RHEP's founders decided from the start to organize interdisciplinary think tanks, symposia, and seminars. The think tanks have purported to lay the ground for a fertile intellectual discourse on key issues in Israeli higher education which could lead to the establishment of a scholarly community on higher education, as well as have an indirect impact on decision making in crucial policy matters. Three think tanks have operated within RHEP since 1995: the first dealt with *Access to Higher Education;* the second focused on *Excellence in Academic Management;* and the third discussed the *Intricate Interrelations between the University and Non-university Sectors.* Each of the teams was composed of some twenty to thirty members from diverse backgrounds who had different academic expertise, e.g. history, sociology, education, economics, political science, business administration, statistics, psychology, assessment and evaluation, natural sciences, mathematics, geography, etc. The end products of the think tanks were position papers and symposia which were open to a wide public. Some of the position papers were published (Guri-Rosenblit forthcoming; Ministry of Education 1997). The background of the participants helped to present a rich spectrum of standpoints which were studied from different angles.

10.2.4 Enhancement of university research

RHEP was not established as a research centre. It was agreed that re-search is a university function and that one of RHEP's tasks was to enhance research by individual scholars or by groups of university scholars. The enhancement of higher education as an academic field of study was promoted by: the preparation of position papers based on interdisciplinary scholarship and which deal with present central policy issues; the coordination of a data-base on higher education literature and documentation; the launching of special fellowships for graduate students who focus their theses or disserta-tions on themes related to higher education (the funds are transferred directly by the Council for Higher Education to the universities); and invitations of scholars for short visits to deliver lectures and conduct symposia.

The generous fellowships for graduate students who focus their research on higher education have already encouraged a greater number to submit proposals on various issues related to the Israeli higher education system. In 1998 and 1999, they submitted proposals to the Higher Education Fellow-ship Committee on a plethora of topics, such as the impact of the foreign extensions on the Israeli higher education system; factors that stimulate the creation of private and public higher education institutions; the parameters of psychometric testing; the history of research and teaching of micro-biology in Israeli universities; the history of the humanities in Israeli universities; the economic factors of higher education systems, etc. The number of graduate students specializing in various aspects of higher education will probably grow with the creation in the near future of a graduate program in this field in one of the universities.

Inviting scholars to stay at an Israeli university for a semester or a year has not yet materialized, although special funding was allocated for this pur-pose in 1997. Since it was difficult to recruit eminent scholars for a whole semester on account of their busy schedule, it was suggested that the possi-bility of a joint teaching responsibility between an Israeli and an external scholar be explored. The Council for Higher Education has agreed to spon-sor visiting professors who will be responsible for seminars leading to aca-demic credits. Short visits are funded by the Van Leer Jerusalem Institute and the Academy of Sciences and Humanities.

10.3 Collaboration between academics, administrators, policy makers, and practitioners

From the outset, RHEP aimed to enhance collaboration between scholars, practitioners, policy makers, and administrators. For instance, the think tanks were composed of representatives from the Council for Higher Education and the Planning and Budgeting Committee, former and current presidents and rectors of universities and colleges, deans of schools and departments, scholars in the field of higher education from both universities and research institutes outside the universities (e.g. the Institute for Social Research, the Institute for Aptitude and Psychometric Testing, task forces of the Ministry of Education, Adva Center), administrators, etc. RHEP willingly cooperated with research groups from various bodies. For instance, the Ministry of Education and Culture nominated a Research Group in 1995 to study the interrelations between formal schooling, and more particularly secondary education, and higher education. The coordinators of this research group approached RHEP and offered their collaboration. Members of this group were invited to join the think tank on *Access to Higher Education.* The cooperation with this group ended in April 1997 with a public symposium at the Van Leer Jerusalem Institute. The position papers were co-published by RHEP and the Research Group on the Interrelations between High Schools and Higher Education (Ministry of Education 1997). The *Adva Center*, which is supported by grants from the Ford Foundation and the New Israel Fund, approached RHEP members in 1996 to participate in the preparation of a comprehensive report on the emergence of new colleges and their impact on access and social equity in Israeli society (Svirsky and Svirsky 1997).

10.4 Future prospects of higher education research

Higher education research in Israel has developed steadily in recent years, thanks to initiatives of RHEP members and other actors in Israeli academia. Future trends are likely to progress in the following directions: the creation of think tanks on "burning issues"; the institutionalization of a graduate program on higher education at one of the universities; the establishment of an inter-university and interdisciplinary higher education research centre; the promotion of international collaboration ventures and research projects; and the creation of a scholarly journal on higher education.

10.4.1   New think tanks on "burning issues" in Israeli higher education

1998-1999 was a stormy year in the history of the Israeli higher education. The Council for Higher Education decided to authorize certain colleges to teach towards master's degrees, a right that was reserved until recently to universities. This gave rise to a large debate, both in academic circles and in the public, through the mass media. The members of the International Advisory Committee of RHEP were asked to give their opinion on this issue and their suggestions were transmitted to all the members of the Council for

Higher Education. Although all the heads of the universities were against the proposed reform, the members of the Council for Higher Education (the majority of whom are university professors) decided to approve it. This issue and political debates in Israeli society prior to the elections in June 1999 led to the creation of an association of professors, *BaShaar* (The Gatekeepers). Many of its founders are former rectors and presidents of universities. Some participated in the RHEP think tanks mentioned above. One of the proclaimed purposes of this association is to create think tanks on "burning issues" in Israeli society, with a special focus on the development and future agenda of the higher education system. As with RHEP, the aim is to bring together scholars from various institutions and across many disciplines to provide a rich and colourful range of independent standpoints which are not subjected to particular interest groups. The new think tanks will be created around issues such as the economics of higher education; the optimal structure of the Israeli higher education system; differentiation of tuition and salaries in Israeli academia; access to undergraduate and graduate degrees; accreditation of prior and experiential learning, etc. Many of the participants of RHEP will take part in these think tanks. The end-products will be position papers, some of which may have an impact on future policy making on "burning dilemmas" that are high on the agenda of the Israeli universities. Some may also lead to research projects.

10.4.2   Launching a graduate program on higher education

Some of RHEP's participants have expressed their willingness to establish a program on higher education at master's level. It will probably begin in the year 2000 at the School of Education of Tel-Aviv University, where a cadre of seven faculty members are already engaged in research on various higher education topics. Negotiations are already under way. The program will be interdisciplinary in nature and will study issues in Israel and in the broader international context from various disciplinary perspectives. Ideally, the courses and seminars will also be open to graduate students of other departments and schools at Tel-Aviv University and to students from other universities.

The participation of eminent scholars from abroad in the framework of short sabbaticals will be crucially important to establish the academic reputation of this new venture. Members of RHEP's International Advisory Committee and other scholars will be invited to lecture and give seminars. New advanced technology, such as interactive video conferences through satellites and computer teleconferencing, will be mobilized to enhance international participation. The new program will probably collaborate with other centres of higher education and graduate programs on higher education, such as the one that is offered jointly by the Open University in Britain and Twente University in the Netherlands.

10.4.3   Founding an inter-university research centre

RHEP's three-year existence and the gradual creation of a community of scholars on higher education have laid the ground for the establishment of an inter-university higher education research centre at one of the universities. The Council for Higher Education and the Planning and Budgeting Committee have expressed their readiness to sponsor such an endeavour. The centre could eventually replace RHEP and institutionalize higher education research. Clearly, RHEP's initiators and participants will be active actors in its creation. There is one precedent in Israel. It is an inter-university research centre on oceanography, which is very successful. The inter-university character of the new centre will encourage the active participation of scholars and graduate students from different universities. The Council for Higher Education suggested that it might start as a "virtual centre", in the sense that its activities would be disseminated in several universities and its coordinators would move from one university to another every four to five years. It intends to carry out research projects in a rich spectrum of disciplines.

10.5 International collaboration and research projects

The Israeli academic world has always been very internationally orientated. Academics participate in international research projects, forums and conferences. Mechanisms have been built into the career ladders of the senior academic faculty that encourage them to go on sabbaticals, launch cooperative research projects and publish in international journals. As higher education research will become more institutionalized through a graduate program in one of the universities and a research centre, the orientation of many projects will certainly be international in scope. Some of RHEP's members already participate in international research groups, such as the one on the implementation of new advanced technologies in higher education systems under the auspices of the Center for Studies on Higher Education at the University of California in Berkeley. The Euro-Med conference on "Technology in Learning Environments" is planned to take place in Israel at the end of October 1999 in cooperation with the Open University of Israel. Other international research themes that are being planned relate to: accreditation policies worldwide; Israel as a melting pot of academic cultures; tuition and salary policies in various academic settings, etc.

10.6 Founding a scholarly journal on higher education

At present, only the Committee of the Universities Heads ("VERA" which is composed of the seven older research universities and institutes) publishes a biannual journal, *Academia*, which is devoted to various issues related to the seven research universities. The time seems right to create a scholarly journal on higher education which would include research papers, position papers, symposia summaries and exchange of ideas.

The *BaShaar* association has recently joined forces with another journal on academic issues of social relevance. The aim is to lay the ground for both scholarly and "popular" presentations on relevant issues in academia and society. This new endeavour could develop into an interdisciplinary journal on higher education. In addition, the institutionalization of the graduate program on higher education and the establishment of an inter-university higher education centre in the near future will almost certainly lead to a scholarly journal in this field.

REFERENCES

Guri-Rosenblit, S. (ed.) (forthcoming). *Access to Higher Education: Selection Criteria and Social Perspectives*. Jerusalem: Van Leer Institute (in Hebrew).

Guri-Rosenblit, S. and Sultana, R. (eds.) (1999). Higher education in the Mediterranean, a special issue of the *Mediterranean Journal of Education Studies, Vol. 4 (2)*.

Herskovic, S. (ed.) (1997). *The Higher Education System in Israel: Statistical Abstract and Analysis*. Jerusalem: Council for Higher Education (in Hebrew).

Ministry of Education (1997). *The Interrelations between the High School and University Position Papers*. Jerusalem: Ministry of Education and Culture and the 'Rethinking Higher Education Program' at the Van Leer Jerusalem Institute (in Hebrew).

Rothblatt, S. (1995). *Summary Report of the International Advisory Committee of the Rethinking Higher Education Program*. University of California at Berkeley. An internal document.

Svirsky, S. and Svirsky, B. (1997). *Higher Education in Israel*. Tel-Aviv: Adva Center (in Hebrew).

Chapter 11

Higher Education Research in the Czech Republic

HELENA ŠEBKOVÁ
Centre for Higher Education Studies, Prague, Czech Republic

11.1 Introduction

For four decades, higher education in the Czech Republic (CR) developed under very rigid regulations imposed by the State. The institutional autonomy, academic freedom and self-governance of the universities were minimal. Any important measure concerning higher education institutions was decided by top government authorities and the content of studies and research were deeply marked by the ideology of the Communist party which played an essential role in their planning. So it is clear that the results of higher education research were not needed in the decision making process.

We are now at the end of a ten-year transition period. The 1990 Higher Education Act gave back autonomy and academic freedom to the universities and changed the role of the State which coordinates and indirectly governs higher education through funds allocated from the state budget. The 1998 Act approved the positive aspects of the former legislation, improved the balance of competencies and responsibilities both at the state (relationship between institutions and state authorities) and the internal institutional level (between institutions and their units) and opened the way for a broad diversification of higher education which included the creation of private institutions.

The context described above needs very good management and strategy planning at the top government level, based on the results of higher education research. This is why there is a continuous development of institutional higher education research which is supplemented by the development of smaller units, usually within universities, and a network of independent researchers in this field.

S. Schwarz and U. Teichler (eds.), The Institutional Basis of Higher Education Research, 167–174.
© 2000 *Kluwer Academic Publishers. Printed in the Netherlands.*

11.2   Institutionalised research

11.2.1   Centre for Higher Education Studies (CHES)

The Ministry of Education, Youth and Sports founded the Institute for Higher Education Development in 1981. It was quite a large institution (about 100 employees) whose main aim was to elaborate ministerial plans and decisions. In 1991, it was completely reorganised. The number of staff fell to 29 persons and it was renamed the Centre for Higher Education Studies (CHES). A new statute determines that its main mission is to carry out research and pedagogical activities in the field of higher education. It is funded by the Ministry of Education.

A further significant change was new partnerships. The main partner of CHES remains the Ministry of Education, but close collaboration has been established with the Council of Higher Education Institutions (representatives of academic senates) and the Czech Rectors' Conference which jointly form a representative body of all the institutions in the country. Other partners include the Accreditation Commission of the CR, Czech and foreign higher education institutions, foreign research institutions and students.

It was proposed to develop CHES's mission. First, it was decided to establish a TEMPUS Office as a second department which recently became the Agency for Educational Programmes of the European Union. It administers and coordinates activities required by the TEMPUS and SOCRATES Programmes. A further extension was the creation of a third department, the National Centre for Distance Education, which is responsible for the coordination of distance education provided by tertiary institutions of education. It was created in 1997. The Centre for Equivalence of Documents about Education was founded in accordance with the Convention on the Recognition of Higher Education Qualifications in the European Region. It also assumed the tasks of Network of European National Information Centres (ENIC), Network of National Academic Recognition Information Centres (NARIC).

CHES is a member of research organisations (Consortium of Higher Education Researchers [CHER]; European Higher Education Society [EAIR]), of educational organisations (European Distance Education Network [EDEN]; European Association for International Education [EAIE]; Association of Teacher Education in Europe [ATEE]; *Internationale Gesellschaft für Ingenieurpädagogik* [IGIP]), and of other international organisations (Institutional Management of Higher Education [IMHE/OECD]; Global Alliance for Transnational Education [GATE]; International Network for Quality Assurance Agencies in Higher Education [INQAAHE]; Network of European National Information Centres [ENIC] and Network of National Academic Recognition Information Centres [NARIC]).

CHES now carries out many new tasks, but the increase in the number of staff to 38 full time employees is not very significant.

The *Research Department* undertakes analytical and comparative studies on higher education and research policy, diversification of the tertiary education system, higher education legislation, quality assessment and assurance, management and strategic planning of higher education institutions, relationship between the institutions and the state, staff development and student affairs. It is establishing a national network of academic guidance and career centres and in-service training for academic personnel to improve their pedagogical skills. The department also offers services to the Ministry of Education, the representation body of higher education institutions and the Accreditation Commission.

Other activities include the organisation of seminars to disseminate research outcomes and to launch debates on issues that are important for higher education institutions at the national level (e.g. problems linked to the implementation of the new Higher Education Act). The department also organises international seminars or workshops, usually in collaboration with foreign partners (Council of Europe – Legislative Reform programme, OECD, etc.) or in the framework of projects under PHARE, TEMPUS, SOCRATES and other programmes.

Even if the composition of the institution does not seem very coherent, it has proved to be useful.

The *National Centre of Distance Education* uses researchers' expertise to provide consulting and counselling services as well as information in the area of distance and lifelong education. It also supplies researchers with information on quality assessment methodologies in distance education in the Czech Republic and abroad, issues of legislation related to distance and lifelong education, etc.

The *Centre for Equivalence of Documents* about Education provides information on the quality of higher education in the country in comparative studies on students, teachers, quality assessment, etc. carried out by the research department. It supplies researchers and other staff with data on the quantitative problems of higher education in the CR and other countries.

The CR became a member of SOCRATES in late 1997. The experience of the TEMPUS office can be used here. ERASMUS, ODL, AE, and NARIC are closely connected with higher education. Hence, advice, consultation and debates with those who are interested in submitting a project are very useful.

The performance of any department can benefit from the results of other departments. Staff members participate in different teams that have been created to provide solutions to specific problems or in respect of on-going projects.

CHES has recently participated in a number of international projects, either as a coordinating institution or as a collaborating member. The most important focused on quality in higher education (Evaluation and Assessment of Higher Education Institutions, Programme of the Institute for Local Government and Public Service), quality and strategic management (Strategic and Internal Management of the Czech Universities: Design and Implementation of a Quality Assurance System at Institutions of Higher Education in the Czech Republic, TEMPUS), evaluation of quality in connection with the recognition of studies (PHARE, the pilot and follow-up projects), guidance and counselling (Development of Careers Services at Czech Universities, TEMPUS) and distance education (Multi-Country Cooperation in Distance Education, PHARE, the pilot and follow-up projects).

Research results are very important for the *pedagogical activities* of CHES which is preparing a course for academics who hold leading positions in the institutions or for those who are preparing for this type of career. This course is developing at an international level in the framework of the PHARE Programme.

Research projects at the national level are mostly sponsored by the Ministry of Education which runs its own modest grant agency. Current projects are mostly in the field of sociology and relevant methods. Obtaining significant results is expensive and needs an additional research grant.

There are biannual projects on students' social background. Another important project is devoted to staff development in the Czech higher education institutions which aims at making the conclusions comparable to those of international research. Comparative studies (university management in selected countries, engineering education, etc.) can also benefit from additional funds. These activities can be found on CHES's *Internet homepage: www.csvs.cz. The Information Bulletin* publishes abstracts of publications by the staff members of CHES (in Czech). It is available on the Web. *CHES publishes AULA,* a quarterly *Review for Higher Education and Research Policy* (in Czech). Its English version is published as an annual digest.

11.2.2   Centre for Educational Policy (CEP)

This is an autonomous centre of the *Institute for Research of Educational Development* (IRED) at the *Faculty of Education of Charles University in Prague*. It was established in 1994, following an agreement between the Ministry of Education, Youth and Sports and the dean of the Faculty of Education. IRED focuses primarily on the needs of school education, whereas CEP deals with the tertiary sector as a whole, but more especially professional higher education. Its *research activities* are funded by the State through the university budget.

CEP is only a small unit of six persons, *both nationals and foreigners*. Its mission is to carry out tasks for the Ministry of Education which call for an independent approach and flexibility. Activities include international (mainly European) comparative studies on the importance of educational policy for the development of other sectors of society. CEP uses interdisciplinary approaches and studies problems from the pedagogical, sociological, economic and political angle.

CEP is also the *coordinator of the Czech participation in OECD education programmes*. It takes part in the meetings of the *Education Committee* and its two programmes – *Centre for Education and Research Innovations* and the *Programme on Educational Building* (connected with IMHE). It plays an important role in the INES Programme. Even if the coordination of the Czech participation in this programme is ensured by the Institute for Information in Education, members of CEP participated in the meetings of the *Network C of the Technical Group*. The INES programme focuses on information. Descriptive and analytical studies constitute an extremely important tool for comparative research, not only at CEP, but also at CHES and other organisations.

CEP was the main coordinator of a joint Czech/OECD project on the evaluation of the Czech educational system. The final recommendation of the OECD experts in secondary education leaving examinations and access to tertiary education are very important for higher education research.

Great attention was paid to the first years of tertiary education with respect to the transition of graduates to work. With the support of the Ministry of Education, CEP organised an *international seminar* on this topic. Relevant studies were prepared and a seminar was organised at the national level.

Research is used for the *teaching activities of its staff* and the Faculty of Education disseminates the outcomes. *Regular meetings* for researchers, decision-makers and expert public are a good platform for discussions on a wide range of topics. A number of *publications*, including translations of OECD reports, etc., are available in the form of books, reports, articles, etc.

11.2.3   Collaboration of research institutions

There is informal *collaboration between CHES and CEP primarily in the field of tertiary education*. Bachelor programmes and postgraduate professional education are the most important topics for researchers and decision makers in the Czech Republic. Transparency and recognition between institutions providing these studies, strategy planning, legislation and evaluation of quality are issues which call for close collaboration between CHES and CEP.

Joint information and participation in events that are relevant for certain OECD's activities represent another type of collaboration. While CEP is the main coordinator of collaboration with OECD, CHES is responsible for the OECD/IMHE Programme. CHES's publication *AULA* is also used by CEP staff to publish research articles.

Two other research institutes, the *Research Pedagogical Institute* and the *Research Institute of Professional Education* were established by the Ministry of Education and are responsible for research and expert service for the Ministry in the area of primary and secondary education. Both CHES and CEP entertain good relations with them. They collaborate on topics that are on the border of secondary and higher education and professional education in the tertiary education sector. Several other non-state institutions (Jan Amos Komensky Academy, National Education Fund, etc.) are active in research which is not exclusively devoted to higher education.

11.2.4   Network of researchers in higher education

There are also researchers in higher education who are *teachers at various faculties* of higher education institutions. Much research focuses on pedagogical topics. Other research fields are of interest to researchers at the faculties of humanities (mainly the faculties of philosophy or social sciences) and there are also specialised faculties, such as the faculty of mathematics and physics or the faculties of physical education and sport, which are able to concentrate human resources and funds to solve research problems that are important for them.

11.3 Research mission in higher education

Institutional research funded by the State can cover many important topics but mostly at the elementary level. Some research methodologies are expensive, extensive comparative studies need support for travel expenses, research that focuses on new information and communication technologies need capital investments, etc. In order to obtain additional support, researchers can elaborate projects and submit them to any of the grant agencies below.

11.3.1   Grant agency of the Czech Republic

It is the largest State-sponsored agency. It is open to any institution or researcher but the submitted project must correspond to its priorities. Unfortunately, very little attention is given to interdisciplinary topics concerning educational research. In this respect, this agency is not very useful for the type of research mentioned above.

11.3.2 Grant agency of the Ministry of Education, Youth and Sports

This agency has a very modest budget, but priorities, which are selected on an annual basis, are oriented towards the needs of the Ministry and therefore linked to most institutional research topics. Every year, several research projects (the agency is open to any institution or individual researcher) are financed by a shared budget consisting of institutional funds and additional funds from this agency.

The following priorities have been identified in the last two years: society and education, support for school teachers, professional education in the framework of life-long learning, steering in education – its structure and function –, development of tertiary education, evaluation, youth issues linked to sports, social and international links in education, analytical and conceptual studies in specific educational sectors, mechanisms to improve education, the moral and social development of youngsters. Projects were submitted by research institutions and researchers from various educational institutions (which were previously faculties of higher education), but only rarely by institutions that are not closely linked to education.

11.3.3 Grant agencies of other ministries

There are similar agencies under the responsibility of other ministries. They are usually oriented towards specialised topics and higher education researchers can only occasionally apply for support for their research topics (e.g. research on graduate employment, sponsored by the Ministry of Labour and Social Affairs).

11.3.4 Fund for the development of higher education institutions

This fund is very specific because it is part of the higher education budget allocated on the basis of agreement between the Ministry of Education, Youth and Sports and the representation of higher education institutions to mandate priority development issues determined by both parties. Obviously, it does not only support higher education research, but researchers from higher education institutions (it is not open to other applicants) may ask for funds.

11.4 Conclusion

The priorities and issues evoked in this article are very important for the development of higher education in the Czech Republic. The new context of freedom and decentralised steering of higher education is very demanding as far as good theoretical expertise and relevant research outcomes are concerned. Yet higher education research is underestimated because of our educational heritage. But successful results have been obtained.

An important issue, which has not yet been solved, is education. There are no courses in higher education at any level (undergraduate, postgraduate) and it will be a challenge to introduce this type of studies in the Czech Republic.

Chapter 12

A Comparative Study of the Institutional Basis of Higher Education Research in Hungary and the Czech Republic

TAMAS KOZMA & IMRE RADACSI
Hungarian Institute for Educational Research, Budapest, Hungary

Higher education institutions are developing as centres of research in Hungary and the Czech Republic. There is greater professionalism and conducting research as an independent professional activity has become accepted. Carrying out research for public purposes has gained greater significance. Team research has replaced individual research and a network of researchers has emerged. In becoming independent from other higher education activities, research has emerged as a distinct process that can be planned as a result-oriented activity. The need for learning and teaching research methods has also become accepted. A new structural framework for research and qualifications has been introduced in both countries. Research has become reflexive and related areas have begun to develop, e.g. the philosophy of science, sociology, economics, and research management and administration. We shall try to describe the similarities and difference in both countries.

12.1 Hungary[1]

Today, higher education is the main venue of research in Hungary. Its infrastructure and human resources, structure and management have remained virtually unchanged. One can conclude that old-fashioned, rigid structures have become fossilized. This is seen in the technical equipment and other resources that were developed to serve lecture-based teaching that neglected the need for individual experiential learning and research. The role of the researcher was tangential to teaching activities. Hungarian higher education does not encourage specialization, rather it emphasizes comprehensive and

S. Schwarz and U. Teichler (eds.), The Institutional Basis of Higher Education Research, 175–180.
© 2000 *Kluwer Academic Publishers. Printed in the Netherlands.*

general education. The structure of the institutions does not correspond to the demands of the funding bodies and the objectives of a professionally oriented educational system. The institutions offer free services and resemble institutions that offer social services. Thus, the system has a buffer function in the social sense and does not train high quality professionals. Above all, it produces degrees and titles, instead of focusing on the production of knowledge. One must redefine the position of research within higher education, otherwise the "mass-production" of higher education may represent a time bomb for the future.

There are three models:

a) Mediterranean: Tertiary education is provided by universities, which produce mass education. Hence, research is concentrated in the Academy of Science, in independent research institutions and in industrial and agricultural research institutions.

b) Central European: Tertiary and scientific education are offered in separate institutions. Tertiary education is provided by colleges which offer certificate courses. Research remains within the confines of universities and academic institutions.

c) Trans-Atlantic: Tertiary education is at a lower level than university education, which remains élitist, its predominant activities being scientific/academic research.

12.1.1   Research Centres[2]

Higher education research centres in Hungary are affiliated to the universities and colleges where their activities take place along with educational/teaching activities. There are a few separate institutional units. Research is carried out in the framework of plans.

The types of institutional units include
– research institutes,
– laboratories,
– research units within departments,
– independent research centres.

The following are well-established state institutions of national and international reputation:
– Eötvös Loránd University (ELTE), Budapest;
– Technical University (BME), Budapest;
– University of Economics (BKE), Budapest;
– József Attila University (JATE), Szeged:
– Kossuth Lajos University (KLTE), Debrecen;
– Janus Pannonius University (JPTE), Pécs.

Of the medical schools, Semmelweis Medical School, Budapest, Imre Haynal Health Medical University, Budapest, and Albert Szent-Györgyi Medical University, Szeged, enjoy international reputation.

Of the Agricultural Universities, the Georgikon Keszthely University has gained international recognition.

12.1.2   Research on Higher Education[3]

The Hungarian Institute for Educational Research (HIER) is the umbrella institution for research on the integrative and comprehensive issues of education in Hungary. It monitors and analyses the issues of education for young people and adults. Its research results provide the basis for the decisions taken by the educational administrative bodies at the national level.

The research objectives of the Institute are strategically defined, since they concern the analysis of the Hungarian education system as a whole, structural, political, and financial developmental issues and its national, regional, local, and institutional aspects.

12.1.3   Evaluation of Research

The HIER is commissioned by the Hungarian Ministry of Education to conduct the evaluation of research projects that receive grants on a competitive basis.

Some 60 percent of the projects reached their objectives. Some 49 percent of the grants went to research projects in natural sciences; 27percent to the technical sciences; and 24 percent to the social sciences. Some 29 percent went to the Eötvös Lorand University (ELTE), where 43 projects were carried out. 25 projects of the Technical University, Budapest (BME) and 20 projects of Jozsef Attila University, Szeged (JATE) received grants. Hence, the multi-faculty universities were more successful than the specialized universities.

From the evaluation results in regard to the types of institutions and areas of research, it can be said that many applicants were awarded grants on a regular basis in the fields where research was most successful. They sought different forms of support from various sources and are seeking international and national inter-institutional cooperation. They are able to manage the research processes, the research and development support systems, and the administrative aspects of the projects.

The input/output ratio of institutions depends on the status of their areas of research. Those that are considered modern are those that comprise several disciplines and several types of activities, such as teaching, research and science management, or have obtained outstanding results in one particular area.

12.2 Czech Republic[4]

The OECD examiners recommended that changes in this area should be aimed primarily at restoring the significance of research conducted in the higher education institutions and its links with teaching, and more especially at doctoral level. The changes should develop cooperation with the Academy of Science and improve relations with organisations of applied research, as well as with industrial companies.

But research in higher educational institutions cannot be analysed and assessed separately. It is part of the scientific and research system as a whole and proceeds in parallel with other fields of research and development. The problems of research and development in higher education institutions are reflected in the following legislation: since November 1992, the responsibility for state research and technological policy in the Czech Republic has been entrusted to the Ministry of Education.

12.2.1   Research and its links with teaching

The evaluation by the individual institutions and faculties of the development of research in higher education institutions during the last two years differs. Some clearly state that its level, extent and significance have increased. They evaluate the research activity positively, both in terms of quality and quantity, and there is growing awareness that research is an inseparable part of the teachers' mission.

In other institutions, the parameters of research are regarded with a certain circumspection and opinions differ. It is often stated that the quality of research has been enhanced in the last two years. The main obstacle is a lack of financial resources to renew obsolete equipment.

The main examples of developments are[5]:
– progress in doctoral studies at higher education institutions,
– development of the funding system that supports research,
– greater international academic and research cooperation.

12.2.2   Relationships between the Academy of Science and the higher education institutions[6]

In April 1993, the Government accepted a transformation programme for the Academy of Sciences. The objective is to build a modern, efficient, national scientific and research centre that will be able to stimulate research at a level that corresponds to international standards. The transformation should take place in accordance with state scientific and research policy and with the changes in higher education. It should lead to greater openness on the part of the Academy towards research and development and to the mobility of researchers within the Academy, between the Academy and higher education institutions and at the international level.

The collaboration between higher education institutions and the Academy of Sciences is developing according to OECD recommendations. There are already many agreements on mutual help, and the joint training of post-graduate doctoral students should influence the new legislation in this area.

This cooperation is also implemented through contracts between individual workplaces to pursue joint projects, found joint workplaces, use common grants, equipment and facilities, and contracts whereby the Academy researchers teach at higher education institutions. An overwhelming majority of officials and ordinary employees at both institutions are seeking effective and beneficial cooperation.

12.2.3 Creating social demand for research and researchers

Research companies in the economic sphere still have many problems and do not pay much attention to the results of research and development in higher education institutions.

Cooperation between higher education institutions and applied research has collapsed. This means that the higher education institutions could take over some of the demands made for non-higher education applied research. This has already been put into effect. Institutes of applied research which are not threatened with abolition are strengthening their links with higher education institutions.

Direct cooperation between higher education institutions and industry in the area of research is developing. It is still only potential, since companies do not show much interest in research results because of their economic problems. There is little innovation in the Czech Republic, yet the first scientific-technical parks are being established. One example is the scientific-technical park Agrien in Ceske Budejovice which opened 1992. Another is the Technoligical Park in Brno. Their creation and development are progressing slowly because of a lack of financial resources and the space capacity of the higher education institutions. Prospects will improve with the future legal definition of the status of non-profit organizations.

NOTES

1 Kozma, T. *et al.* (1997). *Higher Education in Hungary.* Bucharest: UNESCO Office.
2 Setényi, J. (ed.). (1992). *State Control in Higher Education: New Patterns.* Budapest: Educatio
3 Végvári, I. (1992). 'Hungary', in Clark, B. R. and Neave, G. (eds.). *The Encyclopedia of Higher Education.* Oxford: Pergamon Press.
4 Centre for Higher Education Studies (1993). *Higher Education in the Czech Republic.* Prague: Centre for Higher Education Studies.
5 Šebková, H. *et al.* (1993). *Research Training in the Czech Republic.* Prague: Centre for Higher Education Studies
6 Šebková, H. (1994). 'Institutions of Higher Education and the Academy of Sciences in Transitional Period', *European Journal of Education* 1, pp. 109-130.

Chapter 13

Relationships Among Higher Education Research, Policy and Practice in South Africa

MAGDA FOURIE & KALIE STRYDOM
Unit for Research into Higher Education, University of the Orange Free State, South Africa

13.1   Preamble

Developed countries, in our current post-modern era, have in many cases already become "knowledge societies", while developing countries are still struggling to cultivate the human potential needed for the growth of their ailing economies. It is generally accepted that the generation and dissemination of knowledge is an important facilitator of economic and social progress. "… (W)e are living at a time when without good training and research at the higher level, no country can assure a degree of progress compatible with the needs and expectations of a society in which economic development is carried out with due consideration for the environment and is accompanied by the building of a 'culture of peace' based on democracy, tolerance and mutual respect, in short – *sustainable human development*" (UNESCO 1995, p. 13). Particularly in developing countries it is crucial to cultivate the potential of their human endowment, which is still largely untapped. According to a UNESCO policy paper "(t)he gap between the developing and the developed countries with regard to higher education and research, already enormous, is becoming bigger" (UNESCO 1995, p. 3). Struggling as they are with a multitude of social problems - many of which arise from economic conditions, cultural differences and underdevelopment - developing countries all the more need systematic knowledge development and dissemination in those spheres of life where major problems are observed, and noticeable efforts are required to improve the situation (Teichler 1997, p.1).

In spite of the fact that knowledge production and dissemination in developed countries take place in a multitude of sites, only one of which is

S. Schwarz and U. Teichler (eds.), The Institutional Basis of Higher Education Research, 181–191.

higher education, the latter is still regarded as the "heart of the knowledge society" (Teichler 1997, p.1). However, in some developing countries the sad truth is that not even higher education is sufficiently generating and disseminating knowledge to address the many complex problems which these societies are facing, and virtually the only new knowledge which researchers and practitioners can draw upon, comes from highly developed and industrialised countries. "UNESCO's *World Science Report 1993* shows that more than 80 percent of world research and development (R&D) activities are carried out in just a handful of industrialized countries" (UNESCO 1995, p.15). Research and consultation have also shown that the rigid transmission or adoption of foreign models and structures, and the neglect of regional and national cultures and philosophies in development efforts are bound to lead to failure. In developing countries the aim should therefore be to make higher education more responsive to and relevant in the context of a specific region, country or community by overcoming intellectual over-dependence on more developed countries. Universities should also make a concerted effort to make their presence felt and to present their skills and special abilities to policy-makers and practitioners for the development of the country.

13.2   Policy investigations

As far as developing countries are concerned, South Africa is probably one of the most recent examples of comprehensive policy studies having been done for education in general, and for higher education specifically. Because of the particular political system reigning in the "old" South Africa, previous policy investigations into higher education (such as the Van Wyk-De Vries investigation of 1974) never concentrated on the entire system, but only focused on some sectors or aspects. These investigations were also often commissioned purely as a reaction to outside pressure and aimed at verifying existing government policy.

Following on the political transition to a democracy in 1994, the National Commission on Higher Education (NCHE) (established in 1995) constituted the first ever comprehensive analysis, evaluation and redirecting of South Africa's entire higher education system. The Commission comprised of 13 commissioners. It had 14 terms of reference and for this purpose set up five Task Teams (Current Situation; Future Needs and Priorities; Governance; Finance; Programme, Institutional and Qualifications Framework). The Task Teams were assisted by Technical Committees, and working groups were established in order to ensure that their tasks were carried out efficiently. In spite of criticism to the contrary, the Commission adopted a participative and consultative *modus operandi, inter alia,* by inviting written submissions; consulting with local and international experts; holding stakeholder forums in all nine provinces of South Africa; having site visits, and national and international conferences. After its draft discussion document had been released, comments and inputs were invited, which were taken account of in the final report, published in September 1996. The proposals of the NCHE were also informed by a variety of official publications emanating at the same time from other departments or ministries, e.g. the Draft Constitution, the Reconstruction and Development Programme, the Green Paper on Science and Technology, and the new Labour Relations Act.

The NCHE drew extensively on the expertise of the staff members of the few research and/or academic development units at higher education institutions by appointing them on Task Teams and Technical Committees. During this time too a higher education policy unit was established to support higher education policy development through research. (In the past no South African research unit focused on policy studies. Because of the political situation in the country policy-making and -development were not done in a transparent or consultative manner.) Another important source of expertise for the NCHE was higher education specialists from various other countries who either prepared reports, formed part of Task Teams and Technical Committees, participated in conferences, or gave feedback on draft reports, once again emphasising South African higher education's dependence on outside expertise - a characteristic it shares with many other developing countries.

An examination of the Green Paper and White Papers on Higher Education, as well as the Higher Education Act of 1997, reveals that the NCHE investigation greatly influenced higher education policy. Many of the recommendations of the Commission were adopted or only slightly adjusted in the new higher education policy and legislation. There is general consensus that the new South African higher education policy is particularly well-suited to the new socio-political circumstances of the country and aims at addressing socio-economic needs and challenges. Whether the country and its people have the required human and material resources to give full implementation to this policy, still has to be demonstrated. It should also be kept in mind that policy-making in South Africa is an inclusive, transparent process, involving various groups of stakeholders. The influence of "experts" such as higher education researchers, is therefore greatly diluted.

13.3   Problems of higher education research practice

At the institutional level the influence of researchers in higher education research units has been minimal. Only of late have higher education institutions been looking at creating posts for specific important priority areas (according to national policy) such as programme planning and quality assurance. Most of these researchers are so heavily involved in institutional development work that they have very little time for sustained, meaningful research. Very often higher education researchers have to be appointed from candidates with no particular higher education research experience or expertise, but only practical experience in the higher education sector.

Other problems which higher education researchers have to cope with include:

- The lack of an independent disciplinary base. Mostly researchers and research units or centres in higher education are attached to faculties of education whose prime focus area is pedagogy, and who often have little understanding or sympathy for the interdisciplinary nature of higher education as a field of study. Bawa (1997, p.48) points out that "... we have developed a generalist approach to knowledge production. The cutting edge that the disciplines of sociology, psychology, philosophy, and the like instils in research has declined".
- The lack of research training and development of young researchers. Many South African universities provide students with very little research training and experience at the undergraduate or basic degree level. Students who want to pursue higher education studies at a master's or doctoral level therefore have almost no research expertise and research capacity building should therefore be an important ingredient of these programmes. Because of the smallness of the field in South Africa, there is unfortunately often also a lack of experienced senior staff members or researchers who can provide good supervision to post-graduate students, particularly in terms of research design and methodology. Limited provision of training courses in social sciences research in general and higher education research in particular compounds the problem.
- The lack of specialists in the field of higher education. For example, virtually no single institution in South Africa has the capacity to, by itself, present a good, well-balanced post-graduate course in higher education. Specialists in the field are hard to find. Because so few people are working in the field and the needs are so great, higher education researchers are forced to cover a wide spectrum of research topics, with an inevitable decline in the quality of research. The adverse effects of the brain drain are also felt in the field of higher education research as in many other specialised fields in South Africa, and the following warning pertaining to African countries in general, is also true of South Africa in particular: "Brain-drain is perhaps the single most important problem that needs to be tackled by African universities... Universities, in consultation with their governments, will have to revise their salaries and conditions of service in order to attract and retain well-qualified staff" (Mohamedbhai 1995, p.28).

- The lack of collaboration among higher education research units and individual researchers. No active network of higher education researchers exists, and collaborative ventures between research units are rare. Not only national and regional networks of higher education researchers, but also international cooperation in this regard, particularly in the southern hemisphere, is important. "An interlocking system of international postgraduate and research centres can provide an important boost to higher education within a given region and can help to promote South-South cooperations, especially when such arrangements are based on common interests and adequately shared financial responsibilities" (UNESCO 1995, p. 36).
- The lack of a widely accepted and well-articulated theoretical framework and methodology which are suitable for the diverse higher education scene in South Africa. Higher education researchers come from a wide variety of historical, cultural, academic and disciplinary backgrounds and their personal and scientific frames of reference can hardly be reconciled. This further impedes collaborative efforts.
- A shaky funding base. In the past higher education research was funded by the Human Sciences Research Council, more specifically, the Centre for Science Development of this Council. New legislation has, however, brought about a totally new dispensation for the organisation and funding of research at a national level. The new funding agency, the National Research Foundation, will fund research in not only human and social sciences, but also medical, agricultural and natural sciences. The emphasis on the value of natural sciences and technology for a developing economy such as South Africa's, predisposes funding agencies towards research in these fields, to the detriment of human and social sciences research (including higher education research).

For higher education research to play a meaningful role in shaping policy, in making a contribution to arriving at solutions for the many social, economic and development problems besetting the young democracy and in improving higher education practice, many of these problems will have to be tackled and overcome. These efforts will have to emanate from the higher education research community itself, but will flounder without solid financial and institutional backing.

13.4   New challenges for higher education research

The new higher education policy and legislation pose significant new challenges to higher education research, in particular to institutional research. These challenges emanate from the policy and they have major implications for the practice of higher education in institutions.

13.5 Council on Higher Education

A major new role-player in the higher education scene in South Africa is the Council on Higher Education (CHE), which was established as an advisory body, and is expected to play a pro-active role in steering the higher education system towards the achievement of the policy goals set by the government. These policy goals include:
– promoting equity of access and fair chances of success;
– meeting national development needs for high level personpower, especially those related to the demands for economic growth;
– supporting a democratic ethos and the development of an enlightened, critical and responsible citizenship;
– contributing to the advancement of all forms of knowledge and scholarship particularly related to local, national and regional needs and demands.
These policy goals for higher education have much in common with what many other developing countries envisage for their higher education systems. Many new democracies see in higher education "… a key instrument not only for their future economic development but also for the social, cultural and political change required to remove the vestiges and inheritance of colonialism and other undemocratic systems, to foster national identity and to develop local human resources and capacities to receive and apply knowledge and technology" (UNESCO 1995, p.15).

Policy goals are, however, not achieved of their own accord. Stumpf (1998) believes that one of the pro-active approaches of the CHE will entail monitoring the extent to which these policy goals are being realised. He argues further that this monitoring role can only be performed effectively by the CHE if a set of impact measures or indicators is developed to assist in evaluating overall progress in achieving the policy goals and objectives. Some of these impact measures will be quantitative in nature such as equity profiles, completion rates, job placement rates, etc., while others may be more qualitative in nature and would require different forms of assessment. In any case, the steering and monitoring roles of the CHE will require new and different forms of information from higher education researchers, particularly at the institutional level.

13.6 Quality assurance

According to the Higher Education Act (Act 101 of 1997), one of the major roles of the CHE pertains to the quality assurance of higher education through its permanent committee, the Higher Education Quality Committee (HEQC). The act requires the CHE to:

– promote quality assurance in higher education;
– audit the quality assurance mechanisms of higher education institutions;
– accredit programmes of higher education.

The CHE through the HEQC thus has a clear policy as well as an operational responsibility as far as quality assurance of higher education is concerned. This body will, however, have to deal with a fragmented system of quality arrangements that differ significantly between universities and technikons. Each university, through the private act by which it was established, acts as its own accreditation and certification body. This is complemented by a fairly well established system of external examination, particularly at the higher levels of study. In addition, universities are subject to some form of accreditation by professional boards in many of the professional fields included in the institutions' programmes. The establishment of the Quality Promotion Unit (QPU) of the South African Vice-Chancellors' Association (SAUVCA) in the early 1990s continued and formalised the quality assurance arrangements adopted by some institutions previously, *viz.* self-evaluation exercises followed by an external peer evaluation. The QPU audits mechanisms and procedures for quality assurance which exist (or should exist) at the institutional level.

Quality assurance of technikons, on the other hand, is done under the auspices of the Certification Council for Technikon Education (SERTEC), a statutory accreditation body for technikon education, and these arrangements should be seen against the background of a far greater degree of programme or curricular standardisation characterising technikon programmes than university programmes. SERTEC performs its programme accreditation functions in conjunction with a wide variety of stakeholders, such as industry, employers and professional boards. "SERTEC's statutory powers mean that technikons have to implement the recommendations emanating from SERTEC's evaluations or face the consequences of offering 'non-recognised' diploma/degree programmes" (Stumpf 1998, p. 3).

One of the primary goals at the national or system level being "to conceptualise, plan, govern and fund higher education in South Africa as a single, coordinated system" (RSA DoE 1997, p. 7), presupposes that the new system for the quality assurance of higher education should be an integrated and coordinated system, i.e. one system for both universities and technikons, which at the moment is not only performed by two different bodies, but also has divergent purposes (i.e. institutional audits and programme accreditation). The policy implementation process in terms of the establishment of the HEQC and the performance of the quality assurance functions by the CHE are still developing, and the final outcomes are unsure. However, these developments have major implications for higher education researchers. Not only will researchers at the national and institutional levels have to acquaint themselves with the newest developments in the field of quality assurance world-wide, but institutional researchers in both technikons and universities will have to start preparing their institutions for comprehensive self-evaluation exercises; universities for rigorous programme evaluation, and technikons for intensive audits of their institutional quality assurance mechanisms and procedures.

13.7   Institutional plans

The key instruments that the government will be employing in planning a single coordinated higher education system will be the development of an overall national plan and institutional three-year rolling plans. Three-year rolling plans of institutions should include the vision, mission and values of the institution, the size and shape of the institution including participation rates by population group, gender, under-/post-graduate, field of study, etc. Institutions should also indicate how they propose to or are addressing equity, redress and efficiency demands, and provide particulars on their involvement in inter-institutional cooperation. The first round of three-year rolling plans having been prepared and submitted by institutions recently brought new research needs and challenges to light. Some institutions found themselves relatively well equipped in terms of institutional information databases and expertise to produce well-prepared plans, while others experienced great difficulties in doing so.

The critical importance of these institutional plans, apart from the obvious benefits for the smooth running and management of the institution, lies in their close linkage with the funding of institutions -- "the approval of institutional plans will lead to the allocation of funded student places to institutions for approved programmes in particular levels and fields of learning" (RSA DoE 1997, p.13). The improvement of institutional capability in developing three-year rolling plans and in establishing and utilising effective institutional information databases, are therefore major challenges for higher education research in this country.

13.8   Institutional governance

The new higher education policy and legislation brought about new governance structures not only on the national level (such as the Council on Higher Education mentioned above), but also at the institutional level. The Higher Education Act stipulates that every public higher education institution must, in addition to the more "traditional" governance structures such as the council and the senate, also establish an institutional forum as a permanent advisory sub-committee of the council. By this legislation statutory status is given to these bodies which were established in many institutions during the transition phase, and were mostly called transformation committees or broad transformation forums.

Higher education researchers have at least two roles to play with regard to institutional forums. On the one hand, these forums will only be able to avoid the pitfalls of power-play and unhealthy conflict if they dispose of reliable information based on solid research results, particularly as far as institutional issues are concerned. Many institutions are at present revising their private acts, statutes, institutional vision, mission and goals, and these matters are debated by institutional forums. Because of the representativeness of these bodies, however, members often lack the necessary knowledge and expertise in terms of these technical and complicated matters. Higher education researchers can make an invaluable contribution to the effective functioning of these bodies by providing relevant information, also of a comparative nature.

A second role for higher education researchers related to institutional forums concerns evaluative research into the role and function of these forums. Institutional forums are relatively unique to the South African higher education system, and investigations into their effectiveness and particularly their contribution to the transformation of the institutions could lead to fresh perspectives on higher education transformation, also in other countries.

13.9   The structure of the system

Higher education in South Africa has for many years been a binary system with a clear distinction between universities and technikons. The difference between these two types of institutions could be seen as one of emphasis and approach, rather than programmes and courses. Whereas the teaching approach of universities is more academic, technikons emphasise applied knowledge and are directed towards career training. Although both types of institutions have the fundamental task of producing high-level personpower, the university focuses on the acquisition and development of pure knowledge, and the technikon concentrates more on the application of knowledge, rather than on its development. However, a careful analysis of the teaching and research activities of universities and technikons at present reveals a considerable degree of academic drift in both directions. The generation of new knowledge at a mind-boggling rate has rendered rigid distinctions between "pure" science and technology, and between "academic" and career education, largely obsolete.

Decisions on the shape, size and structure of the new higher education system for South Africa cannot, however, be taken without basing these decisions on valid and reliable research information. "The crucial issue is that of establishing and maintaining acceptable levels of institutional diversity in a single integrated South African HE system" (Stumpf 1998, p.7). Achieving this ideal will require much concerted research effort at both institutional (practice) and national (policy) level.

13.10 The way forward

What is then the way forward for higher education research in South Africa with regard to policy and practice? At national and institutional level there are now concerted efforts to establish capacity-building projects and higher education support units to address a range of needs and support policy development projects. Examples are:
– the coordination of programmes for addressing the management and leadership capacity challenges;
– a programme for the development of the capacity of council (governing board) members;
– endeavours in the field of curriculum transformation and restructuring;
– a project for the development of a set of transformation indicators and institutional case studies in higher education;
– the establishment of a website for women in higher education;
– projects for capacity-building in the field of quality assurance;
– the development of regional consortia (CHET 1997).
Other projects include the development of an inter-institutional programme in higher education studies at diploma and Master's degree level, networking nationally and internationally. Support for national research associations such as the SA Association for Academic Development, the SA Association for Institutional Research, and the SA Association for Research and Development of Higher Education with its one accredited journal, the *SA Journal for Higher Education* seems to be growing and will hopefully contribute to the recognition of the value of higher education studies and research.

In the past higher education research in South Africa focused almost exclusively on investigating and improving practice. The new democratic dispensation brought about challenges and opportunities for higher education research to play a stronger role as a provider of policy options. For its voice to be heard, however, higher education research will, like every true science, have to engage in continuous critical discourse with policy-makers and practitioners across disciplines and contexts.

REFERENCES

Bawa, A. C. (1997). Knowledge production and curriculum research strategies in South Africa, in Cloete, N., Muller, J., Makgoba, M. W. and Ekong, D. (eds.). *Knowledge, Identity and Curriculum Transformation in Africa*. Cape Town: Maskew Miller.

CHET (Centre for Higher Education Transformation) (1997). *A draft framework for creating management capacity and a culture of leadership in higher education institutions*. Pretoria: Centre for Higher Education Transformation.

Mohamedbhai, G. T. G. (1995). *The Emerging Role of African Universities in the Development of Science and Technology*. Accra: Association of African Universities.

NCHE (National Commission on Higher Education) (1996). *A Framework for Transformation. Report*. Pretoria: NCHE.

RSA DoE. (Republic of South Africa. Department of Education) (1997). *A Programme for Higher Education Transformation. Education White Paper 3*. Pretoria: Department of Education.

RSA (Republic of South Africa) (1997). *Higher Education Act, No.101*. Pretoria: Government Printer.

Stumpf, R. H. (1998). *The Higher Education Act and institutional research*. Paper presented to the SAAIR Conference, Pretoria.

Teichler, U. (1997). *The relationships between higher education research and higher education policy and practice: the researchers' perspective*. Keynote speech to the Roundtable "The relationship among research, policy and practice in education", Tokyo, 3-5 September 1997.

UNESCO (1995). *Policy Paper for Change and Development in Higher Education*: Paris, UNESCO.

Chapter 14

Improving Higher Education Research at African Universities: The Study Programme on Higher Education Management in Africa

AKILAGPA SAWYERR
Director of Research, Association of African Universities, Accra-North, Ghana

14.1   Introduction

To close the gap created by the absence of African scholarly input into the search for solutions to the African higher education crisis of the late 1980s, the Association of African Universities set up a Study Programme for Higher Education Management in Africa to develop local capacity for undertaking systematic research on issues of higher education policy and management, and increase the indigenous knowledge base of African higher education policy-making. This programme is supported by grants from the Dutch Ministry of Foreign Affairs and the Swedish International Development Cooperation Agency.

It was appreciated from the start that the broad objectives of the programme could not all be met immediately. The design and implementation of programme activities were, therefore, guided by a long-term perspective. The initial concern was to identify African researchers working on higher education issues, and to give them technical training and financial support to enable them raise the quality of their work and promote its greater dissemination. The second concern was to foster relationships among such researchers and, over the course of the programme, open them up to the work of established higher education researchers and institutions in Africa and elsewhere.

A Scientific Committee was established to provide leadership and ensure the scientific quality of both the training and the research output of the programme. Membership of the committee was drawn from among representa-

S. Schwarz and U. Teichler (eds.), The Institutional Basis of Higher Education Research, 193–199.

tives of higher education institutions, established higher education researchers, and social scientists within Africa and from outside.

14.2   The research grants scheme

A Research Grants Scheme took off in 1993. On the basis of the deliberations of the leaders of African universities at the General Conference of the AAU in 1993, and elsewhere, it was decided that the first batch of projects under the scheme should concentrate on issues to do with the financing of higher education in Africa, then considered the most pressing issues facing African universities. Since there were hardly any specialist higher education researchers or institutions on the continent, the decision was taken to start the programme by providing support for on-going work within the general theme of higher education financing, rather than assigning fresh topics for study or commissioning specific projects.

A large number of proposals was received in response to invitations sent to all member institutions of the AAU. These were screened by the Scientific Committee which selected 15 for funding, on the basis of their quality and promise, due account being taken of the need to ensure proper gender, geographic and linguistic balances in all AAU programme activities. The Research Grants Scheme thus started with 15 teams made up of 28 individual researchers, of whom only three were women.

A second batch of grants was awarded in 1996. This time 22 research teams, consisting of 49 researchers, of whom 14 were women, were selected. The chosen projects fell under four sub-themes, namely: institutional culture, decision-making processes, financing modes, as well as higher education and work.

As the majority of grant recipients were not specialists in higher education research, there was a very heavy emphasis on research training. Thus, release of tranches of the grant was conditioned upon attendance at training seminars and workshops organised as part of the programme and the submission of progress reports by all research teams. Members of the scientific committee as well as resource persons engaged for the purpose, provided advice on the research proposals in the first instance, and acted as resource persons throughout, guiding the research process from inception to completion.

14.3   Training

As indicated above, a central feature of the programme was a series of training workshops designed to improve the quality of the design and conduct of the funded projects, strengthen the research capacity of the teams and expose work-in-progress to critical peer review. At least one member of a research team attended each training workshop. In addition to improving the research capacity of the researchers and the quality of the research, these workshops provided opportunities for developing relationships among researchers, laying the basis for future higher education research networking across the continent. The workshops were of two main types:

Methodology Workshops were intended to: help clarify the research objectives of each project; isolate and develop researchable topics; and improve the formulation of the projects and the methodology for their prosecution.

The principal characteristic of these workshops has been the emphasis on group work. This ensures substantial peer contribution and self-correction, under the guidance of resource persons. Towards the end of each workshop, each participant writes a summary of their projects to reflect the impact of the workshop. These summaries have proved extremely valuable both in the refinement of the research objectives and methodology of the projects, and as a means of bringing together persons working on similar topics.

Data Gathering and Analysis Workshops: After about six months of preparatory and initial field work, the researchers are brought together at a workshop on data gathering and analysis. The objective at this stage is to advise on data collection and analysis, as well as report preparation. The approach adopted is broadly similar to the methodology workshops, except that owing to the variation in the subject-matter of the projects, and the different stages reached by the various projects, group work is heavily supplemented by individual work with resource persons.

A critical part of the entire process are the relationships that develop between researchers and the resource persons designated to supervise the projects. The closeness of the relationships has varied considerably, but overall, the researchers have derived great benefit from the contact with experienced higher education researchers.

Participation in these workshops and close supervision by established researchers have had many significant effects. Apart from the improvement of the final quality of the research projects, there was a marked sharpening of the focus of virtually all projects, and a strengthening of the capacity to define a researchable topic. Overall, there were observable improvements in the technical competence of virtually all the researchers, especially in dealing with the difficulties of data quality and accessibility under the specific conditions of their countries. In addition to this enhancement of research capacity, several of the researchers have acquired some capacity to advise on aspects of higher education policy in their countries – though this cannot be a major consideration at this early stage of the programme.

Whether as part of future phases of the study programme or outside it, most of the participants in the first two batches of grants under the programme have acquired increased capacity to make a sustained contribution to the understanding and development of higher education in Africa. One of the objectives of the future phases of the programme must be to help sustain their interest, and help them keep up and enhance the skills acquired under the programme. To this end, the strengthening of community among past grantees through more effective networking will be one of the objectives of the next phase of the programme. Also of great promise is the notion of using the more accomplished of the past grantees in such AAU activities as the on-campus workshops and seminars which have been proposed as part of the next phase of the programme.

14.4   Research

Up to 1998, nine research projects under the first batch, and eight under the second had been completed. The themes of these were:
– Resource utilisation in public universities in Kenya;
– cost-recovery in Nigerian university education;
– cost and financing of university education in Nigeria;
– resources for enhancing university research and postgraduate training in Ghana;
– funding and management of higher education in Benin;
– modelling for resource allocation to departments and faculties in African universities;
– the social background of Makerere University students and the potential for cost-sharing;
– statistical data as a tool for higher education management – the case of Makerere University;
– government-University relations in Sudan;
– communication culture and the work role of academics within Nigerian universities;
– l'évaluation de l'université par les diplômes;
– mode de financement et de gestion dans les institutions d'enseignement supérieur;
– gender differences towards the study of mathematics at university level in Swaziland;
– women in academic and senior management positions in the universities in Nigeria;
– the institutional culture of the University of the North, South Africa;
– le suivi des diplômés des universitiés sénégalaises dans le milieu du travail;

– higher education and the demands of manpower development in Nigerian manufacturing sector.

These reports represent a very encouraging beginning to the scientific work of the Study Programme. Though their quality varies considerably, each report adds to our knowledge and understanding of some aspects of higher education in Africa. In a very general sense, they tend to confirm positions previously advanced, though not always on the basis of this sort of research. But beyond that, the reports contain much useful documentation in relation to specific cases and countries.

In several instances, the reports have produced new material or cast new light on old material. These include the very instructive examination of the social background of university students (Mayanja 1998), and the role that improved data storage and retrieval could play in strengthening management capacity, thereby saving costs at universities (Nakabo-Ssewanyana 1999). Also of very great interest and practical value to universities all over Africa is the presentation on how universities could get at the untapped resources potentially available in the budgets of government departments. Finally, mention has already been made of the innovative proposal of a global funding model for budget preparation and fund allocation (Liverpool et al. 1998). These reports are listed at the AAU Website on the Internet (www.aau.org), and means for obtaining them are there indicated.

The value of the research undertaken within the study programme and the capacities developed in the process, go beyond the preparation of reports and papers. For, many of the researchers occupy positions in their institutions and countries which make it more than likely that their increasing insights and capacities will feed directly into higher education policy-making and administration. Additionally, their work will have other less direct effects – through the dissemination of their findings and their participation in national and international policy debates.

As a particularly interesting and promising departure from the pattern of the first batch, seven of the projects of the second batch grouped under the sub-theme, 'Higher Education and Work'. These, together with three others set up under another AAU programme, involve graduate and employer surveys in seven countries – Benin, Ghana, Kenya, Malawi, Nigeria, Tanzania, and Uganda. Using a common core questionnaire and very rigorous survey and analytical techniques under the supervision of the leading authorities in the field, these projects are expected to yield valuable material, on the basis of which a major comparative analysis of the graduate employment situation in Africa will be undertaken. The results of both the individual studies and the comparative analysis should substitute for the often impressionistic assessments of the vexed question of graduate unemployment, and thus be of the greatest theoretical and practical interest to African higher education policy-makers.

14.5   Dissemination of research results

Expectations about the scientific quality and the immediate applicability of the results of the initial projects were rather modest, given the background of the researchers. It was, nevertheless, considered necessary to ensure the dissemination of the work as it emerged, through publication and presentations at seminars and workshops.

Articles based on the results of four of the projects have been published in the journal *Higher Education*. The other researchers are being encouraged to publish their reports or papers on them in other journals. In addition, a collection of essays based on the reports of seven of the completed projects is being brought out in the newly-introduced *AAU Study Programme Research Paper Series*.

Various seminars and workshops were arranged for presenting the results. It is hoped, by all these means, to bring the research product of the Study Programme to the attention of higher education policy-makers and administrators throughout the continent, and to make a contribution to the on-going debates about higher education financing and policy generally.

14.6   Linkages

The development of a cadre of higher education researchers within Africa requires the building up of links among African researchers, and between them and researchers outside Africa. Links have begun to be developed among the researchers during the workshops and in follow-up contacts. In addition, the researchers have established relationships of varying effectiveness with the resource persons and their institutions. Modest as these relationships are, they contain the elements of future professional collaboration.

REFERENCES

Abagi, O. (1998). *Revitalising Financing of Higher Education in Kenya. Resource Utilisation in Public Universities.* Accra: Association of African Universities, World Wide Press Ltd.

Babalola. J. B. (1998). 'Cost and financing in university education in Nigeria.' *Higher Education*, 36 (1) 43-66.

Liverpool, L. S. O., Eseyin, E. G. and Opara, E. I. (1998). 'Modelling for resource allocation to departments and faculties in African universities', *Higher Education*, 36 (2).

Mayanja, M.K. (1998). 'The social background of Makerere University Students and the potential for cost sharing', *Higher Education*,36 (1) 21-41.

Nakabo-Ssewanyana, S. (1999). 'Statistical data: The underestimated tool for higher educa-
    tion management. The case of Makerere University', *Higher Education*, 37 (3), 259-279.

Chapter 15

Thinking about Advanced Learning Systems

KATHRYN M. MOORE
Center for the Study of Advanced Learning Systems, Michigan State University, East Lansing, USA

My purpose in this paper is to describe our new research group at Michigan State University, called the Center for the Study of Advanced Learning Systems (ALS) and also to provide a few thoughts on how, from an advanced learning systems perspective, we might develop ways to work together to study and to improve higher education world-wide in the next century.

15.1 Concepts underlying the study of advanced learning systems

As we have already noted during this symposium, many institutions of higher and post-secondary education around the world are undertaking various reforms designed to revise their missions and better use their intellectual resources to meet the demands of the next century. Many forces, forces that we took some time during this symposium to define and discuss, have prompted such efforts. The ones that we in the ALS take particular note of include: demographic shifts in student populations; widespread adoption of electronic telecommunications and computing for both instruction and institutional operations; large-scale alterations in fiscal and governmental linkages; the acceleration of knowledge creation, and the emergence of a complex market of knowledge providers and learners world-wide. In particular, these trends have arisen from changing conceptions of the learner and of learning beyond high school.

For the most part, although we acknowledge these forces and trends as being global, as scholars, most of us tend to localize them to our own country and even to our own state and university setting. (I will return to the no-

S. Schwarz and U. Teichler (eds.), The Institutional Basis of Higher Education Research, 201–210.

tion of global trend analysis later when I address ways that we can work together.) Nevertheless, in ALS we believe that these changing circumstances are reshaping and reconceptualizing higher education. So we have begun to direct our inquiry and practice both in research and in our degree offerings toward these changes.

We call this new orientation to our work *advanced learning systems*. This phrase is intended to focus attention on the processes and environments that are emerging around the globe which are connecting learners with knowledge and learning processes in new ways. The idea reflects a mixture of concepts borrowed from higher, adult and lifelong education as well as organizational theories, particularly systems thinking, all of which view both individuals and organizations as dynamic and complex open systems marked by a high degree of interdependence (Senge 1990; Schon 1995; Checkland and Scholes 1990). Constructively ambiguous, the term *advanced learning systems* encourages the inclusion of a variety of venues where teaching and learning beyond high school take place, such as corporations and other workplaces, private homes, media, libraries and museums, as well as four-year and two-year colleges and universities. Additionally, the term acknowledges new forms of delivering education such as on-line and distributed learning.

With *advanced learning systems* as our focus, we want to examine the connections between and among institutions, individual actors and knowledge areas; i.e., the "systems" that serve to bridge the many components of higher learning. We are looking for linkages, for dynamism, for interactions among structures, learners, content and context where new forms of learning and knowledge generation are emerging (Dolence and Norris 1995).

In sum, we selected the term, *advanced learning systems*, as a way of helping us to view the world of higher education through new lenses. Although traditional views of institutions and actors such as faculty, students and administrators will still be present, we have challenged ourselves both to look in new ways at the phenomenon of higher education and also to look for new developments and innovations. In these activities we seek to link ourselves with others who are interested in studying and understanding what these developments portend in the coming century.

I refer you to the following Figure for a diagram of how we are conceptualizing our work. You will note that arrayed around the concept of ALS are three relatively traditional ways of understanding higher education: teaching and learning, leadership and organizational development, and policy and environmental analysis, but we are schooling ourselves and our students to think of these areas in very broad terms initially – to ask, for example, who are the learners? What are the new types of organizations that are offering advanced learning opportunities, and how are they organized? What are the policy environments that are fostering the emergence of new types of providers of higher education?

Figure:

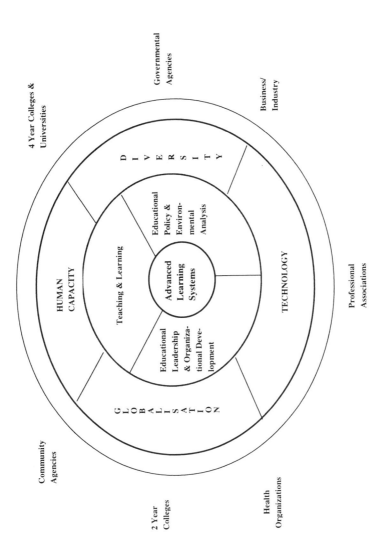

We recognize and appreciate that these three areas of study reflect extensive knowledge bases that already undergird the field of higher education. However, to be successful, we also believe that scholars and practitioners within the emerging learning environments of the early 21st century must do more than merely comprehend certain knowledge domains; they must develop complex problem-solving skills, a high degree of creativity, and advanced conceptual abilities. So to aid our own creative problem solving and conceptualizing abilities, we have selected four issues of current concern and interest that crosscut the three knowledge domains. These are depicted in the figure as the outer ring: human capacity, including leadership, diversity, and technology and global awareness. While there are many ways to explore these concepts, what follows are our beginning approaches.

Human capacity. In a world that is changing rapidly in so many ways, we are concerned with how higher education assists people to form and maintain their individual and collective identities. In the United States, at least, institutions of higher education have long held the responsibility for the education and socialization of a large proportion of our youth and a growing sector of adults for productive work and citizenship. But intimations of the next century suggest that both work and citizenship are likely to, indeed, already are undergoing substantial change in the context of the "Knowledge Age". How shall our colleges and universities respond?

Moreover, while many analysts say that in the new century the ability of people to adapt will be at a premium, other analysts are equally vehement about people's countervailing need to claim or reclaim values and traditions that help define their lives. These debates and others are already at play in many institutions and national systems. Learners seeking their places in the emerging social and work environments of the new century will seek educating institutions that are knowledgeable and skilled in helping them develop along many dimensions. But what are these dimensions of knowledge and skill that educating organizations need in order to develop human capacity in the Knowledge Age? And who is making that determination?

The challenge of change affects us all, but some individuals, groups and organizations will step forward to offer new ideas, directions and opportunities for meeting these challenges. Our work in leadership focuses on enhancing the abilities of individuals and organizations to create more humane, inventive and vital *advanced learning systems.*

Diversity. The changing demographics of the US and other societies pose significant challenges for organizations of higher learning. Within the borders of the US, cultural diversity is more than a trend; it is a reality of social and organizational life in the 1990's and will continue to shape it in decades to come. Key challenges face both educational practitioners and scholars in implementing effective teaching and learning processes in the light of the growing diversity of students and faculty. These challenges call for the construction of new theories and perspectives on student and faculty development and a better understanding of how diverse groups make sense of their educational experiences. It should also be noted that diversity could refer to other important aspects of higher education, such as type of institution and the design of educational systems. In ALS, several of us have research interests that involve exploration of developmental issues of students, and others are quite interested in issues involving faculty. We all interest ourselves in various questions of organizational diversity and design.

Technology. The pace of technological change in postsecondary education has already affected how and where individuals engage in learning. No longer are learning opportunities confined to certain institutions; indeed, millions of learners throughout the world already utilize distance and other technologies to access information, to connect with other learners, and to participate in "virtual" learning environments (Daniel 1996). However, the development of the technologies that enable these exciting developments is in many ways outpacing our understanding of how to organize learners and the learning experience. At ALS we seek to understand the various opportunities and challenges that face learners, teachers and leaders who are seeking to use these new technologies and in so doing to create 21st century *advanced learning systems.*

Global awareness. At ALS we must be mindful of our place in a land-grant university of the State of Michigan, but we are equally concerned for the larger global context in which our students, clients and we ourselves carry out our work. There is much to learn from the changes that are occurring in post-secondary education in other countries and many ways we can benefit by working more closely with scholars and educational leaders from other countries. Our faculty has a history of working both individually and collectively in a variety of international venues. We intend to continue this practice but also to do much more by way of infusing global awareness and international connections into our educational work on campus as well as taking our work abroad. We are increasingly mindful that in the future through telecommunications, we will be able to work in new, more closely connected ways with students and colleagues from many countries.

If you will refer again to the Figure, you will note that we view this outer ring of issues as moving and changing so that they can align with any one of the three main knowledge domains. For example, we can examine technology in teaching and learning but also in policy and environmental analysis, or we can combine one or more issues in a knowledge domain, such as technology and global awareness as they pertain to teaching and learning, etc.

Finally, the outer periphery of the Figure shows a set of target groups from which we gain students, clients and stakeholders. These groups can influence how we view the issues and help us change the content of the various knowledge domains. This outer ring also illustrates that post-secondary education is no longer synonymous with traditional higher education. People now learn in a variety of organizational contexts, and we must consider these contexts and providers in our research and teaching (Dolence and Norris 1995; Daniel 1996). Indeed, it is the emergence of this more diverse, technology-enabled, globe-spanning set of educating organizations that first got us thinking about the notion of advanced learning systems. It was only as we began to break out of our traditional mindsets and knowledge frameworks to take seriously the presence of these innovators that we began to see that these additions to the higher education cosmos as not merely temporary perturbations or interesting but insignificant alterations; rather, they are true frame-breaking innovations. A new term was needed that captured the sophisticated, demanding, knowledge-generating aspects of higher education – hence, advanced learning – and that also captured the dynamic, telematic connectedness of these new forms of teaching, learning and knowledge generation; hence, advanced learning systems.

15.2 An advanced learning system for the field of higher education

Now let me briefly share some thoughts on how we as higher education scholars might go about building our own *advanced learning system*. To do so, I would like us to consider the development of a sister discipline, meteorology.

According to the *Encarta Encyclopedia* (1997), in about 400 BC Aristotle wrote a treatise called *Meteorologica,* which dealt with the "study of things lifted up". About one third of the treatise was devoted to atmospheric phenomena, and it is from this that the modern term meteorology is derived. Weather forecasting has been of interest to humans for centuries. As early as the 14th century, certain localities kept weather records. But it was not until the 17th century that there were any systematic observations over an extended area. The invention of the telegraph in the middle of the 19th century permitted weather data from an entire country to be transmitted to a central point and correlated for the making of forecasts.

Modern meteorology is the product of the work of scientists from many nations. During World War I, Norwegian meteorologists studied the behavior of air masses in generating cyclones. A British mathematician, Lewis Fry Richardson, made the first attempt to mathematically calculate atmospheric equations. And the invention of a radio-sounding device made it possible to investigate conditions at extremely high altitudes. Finally during World War II, Swedish scientists and US collaborators discovered the jet stream, a truly global phenomenon. Subsequently, the application of electronic computing capacity using hydro- and thermodynamic equations coupled with the introduction of weather satellites brought us the highly sophisticated weather tracking and analysis system that many of us witness when we view the Weather Channel on television or track El Niño across the globe by Internet (Encarta 1997).

The point is that against the frame of developments in meteorology, we in higher education are in the 19th century. We are able to report local higher education "weather conditions" for our countries and sometimes for a somewhat larger region, but we have yet to begin working together on a full-scale global research system, nor are we very far advanced in exploring whether there are metaphorically equivalent hydro- and thermodynamic conditions in higher education. Moreover, we are a very long way from studying higher education in the way "cloud physicists" contemplate the prospect, through seeding clouds with various substances, of changing the atmosphere to increase rain in an area or reduce fog or hail. We have yet to understand how higher education works world-wide, much less attempt to influence it for the better (see Banathy 1992; Vaill 1996).

I introduce this metaphor of meteorology somewhat playfully, but also in the belief that in the 21st century we need to operate on the notion of a more globally connected system of higher learning than we ever conceived of in the 20th. Many higher education innovators already believe that their market for learners is a global one in which students' differing languages and educational backgrounds are merely challenges, not insurmountable barriers, which can be resolved through expert systems, "smart tutors," and customized attention. And many of the innovators' financial backers, both private sector and governmental, already believe that traditional concepts of higher education as place-bound, tradition-laden professorial preserves need to be replaced by a variety of new modes of delivery.

Let me hasten to add that I do not argue here that older modes of higher education will disappear anytime soon. Many will have the prestige and financial power to remain as is; some will be far-sighted and agile enough to adapt or co-opt some of the most important innovations, and some will have their sphere of influence curtailed but still remain in tact. There will almost certainly be a need for some higher education scholars to work on subjects pertaining to these established organizations. But my larger point is that we, as a community of scholars dedicated to the study of higher education across space and time, need to enlarge our view of our work more along the lines of our colleagues, the meteorologists. We need to see our local higher education institutions within a much larger global context of forces and circumstances that are becoming increasingly interconnected and dynamic. Just as we are learning that Japan's financial actions affect our own in the US, so we need to work more vigorously together to understand the dynamic forces that are affecting all of our higher education institutions, our students, as well as other participants and stakeholders.

15.3 Dynamic forces in higher education

Let me introduce the metaphor of "trade-winds". Various "trade-winds" may affect higher education world-wide. Although they may operate at different altitudes, and with differing velocities in various locations, with proper co-ordination and collaboration, is it possible that we could discern such general phenomena? Like meteorologists, we would need to establish observation stations around the globe which are geared to observing and measuring the same things with the same tools and sharing that information with each other. In addition, we also would need to communicate changes in local conditions that might affect others down the line. For example, the emergence of the European Union and its subsidiary educational co-operation programs are beginning to take on some of these aspects. Certain observation posts might specialize in specific phenomena much as the National Hurricane Center in Florida or the European Center for Medium Range Weather Forecasting in Bracknell, England. For example, rather than trying to study all topics at once, certain higher education centers could focus on a large topic to which the rest of us would connect and contribute.

Over time, with effective communication and collaboration, we might be able to discern some important prevailing conditions or global forces. If we did, we might then be able to ask new questions and gain new insights about higher education. Only a relatively simple alteration in our thinking and actions will be required. We would need to shift our attention to measuring change and flows, not stasis and fixed entities. Just one example: if we were to consider the flow of humans across the face of the planet in relation to their connection to higher education institutions we might see some very interesting new things about how the world student population is behaving, or the world faculty population. Much like a weather map does, we could track high and low densities of faculty and students and also their shifts. If we examined the student population against the movements of people generally, we might notice that refugees and immigrants compose a large part of the movement of populations, but relatively small proportions of the student population and so uncover a burgeoning market for some institutions to address.

For another example, if we were able to track the stock and flow of ideas in various disciplines, might we come to understand the dynamics of 21st century knowledge generation and faculty behavior in new and constructive ways? The pioneering work of Burton Clark and others over a decade ago have provided a foundation on which we might construct such a body of scholarship world-wide.

Recent analysis by Cohen (1997) of the internationalization of academic scholarship suggests that if higher education scholars were to undertake greater international collaboration, in all probability we would confront issues that other internationalizing fields and disciplines face. For example, we would need to attend to the construction of shared languages of discussion, to mutual values and goals, particularly concerning ways to foster and support our shared work, to shared standards for research, data collection and communication, and perhaps even to shared protocols for the preparation of future scholars of higher education. True international collaboration would engender new problems and issues for us as scholars, but they also could heighten our awareness of, and participation in, the dynamic, global changes that are underway.

These are only suggestions of how we might consider building an advanced learning system among higher education scholars and students world-wide. But I believe such a conceptualization holds the prospect of increasing the creativity of our field and enhancing its contributions in ways more in sync with emerging developments in higher education generally in the 21st century.

15.4 Conclusion

Research in higher education is approaching a watershed in its history. There is a need to consider how best to deploy our intellectual resources to best effect. At ALS, even as we strive to become better and more sophisticated analysts of conditions and dynamics within our own local and national higher education setting, we are determined to move with the times. And the times suggest far more connection and dynamism in higher education on a global basis. The themes we have selected: human capacity with attention to leadership, diversity, technology, and globalization, are only a few of the ones that will be important to understanding the advanced learning systems that are emerging. We believe that one of the best ways to study these innovating systems is to create among higher education scholars an advanced learning system of our own, one that can become a powerful means of understanding higher education in the next century. We look forward to that possibility.

REFERENCES

Banathy, B. H. (1992). 'Designing educational systems: Creating our future in a changing world', *Educational Technology,* November 1992, 41-46.

Checkland, P. and Scholes, J. (1990). *Soft Systems Methodology in Action.* New York: John Wiley & Sons.

Cohen, D. W. (1997). 'Understanding the globalization of scholarship', in Peterson, M. et al. (eds.) *Planning and Management for a Changing Environment.* San Francisco: Jossey-Bass.

Daniel, J. S. (1996). *Mega-Universities and Knowledge Media.* London: Kogan Page Limited.

Dolence, M. and Norris, D. (1995). *Transforming Higher Education: A Vision for Learning in the 21st Century.* Ann Arbor: Society for College and University Planning.

Encarta Encyclopedia 1997. Microsoft 1993-96.

Schon, D. A. (1995). 'The new scholarship requires a new epistemology', *Change*, November/December, 1995, 27-34.

Senge, P. M. (1990). *The Fifth Discipline.* New York: Doubleday.

Vaill, P. (1996). *Learning as a Way of Being.* San Francisco: Jossey-Bass.

PART THREE

TRAINING AND CAREER OF YOUNG RESEARCHERS

Chapter 16

Training Researchers and Administrators in Higher Education Doctoral Programmes in the United States

STEFANIE SCHWARZ
Centre for Research on Higher Education and Work, University of Kassel, Germany

16.1 Introduction

The number of students in the United States reached a record high of over 14 million in 1997, 44,500 of whom completed their doctoral degree. They study in more than 3,500 institutions. Approximately 1.7 million faculty members, administrators and other professional staff provide the man- and womanpower that is needed for the support base of the maintenance and growth of the tertiary education sector (US Department of Education 1997). The career options of faculty and administrators who work in higher education institutions is very diversified. Faculty conduct teaching and research in hundreds of different fields of study. Administrators work in student services, the bursar's office, public relations, the alumni office, etc.

The diversification of the higher education sector has both advantages and drawbacks for those who wish to study for a doctoral degree. Researchers cite the training of specialists as the main advantage. In the doctoral degree in higher education, students are exposed to theoretical and practical concepts, such as administration in higher education, curriculum and instruction, and courses on students in higher education. This specialization is perceived by a number of doctoral students as an advantage because it provides a competitive edge in the labour market in higher education. However, many also see drawbacks in being able to choose between several hundreds of options. Research shows that some feel insecure in their choice, even after they have obtained their doctoral degree. They say they would not study for this degree if they had to begin their studies again. They would choose a

S. Schwarz and U. Teichler (eds.), The Institutional Basis of Higher Education Research, 213–225.
© *2000 Kluwer Academic Publishers. Printed in the Netherlands.*

field such as business administration, which is broader in scope and offers more job opportunities (Townsend 1989).

The author will begin by evoking the creation of higher education programmes, their history, their structure, and their missions and purposes. Then, she will describe a typical doctoral course in a higher education programme. Next, research on career options for higher education graduates will be summarized and discussed. This will be linked to that of the degree of satisfaction with the programmes of higher education.

16.2 The history of programmes in higher education in the US

The United States was one of the first countries to offer courses in higher education for students who showed an interest in a career in this field. G. Stanley Hall, president of Clark University, taught the first in 1893. This relatively long tradition is accompanied by a growth of the field that went in spurts.

At the beginning of the 20th century, the development of these courses was slow. After Clark University offered the first course in the late 19th century, only a few other institutions, such as John Hopkins University and the University of Minnesota, followed suit (Townsend 1989). Three were then established in the 1920s at the University of Chicago, Ohio State University, and Columbia University. While the first were at the undergraduate level, institutions started to offer courses at the graduate level in the 1920s. During the first half of this century, the main goal was to prepare students for faculty positions in the field of education. Most of the universities and colleges offered these positions in the framework of other programmes (Townsend 1989).

This trend changed after World War II. At the beginning of the 1950s, with the massive growth of tertiary education in the US, experts in the field of higher education were in great demand. As a result, a number of institutions started to offer programmes in higher education which emphasized formalized training of researchers and administrators. Hence, external funding was increased (Pemberton 1980; Townsend 1989). In the 1950s, the number of public higher education institutions, especially with the creation and expansion of Community Colleges, created a need for an even greater number of administrators, and more especially for middle level management positions (Semas 1974). Townsend (1989) conducted research on the history of higher education programmes and states that, in the early 1950s, some 30 institutions offered such courses and that by the early 1960s their number had tripled to about 90. Some 53 of these programmes were identified as units, offering courses at the doctoral level (Rogers 1969).

The number of doctoral level courses continued to rise in the 1970s, 1980s and 1990s. Whereas at the end of the 1970s, there were 70, at the end of the 1980s there were 90 (Mason and Townsend 1988). In the mid-1980s, the average number of PhD students per programme was 46, the average number of EdD students was 34 and some 10,000 doctoral degrees were awarded. Enrolment patterns were steady.

16.3 Number of students in doctoral programmes in higher education in the US

Students who obtain their undergraduate degree usually work for a number of years, e.g. as an administrator, before applying to a graduate programme in higher education. The study by Townsend and Mason (1988) shows that, in the end of the 1980s, the typical student in higher education was a non-traditional female student (see also Brazziel and Beeler 1991). About 60 percent of doctoral students were women (see Table 1) and the average age of graduation was 43 (see Table 2). Whereas recently, non-traditional female students constituted the majority, it used to be non-traditional males. In 1972, the typical graduate of Townsend and Mason's study was male (87%) and just over 36 years old on graduation. The number of years to obtain a degree has increased, a phenomenon that can be seen in all fields (Baird 1990; Nerad and Cerny 1993; Bowen and Rudenstine 1992; Ploskonka 1992; Schwarz 1997). Whereas in the early 1970s, 24 percent of the students obtained their doctoral degree in two years or less, at the end of the 1980s this was only the case for six percent (see Table 3). Whereas in the early 1970s, seven percent obtained their degree within seven or more years, at the end of the 1980s, this was the case for 28 percent.

By and large one can observe the following general trends in regard to graduates of higher education programmes in the US: (a) the majority of the graduates are female, and (b) the majority of graduates are non-traditional aged.

Table 1: Student Gender in Selected US Higher Education Programmes

	N	Male N	%	Female N	%
1972	84	73	86.9	11	13.1
1977	134	97	72.4	37	27.6
1982	140	76	84.3	64	45.7
1987	181	75	41.4	106	58.6
Total	539	321	59.6	218	40.4

Table 2: Average Age when Doctorate is Obtained in Selected US Higher Education
Programmes

Year	N	Ave. Age	Male N	Ave. Age	Female N	Ave. Age
1972	84	36.2	73	35.6	11	40.4
1977	129	39.9	95	39.1	34	42.0
1982	138	41.6	75	40.9	63	42.4
1987	180	43.0	75	41.2	105	44.2
Total	531		318		213	

Source: Townsend and Mason, 1990

Table 3: Years to Obtain the Doctorate in Selected US Higher Education
Programmes

Year	N	2 or less N	%	3 years N	%	4 years N	%	5 years N	%	6 years N	%	7 or more N	%
1972	84	20	23.8	36	42.9	10	11.9	5	6.0	7	8.3	6	7.1
1977	132	12	9.1	64	48.5	26	19.7	16	12.1	6	4.5	8	6.1
1982	139	14	10.1	35	25.2	26	18.7	26	18.7	19	13.7	19	13.7
1987	181	11	6.1	31	17.1	38	21.0	27	14.9	23	12.7	51	28.2
Total	536	57	10.6	166	31.0	100	18.6	74	13.8	55	10.3	84	15.7

Source: Townsend and Mason, 1990

16.4 Training researchers and administrators in higher education doctoral programmes

Higher education programmes in the US are not standardized, but many reveal similarities in structure, i.e. the programme is divided into different stages, starting with core courses, moving to specialization by taking electives, sitting for the comprehensive exam, taking the proposal defence and finally completing the dissertation. The author will now analyse a doctoral course of study.

16.4.1   Stage 1: Application

In order to be accepted in a higher education programme, students must start to prepare their application about a year in advance, obtain information about the programme they plan to apply to, and send off the applications to the programme and graduate school of their choice. Generally speaking, applicants are evaluated according to (a) undergraduate junior-senior grade point average; (b) grade-point average in any graduate work; (c) Graduate Record Examination (GRE) or an equivalent graduate entrance examination (e.g. MAT, GMAT); (d) professional and academic references; (e) a written essay. They can hold degrees in a professional field in the social or natural sciences and in the humanities. But most hold degrees in a field that is related to higher education (e.g. education, sociology). Information about the quality of the higher education programmes can be obtained from the ranking lists in the latest edition of the *US News&World Report*. Some applicants visit the universities of their choice before taking a decision. They talk to the faculty of the programmes, meet doctoral students and find out about possibilities of obtaining research assistantships. About six months before the beginning of the semester, they receive letters of acceptance or rejection. The offer of a research assistantship is often a reason for applicants to accept a given programme. It is perceived very positively, both by the students and the faculty, because students on research assistantships are full-time students whose work is directly related to and often constitutes feedback for their studies. In addition, research and teaching assistants have their tuition fees waived and receive a small salary that covers their basic costs of living. Whereas non-traditional students often use part of their savings from former jobs to maintain their standard of living, traditional students sometimes take out loans or find other sources of additional funding to cover their expenses.

16.4.2   Stage 2: Core courses in higher education studies

During the first two years, the programme is very structured. At the beginning, each student is assigned an advisor who usually carries out research in the same field of higher education studies as the student. The advisor helps doctoral students choose their course, as well as with questions related to the overall programme (Bargar and Mayo-Chamberlaine 1983; Smith et al. 1993). In addition, personal matters can be discussed. Usually, the assigned advisors remain with the students throughout the programme of study. They also serve as supervisors when the student holds a research assistantship. But it is possible to change advisors (even though this is often a sensitive issue). This is recommended when students change the focus of their study or when they express discontent.

Full-time students generally start off in the fall semester as a cohort which becomes the central support group for those who are full-time students with a research assistantship. Part-time students, who usually interact less with faculty are far less involved in the work of the cohort. During the first year, doctoral students in higher education typically follow a set of core courses (typically 15 credits). They often include *history of higher education, administration of higher education, curriculum and instruction, organ-*

izational theory, financial management and strategy in higher education, public policy in higher education, and students in higher education. Full-time students follow approximately three to four courses per semester. Their structure is very standardized: Attendance is compulsory, homework is given after each seminar, and midterms and finals are based on a grading scale of A (highest grade) to F (failure). Students work through an extensive compulsory reading list for each course. This reading list, together with lectures and homework serve as material for the semestrial midterm examinations and the finals. It is interesting to observe that certain group dynamics often emerge shortly after a new cohort starts the semester, partly because of the high pressure of homework, midterms and finals, and partly because of constant grading by the faculty. Faculty sometimes are perceived as "teachers" with great power over the academic and personal welfare of the students.

The classes typically consist of a mix of lecture, discussion, case studies and in-class exams. A three-hour class session (3-credit course) requires about six hours of preparation. Generally, the course load requires that doctoral students in higher education programmes, just like doctoral students in other fields of study, work long night hours and weekends and, where it applies, work for the research assistantship, which generally provides valuable experience. Some work for their advisors and help them to prepare a larger research project (e.g. for the National Science Foundation). They must carry out research on the topic in libraries, communicate with researchers across the country who have carried out similar projects, and manage a statistical database. They often co-sign publications with their advisor and present the findings at national meetings of higher education researchers (e.g. Association for the Study of Higher Education, ASHE).

16.4.3   Stage 3: Electives and comprehensive exam

After the first year, students have generally completed their core courses and start following core research courses, such as statistics and research design. Electives in an area of specialization are also pursued (approximately 12 credits). These include for example *teaching in higher education, institutional research, evaluation and assessment, race, ethnicity and gender,* and *capital financing.* Whereas some students at this stage have already decided on a minor or cognate area of study, others follow courses in different fields of study to find a cognate area that is suitable for them. They frequently talk to their advisors about further plans for their doctoral studies. In agreement with the advisor they elaborate a plan of the courses they intend to follow to fulfil the course requirements of the programme and the graduate school.

In the second year, students mainly concentrate on taking electives inside higher education and in other fields of study and on preparing for the comprehensive/qualifying exam, which can be described as a milestone. The requirements for the exam can differ, but generally doctoral students are tested within a given sequence, usually a couple of days, in all the relevant fields of higher education they have studied in the core courses. This exam requires much preparation. It can take more than six months and is a prerequisite to be officially accepted as a doctoral student (not a provisional doctoral student, as before). Those who are successful can move to the next stage. Those who fail can repeat the exam after six months. Generally, if they fail a second time, they are dismissed from the programme.

16.4.4 Stage 4: Specializing in a sub-field of higher education and completing the course requirements

In the fourth stage, i.e. after success in the comprehensive exam, the students and their advisors are given greater freedom to create a course of study that is geared towards meeting the specific research aligned with the professional needs of the student. Some required courses may still be completed, e.g. in research design, multivariate statistics, qualitative and quantitative research methods (approximately 24 credits), if they have not been completed in the previous year, but for most courses it is up to the students, in agreement with the advisors, to choose which path to take. They must generally take some 60 to 90 credits for the completion of the doctoral degree. After completing all the required courses, they can decide which courses to take, in accordance with the rules and regulations of the programme and the graduate school. Table 4 provides an overview of course requirements of a typical higher education programme, the Programme of Higher Education at the Pennsylvania State University, which was ranked in the top three higher education programmes by the *US News&World Report* in the 1990s. The course requirements for the PhD are established for students who plan to pursue a career in research (e.g. as faculty in higher education studies); the course requirements for the EdD are established for students who plan to pursue a career in administration (e.g. as director of student affairs at an institution).

Table 4: Course Requirements of a Typical Higher Education Programme

PhD Degree Requirements	EdD Degree Requirements
Core Area: 15 credits History of American Higher Education Curriculum in Higher Education Students and Clientele Administration in Higher Education Organizational Theory	*Core Area: 15 credits* History of American Higher Eduacation Curriculum in Higher Education Students and Clientele Administration in Higher Education Organizational Theory
Advanced Study: 12 credits Area of Specialization	*Advanced Study: 12 credits* Area of Specialization
Basic Research Skills: 12 credits minimum Statistics through Multivariate Qualitative Methods Research Design	*Basic Research Skills: 12 credits minimum* Statistics through Multivariate Qualitative Methods Research Design
Advanced Research Skills: 9 credits minimum beyond basic skills, usually taken in research skills cognate area	*Internship: 9 credits internship or practice* based courses, based on previous experience
Electives: Optional 12 credits of coursework *to enhance knowledge base were necessary*	*Electives: Optional 12 credits of coursework* *to enhance knowledge base where necessary*
Cognate Area: minimum15 credits	*Minor: Minimum 15 credits (as required by* *the Graduate School)*
Dissertation: Enrol in HI ED 601 or 611. These are non-credit courses used to maintain continuous enrolment, a requirement for the PhD, until the degree is obtained	*Dissertation: Minimum 15 credits for con-* *tinuous enrolment*

Source: Internet homepage, Graduate Programme in Higher Education, The Pennsylvania State University, 1999 (http://www.ed.psu.edu/hied/)

Students complete their course work approximately after their third year. The electives often help them to identify dissertation topics. Doctoral students in higher education do not only have to meet the requirements of the programme, but also those of the graduate school of the institution. Universities provide detailed guidelines for the writing of a doctoral dissertation.

16.4.5   Stage 5: Proposal defence, writing the dissertation, defence of the dissertation and graduation

Doctoral students who have finished most of their course work typically choose a dissertation committee (generally the advisor, two other faculty in the programme of higher education and one faculty in the field of the cognate area). In agreement with the committee, students choose a dissertation topic and start the research on their dissertation topic in the third year (Isaac et al. 1989). After conducting a dissertation literature review and research on the topic (e.g. ERIC-Database search, database search on relevant government documents, etc.), they produce an outline of the dissertation and write a proposal (Zaporozhetz 1987) which serves as the formal outline of the dissertation study. The proposal can be defined as a written plan for a dissertation developed by a student for consideration and approval by the dissertation committee (Schwarz 1997). It can range from a fully fledged outline, including purpose and significance of the study, research questions, literature overview and anticipation of the results, to a brief sketch of the topics they intend to cover. In the first case, the proposal is a major undertaking. Some advisors argue that writing the proposal takes more time and effort than writing the dissertation because every anticipated step of the dissertation should be written down within the proposal. The time students take to write the proposal can take anywhere between a couple of months and more than a year. Mauch and Birch (1993) argue that advising during the proposal writing stage and guidance during the proposal defence could better prepare students for the writing of the dissertation and therefore result in a better quality product and/or shorter time to degree.

After completing the proposal in agreement with the advisor, students schedule their proposal defence. It can be described as a type of "oral exam" before the doctoral committee in which the students should be prepared to answer all relevant questions related to the research investigations of their planned dissertation. Generally, they pass the proposal defence but are given a set of assignments by the doctoral committee, e.g. to change part of the research questions or to specify the methods of the study.

Writing the dissertation is one of the most difficult parts of the studies for a number of doctoral students (Spriestersbach and Henry 1978, Flores and Montemayor 1979, Isaac et al. 1989, Germeroth 1991, Nerad and Cerny 1993, Schwarz 1997). Whereas they have been working and studying in a group with their cohort until the completion of course work, many students see the dissertation writing stage as a difficult time because they feel isolated. Some feel lost in the transition between what they call a "class-taking" person and a "book-writing" person (Nerad and Cerny 1993, p.30).

Once the doctoral students have finished the final draft of the dissertation, they make an appointment for the defence with the doctoral committee. They must give one copy of the final draft to all the committee members about four weeks in advance so that these can evaluate it. The oral defence often has a justification function. After the oral defence, the committee members inform the doctoral student what changes need to be made. Generally, students can take between a few weeks and a few months to make these changes, depending on the comments of the committee members. After the final approval of the thesis by the committee members, students present the dissertation to the graduate school which checks the dissertation for formal structure and informs the students whether or not it is accepted. If the dissertation is accepted, the student has formally met all requirements for the doctoral degree in higher education and is ready for graduation.

After graduation, students are likely to look back at four stages, as out-lined previously. During these stages, doctoral students should have been trained in four skill areas (Townsend 1989): (1) understanding the practical applications of theory in typical areas of administrative responsibility, e.g. enrolment management, curriculum planning and evaluation, budget and finance, (2) technical and communication competences: research and writing skills to manage course work, (3) integrative competence: applying theory to practice, as well as case studies, and simulation exercises, (4) conceptual competence: interpreting and understanding structured paradigms.

16.5 Students' perceptions of career opportunities in the field of higher education

A number of researchers have speculated on the impact of the higher education programmes on the professional lives of the graduates (e.g. Cooper 1986; Grace and Fife 1986). Few have conducted research on the impact of the skills learned in higher education programmes on graduates' work as researchers and administrators. In 1990, Townsend and Mason pub-lished a descriptive, exploratory, national study on careers of recipients of higher education doctorates. They identified 1,053 graduates of higher edu-cation programmes for the survey (four cohorts: 1972, 1977, 1982, 1987). A survey was sent to all identified graduates, and the researchers obtained a 76 percent response rate.

The results of the study show the employment history of graduates in higher education and the perceived value of a doctorate in higher education. Data on the employment history shows that after graduation most graduates (about 80%) spend their entire career in higher education. The majority (42%) are working in middle-level management positions, e.g. director of housing, athletic director, or registrar. About one-fifth (22%) work in faculty positions, twelve percent hold senior administrative positions, about ten per-cent hold positions that report to the CEO (e.g. dean of student affairs), and 3 percent hold chief executive positions (see Table 5).

Over the fifteen years covered by the study by Townsend and Mason, the percentage of graduates who did not find a position in higher education has increased. Whereas it was less than five percent in 1972, the figure rose to 19 percent in 1987. Townsend and Mason (1990, p.71) argue that this rela-tively high percentage seems "to refute the common assumption that most students in higher education doctoral programmes are already higher educa-tion faculty members or administrators getting the degree to become more eligible for promotion", as for example stated in Dressel and Mayhew (1974).

Table 5: Positions of Graduates of US Higher Education Programmes

Year		CEO in HI ED		Reports to CEO		Other Ad- ministrator		Postsec Faculty		Retired		Outside HI ED	
	N	N	%	N	%	N	%	N	%	N	%	N	%
1972	83	4	4.8	14	16.9	26	31.4	21	25.3	8	9.6	10	12.0
1977	134	3	2.2	12	9.0	52	38.8	30	22.4	10	7.5	25	18.6
1982	140	5	3.6	12	8.6	70	50.0	18	12.9	2	1.4	32	22.9
1987	178	2	1.1	12	6.7	74	41.6	48	27.0	2	1.1	37	20.8
	535	14	2.6	50	9.3	222	41.5	117	21.9	22	4.1	104	19.4

Source: Townsend and Mason, 1990

Townsend and Mason also report in their study that an increasing number of graduates are leaving higher education and moving to another field. There are many reasons for this. The most common reason reported was "it was time" for a career change (45%); the second was the inability to find a job in higher education (31%) and better pay outside education (20%).

The most troublesome finding of Townsend and Mason's (1990, p.74) study is the high percentage of graduates "who would not pursue a higher education doctorate if they were beginning doctoral studies again" (57%). Most indicated other fields of study they would consider: business came first (18%), followed by social sciences (12%), nursing/medical sciences (10%), and law (4%). Respondents who were dissatisfied with the programme mainly evoked the low status of higher education as a field of study. However, even though more than half the graduates would choose another major if they were to do it over again, the study also indicates that more than 70 percent regarded their doctoral studies in higher education as highly relevant or relevant for their current profession.

Last, but not least, the job situation for graduates of higher education programs improved significantly since the mid 90s. The author expects that this is likely to positively effect the perception of graduates in higher education, regarding their choice of study.

ACKNOWLEDGEMENTS

The author wants to thank Lynn Hunter, Distance Learning Program Coordinator at the Advanced Technology Education Center, University of

Maine System and Betsy Palmer, Assistant Professor at the Higher Education Program, University of Alabama for their valuable information on higher education programmes in the United States.

REFERENCES

Baird, L. L. (1990). 'Disciplines and doctorates: The relationships between program characteristics and the duration of doctoral study.' *Research in Higher Education* 31, No 2.

Bargar, R. R. and Mayo-Chamberlaine, J. (1983). 'Advisor and advisee issues in doctoral education.' *Journal of Higher Education,* 54 (4).

Bowen, W. G. and Rudenstine, N. L. (1992). *In Pursuit of the PhD.* Princeton, N.J.: Princeton University Press.

Brazziel, W. F. and Beeler, K. J. (1991). *Doctorate Production and Changing Demography.* Paper presented at the annual meeting of the Association for the Study of Higher Education, Boston.

Cooper, J. H. (1986). *Education as a Field of Study: Some Future Prospects.* Paper presented at the annual meeting of the Association for the Study of Higher Education, San Antonio, Texas.

Dressel, P. L. and Mayhew, L. B. (1974). *Higher Education as a Field of Study.* San Francisco: Jossey-Bass.

Flores, E. Y. and Montemayor, J. (1979). *Beyond Survival in a Doctoral Program: A Guide for Graduate and Doctoral Students in Education.* ERIC Doc # ED 196392.

Germeroth, D. (1991). Lonely Days and Lonely Nights: Completing the Doctoral Dissertation. *ABA Bulletin,* pp. 60-87.

Grace, J. D. and Fife, J. D. (1986). *A Profile of Student Expectations of Graduate Programs in Higher Education: A Marketing Approach.* Paper presented at the annual meeting of the Association for the Study of Higher Education, San Antonio, Texas.

Isaac, P. D., Koenigsknecht, R. A., Malaney, G. D. and Karras, J. E. (1989). 'Factors related to doctoral dissertation topic selection.' *Research in Higher Education* 30 (4).

Mason, S. O. and Townsend, B. K. (1988). *Graduates of Doctoral Programs in Higher Education: Demographics and Career Patterns.* Paper presented at the annual meeting of the Association for the Study of Higher Education, St. Louis, Missouri.

Mauch, J. E. and Birch, J. W. (1993). *Guide to the Successful Thesis and Dissertation: Conception to Publication. A Handbook for Students and Faculty.* Third Edition, revised and expanded. New York: Marcel Dekker, Inc.

Nerad, M. and Cerny, J. (1993). *From Facts to Action: Expanding the Educational Role of the Graduate Division.* New Directions for Institutional Research 80, pp. 27-40.

Pemberton, S. M. (1980). *A Brief Historical Review of Research on Higher Education, 1900-1960.* Washington, D.C.: US Department of Health, Education, and Welfare National Institute of Education.

Ploskonka, J. (1992). *An Explanatory Model of Doctoral Completion: A Description of Characteristics and their Relationship to Time to the Degree.* University of Kentucky. Unpublished Doctoral Dissertation.

Rogers, J. F. (1969). *Higher Education as a Field of Study at the Doctoral Level.* Washington, D.C.: American Association for Higher Education, National Education Association.

Schwarz, S. (1997). *Students' Perceptions of the Role of the Dissertation Chair in Time to Complete the Doctoral Dissertation.* The Pennsylvania State University. Unpublished Doctoral Dissertation.

Semas, P. W. (1974). 'Department of higher education caught in an identity crisis', *Chronicle of Higher Education* 42 (March 25), p.4.

Simmons, R. O. and Thurgood, D. H. (1995). *Summary Report 1994: Doctoral Recipients from United States Universities.* Washington, D.C.: National Academic Press.

Smith, S. W., Brownell, M. T., Simpson, R. L., and Deshler, D. D. (1993). 'Successfully completing the dissertation: two reflections on the process', *Remedial and Special Education* 14 (3).

Spriestersbach, D. C., and Henry, L. D., JR., (1978). 'The PhD Dissertation: servant or master?' *ICUT,* W' 78, pp. 52-55.

Townsend, B. K. (1989). *Doctoral Study in Programs of Higher Education: Overview and Prospects.* ERIC Doc # ED 313965.

Townsend, B. K., and Mason, S. O. (1990). 'Career paths of graduates of higher education doctoral programs'. *The Review of Higher Education* 14 (1).

US Department of Education (1997). National Center for Education Statistics, Integrated Post-secondary Education Data System (IPEDS), "Fall Enrollment", "Staff", and "Completion surveys".

Zaporozhetz, L. E. (1987). *The Dissertation Literature Review: How Faculty Advisors Preparae Their Doctoral Candidates.* ERIC Doc # ED 303131.

Chapter 17

The European Higher Education Advanced Training Course

BARBARA M. KEHM
Institute for Higher Education Research Wittenberg (HoF Wittenberg), Martin Luther University Halle-Wittenberg, Germany

17.1 Introduction: Course structure and organisation

The European Higher Education Advanced Training Course was de-signed by some of the founding members of CHER. It was taught for the first time in 1992 and 1993 and consisted of eight one-week modules. The aim was to offer a course to young researchers and administrators in higher education which would enable them to reflect at a more theoretical and sys-tematic level on their everyday practical problems and pending issues in the field of higher education research and administration.

The course attracted young doctoral and post-doctoral researchers and middle-level higher education administrators from some 12 to 15 EU Mem-ber States as well as from Central and Eastern Europe. Participants from the latter countries received TEMPUS funding. Approximately 20 participants took part in each of the eight modules, whilst about 12 to 15 took part in one or more modules. They were between 25 and 40 years old. Their background alone made the course a unique experience for exchange, communication and networking. Many have kept in contact with each other and with the teachers of the course, sometimes through continued personal contacts, sometimes through meetings at conferences, sometimes through the ex-change of e-mails.

Each of the eight modules was organised by a higher education research institute or university department in a different European country. Apart from meeting eminent researchers and scholars in the field who taught the

S. Schwarz and U. Teichler (eds.), The Institutional Basis of Higher Education Research, 227–237.

respective module, participants were also able to become familiar with the focus of different European institutes of higher education research.

Each module had a different theme and was coordinated by two or three teachers, one of whom was from the institute where the module was taught. Researchers from abroad were also invited to teach individual sessions. Hence, a variety of approaches and problems pertaining to the theme of the module could be discussed. Comparisons were possible because the participants and teachers came from different countries. Participants were expected to prepare for each module by working through a reading list and other course material they received beforehand and to reflect on the module by writing a country report on its theme and submitting it to the organisers for feedback and comments. Successful participation was documented by a certificate. In addition, all modules were evaluated by the participants on a daily as well as an overall basis with the help of short evaluation sheets. These were collected and served to provide feedback to teachers and to improve the preparation and organisation of the next module.

17.2 Modules and themes

The course consisted of eight one-week modules, i.e. one every three months, and was taught at eight different institutes of higher education research in eight European countries. Thus, it did not only serve to familiarize students with the existing institutional infrastructure for higher education research in Europe, but the mix of local teachers and invited guests from abroad also contributed to develop the networking between the participants.

17.3 Processes and structures in higher education

The theme of the first module was "Processes and Structures in Higher Education". It took place at the Centre for Higher Education Management of the Anglia Business School in Danbury Park, Chelmsford, UK, and was co-ordinated by Maurice Kogan and Ian McNay. This was a general and introductory module with the following objectives:
- to introduce students to the concept of the course as a whole and give an overview of the themes;
- to familiarize students with the main conceptual frames that can be used in the analysis of higher education systems, structures and processes, the political and other environments within which higher education works, and the broad structures for the pursuit of research, scholarship, teaching and other functions of higher education;
- to help students to place themselves within the structural analyses offered under the second objective;

– to enhance students' knowledge and understanding of the systems of higher education of different European countries.

Exchanges about the various higher education systems the participants came from, their respective jobs within institutions and their experience in research and administration of higher education played an important role. Participants were expected to have gone through a substantial reading list beforehand and write a case study and country report at the end of the module. This was the case for all the modules.

The module began by an identification of key issues from participants' pre-course work and then went on to discuss values in higher education and the nature of institutions. Experience, values and institutional structures were then brought together in a matrix which related structures and processes by analysing the internal and external normative and operative modes of higher education systems, institutions, basic units and individuals. This model provided a framework for discussions on the nature of disciplines and forces leading to change within the institutions, as well as on various political environments pertaining to higher education in various countries.

The module also included familiarisation with other organisational models, for example the Clark matrix, and an attempt to apply norms and operational modes at different levels of structure. In addition, processes were studied in more detail by examining sources of change, responses to them and forms of implementation. Finally, the changing nature of higher education systems was discussed and compared by confronting academic, managerial and market models of governance. To conclude the first module, national groups of participants were formed to prepare case studies of their countries. These had to be completed and submitted after their return to their home countries.

17.4 Steering of higher education systems

The venue of the second module on "Steering of Higher Education Systems" was the Hungarian Institute of Educational Research in Budapest. It was coordinated by Frans A. van Vught and Tamás Kozma. Its objectives were:
– to introduce students to the political context of higher education in national systems in Western Europe;
– to identify and analyse the significance of political factors for the functioning and development of a higher education system in a mixed market;
– to discuss various methods and instruments for government steering of higher education;
– to show the limitations of the various models employed;

– to give students the opportunity of assessing the application of these models through discussion and both group and individual work.

The theme was divided into four sub-themes: governing higher education, the transformation from élite to mass higher education, innovation in higher education, and implementation. The last day was devoted to feedback and a summary of the module. In addition, the transformation of the Hungarian system of higher education served as a focus for case study techniques.

In the first part of the module, participants were introduced to general models of governance, followed by two case studies. Higher education governance in the Netherlands was discussed by analysing whether the government was really stepping back or whether a shift of state control from one area to another was taking place. A concept for higher education development in Hungary provided the second case study. Participants tried to apply the various concepts of governance to the Hungarian situation. Transformation processes and the role of the government were discussed in the second part of the module. This time Hungary, the United Kingdom and the United States served as examples to analyse the various processes of transformation from élite to mass higher education. The third part helped to make participants more familiar with comparative case study methodology by using examples of innovation in higher education in the Netherlands and the United Kingdom. Questions and discussions, lectures and literature studies as well as exercise groups to analyse the comparability of data from a methodological point of view provided opportunities for an in-depth analysis and practical work with case study methodology. The fourth thematic focus dealt with issues of implementation of policies and innovation. The Dutch and Australian examples of institutional mergers provided material for case studies.

17.5 Economic aspects of higher education

"Economic Aspects of Higher Education" was the theme of the third module, which took place at the Institute for Research on Economics of Education of the University of Bourgogne in Dijon, France. The coordinators were Jean-Claude Eicher and Gareth Williams. The objectives were to introduce students to the basic concepts and methods in the field of economics of education; in particular:

– supply and demand in higher education;
– the public and private costs and benefits of higher education;
– the production function of higher education in various institutional settings;
– the finance of higher education institutions and systems.

The module began by introducing participants to the basic concepts and tools of the economics of education. This topic was studied more in-depth by analysing the costs and financing of higher education, followed by case studies of cost assessments. Other parts of the module dealt with topics related more indirectly to costs and financing, for example the impact of technology on higher education and equity issues in higher education. Higher education and the labour market was a further sub-theme which was introduced by a lecture and then studied more in-depth with the help of case studies and discussions. To conclude, participants were presented with new approaches to international comparisons of higher education funding and a summary of what had been studied during the week.

17.6 Higher education and work

The Centre for Research on Higher Education and Work in Kassel was the venue of the fourth module on "Higher Education and Work". It was coordinated by Ulrich Teichler and Maurice Kogan and had the following objectives:
- to introduce participants to key issues of research and research methods concerning the relationship between higher education and work;
- to give an overview of theories, research and range of practice in various European countries regarding the relationships between higher education and employment;
- to make participants familiar with the following topics and enable them to place their own work and experience in their home countries in the frameworks presented: (a) qualitative, structural and substantive relationships between higher education and work, (b) design, methods and operations of graduate survey research, (c) different levels and ranges of the relationship between higher education and employment (national, cross-national, regional, institutional), (d) the role of the links between higher education and work for the higher education system (institutional dimensions, policy making, curriculum development), (e) new research and potential paradigms to shape the relationship between higher education and the world of work (e.g. trends towards a highly educated society).

The module began with two introductions.

The first provided an overview of theories and research, developments and policies regarding higher education and work, including changes in research approaches and the issue of credentials as an example of links between higher education and work. The second was concerned with research on the impact of higher education on employment and work as well as with the implications of relationships between higher education and work for other higher education issues.

On the basis of an introduction to and study of research undertaken in Germany, participants were invited to discuss whether higher education provisions and environment matter for employment and work. Participants who were particularly interested in statistical methods and survey tools were able to familiarize themselves with conducting graduate and employer surveys in a special option. Special issues within the theme of this module were curriculum development and the labour market, disparities between regional labour markets and their challenge for higher education and institutional aspects of the relationships between higher education and work. The module also discussed trends towards a highly educated society and studied new research and potential paradigms to perceive and shape the relationships between higher education and work. The concluding discussion tried to identify possible further studies and research work.

17.7 Fields of knowledge, teaching and learning

The fifth module on the theme "Fields of Knowledge, Teaching and Learning" was taught at the Centre for Higher Education Studies in Prague, Czech Republic. Its coordinators were Tony Becher, Ludwig Huber and Helena Šebkova. The topics of the lectures, case studies, group work and plenary discussions in this module were:
–   the concepts of knowledge fields, disciplines and specialisations;
–   cognitive and social differences between and within disciplines;
–   dimensions of teaching and learning, levels of action, framework conditions, curriculum and learning situation;
–   reflections on the role of administrators and researchers in relation to teaching and learning;
–   conditions and criteria for 'good' teaching and 'good' learning and the interaction of both;
–   disciplinary traditions of teaching and learning (curricular patterns, teaching styles, learning situations);
–   implications of interdisciplinarity for changes in curriculum and teaching;
–   disciplinary differences in research organisation and styles;
–   research funding and management and implications for methodology and training in research;
–   assessing the quality of teaching (possible instruments);
–   assessing students and the quality of learning;
–   assessing quality in research (disciplinary differences);
–   issues of quality control.
Participants were presented with some innovative teaching methods. The topics not only addressed the cognitive dimension, but also interactive and experimental learning. The module began by a brainstorming and an identi-

fication of participants' agendas, followed by a lecture about concepts of knowledge fields, disciplines and specialisations. By separating participants according to their field of research and administration, significant cognitive and social differences between and within disciplines and between the various disciplinary and geographical cultures could be observed. An overview of the module was then provided and desirable changes were discussed.

The module then introduced participants to the various dimensions of teaching and learning, levels of action and framework conditions, curriculum issues and learning situations. Participants were asked to identify their concepts of themselves and to reflect on the role of administrators and researchers in relation to teaching and learning. This was followed by a discussion of conditions and criteria for 'good teaching' and 'good learning' and their interaction, including general assumptions and their limits and a reflection on common fallacies. Historical issues were analysed in a lecture and a seminar on disciplinary traditions of teaching and learning by studying curricular patterns on the one hand and teaching styles and learning situations on the other. The participants then prepared short lectures on the implications of interdisciplinarity for changes in curriculum and teaching.

A second part of the module addressed disciplinary differences in research organisation and styles, their consequences for research funding and management, implications for methodology and training in research and the challenge of interdisciplinarity in research.

A third part was devoted to quality assessment issues. First, assessing the quality of teaching was addressed by again pointing out disciplinary differences and providing an overview of possible instruments. Second, case studies from three national systems of higher education served as examples to introduce participants to issues of student assessment and quality of learning. Third, criteria and methods for assessing quality in research were developed and discussed, also taking disciplinary differences into account. This part of the module included a debate on general issues of quality control. The module ended by discussing the participants' specific concerns and by attempting to anticipate problems and actions once they had returned to their home institutions.

17.8 Institutional decision-making and research

"Institutional Decision-Making and Research" was the theme of the sixth module which was organized by the Center for Higher Education Policy Studies at the University of Twente in Enschede, The Netherlands. It was coordinated by Frans A. van Vught and Ulrich Teichler and had the following objectives:

- to introduce students to models in order to understand and analyse decision-making processes within higher education institutions and to discuss
  the strengths and weaknesses of these models;
- to give insight in the applicability of the concept of strategy in higher
  education;
- to familiarize students with the usefulness of decision-making, strategic
  planning, and information management models and approaches through
  discussion and group and individual work;
- to give students the opportunity to become acquainted with methods to
  gather and analyse data that support institutional decision-making;
- to discuss the nature of research as a scientific activity and as an instrument to support institutional management.

The module focused on decision-making in higher education at the institutional level. Participants were introduced to various models, such as the
'garbage can' model, the collegial model or the political model. These were
discussed from both a conceptual and a practical perspective. Decision-
making in higher education institutions was then related to institutional or
strategic planning which was presented from a theoretical as well as a practical point of view and analysed with the help of scenarios from Western
Europe and Central and Eastern Europe. From a methodological perspective,
the module introduced participants to work with scenarios.

The role of information for institutional decision-making was also studied. Information management and decision support systems constituted important aspects of this issue. Relating to issues of quality assessment in previous modules, information on the quality of higher education was examined
in the light of how decisions are made in the quality assessment process and
how such decisions influence and in turn are influenced by other spheres of
institutional decision-making. Further issues for study and debate were
questions and outcomes of research for institutional decision-making and the
political contexts of institutional decision-making.

Last, the module offered participants a management-oriented and a re-
search-oriented visit to locations of institutional decision-making at the host
university. In a final session, participants discussed designs and issues to be
incorporated in the country reports and reflected on the outcomes of the sce-
nario exercise.

17.9 Management of higher education institutions

The seventh module was organised by the University of Turku in Finland
on the theme "Management of Higher Education Institutions". The coordinators were Kari Hyppönen and Ian McNay. It aimed to relate functional
areas of management, e.g. personnel, finance and marketing, to the chal-

lenges facing institutional managers at the end of the century. It drew on and developed from material of previous modules to examine four main themes in a holistic way:
– managing change and evolution;
– managing an entrepreneurial institution;
– managing equality and diversity;
– managing for excellence.

Part of this module took place on the island of Nauvo in the archipelago south of Turku which is one of the biggest nature reserves in Europe.

The module started with a lecture on an issue of particular interest for the higher education systems in Central and Eastern Europe, namely whether managing institutional change in the new era should be regarded as an evolution or a revolution. The issue of managing for excellence and institutional renewal accompanied almost all the debates and lectures of this module. In a first part, this issue was dealt with by covering the following topics with the help of examples and case studies: the management sequence, patterns of control and regulation, the culture of evaluation and its development, variables affecting internal regulatory patterns, infrastructure for institutional renewal, theoretical and practical considerations, institutional evaluation and processes for internal developmental evaluation. Participants were divided into groups which tried to design renewal and improvement processes. This rather systematic overview was complemented by an introduction to frameworks for the management of enterprise and equality in higher education institutions. It also included a Finnish case study on regional entrepreneurialism.

Issues of distance education, open learning and flexible delivery constituted the second part of the module. Participants were presented with examples from Australia and the UK to widen access and improve opportunities for non-typical groups of students. In the third part, participants were made familiar with research on institutional management, in particular with reference to strategic planning and budgeting and academic staffing. The topic of academic staffing was then studied in depth with debates about trends and policies, qualifications, career and recruitment issues and academic production. The module ended with a lecture by Burton Clark who introduced his work in progress about universities as places of inquiry and the implications of this for management. A panel commented his lecture, which was then discussed by all participants.

17.10 Higher education and international developments in Europe

The eighth and last module on the theme "Higher Education and International Developments in Europe" was organised by the European University Institute in Florence, Italy, and was coordinated by Claudius Gellert, Roberto Moscati and Guy Neave. The objectives were to introduce students to:
– aspects of internationalisation of higher education;
– the place of international higher education organisations;
– the role of interest groups in the formulation of policies on higher education.

After an introduction to the theme, participants were given a historical and systematic overview of internationalisation in higher education. Patterns of change in European higher education constituted the follow-up of this overview which was then analysed in depth in group exercises and discussions. The second part of the module was devoted to recent trends in higher education policy of the European Union. Due to the geographical spread of teachers' and participants' home countries, the issue of centre and periphery influences in European higher education played an important role here. Another issue was how European higher education policy was implemented. In this context, participants studied the general features of programme objectives and administrative problems of EU programmes in higher education. This was followed by a case study of the ERASMUS Programme. A lecture on clientelism in Italian politics completed this part of the module.

The third part dealt with international organisations and interest groups. Five examples of policies of internationalisation in higher education were presented and discussed. They included the perspectives of the International Council of Social Studies, of the European Rectors' Conference, of the World Bank, of OECD and of UNESCO. In order to provide participants with an outlook which went beyond the European Union, information and discussions on changes in higher education in developing countries concluded this part of the module. Finally, reforms in Central and Eastern European higher education and new relationships with Western European systems were studied more closely. This brought the European Higher Education Advanced Training Course to a close. There was also a big farewell party with exchanges of addresses and promises to keep in contact which have been fulfilled in many cases.

17.11 Experiences and perspectives

Participating in the course was a unique experience for all involved. Apart from getting a good overview of the major fields of research on higher education and the active networking, an important outcome for participants was also the first or a better integration in the existing academic community in the field.

Naturally, all participants hoped that such a course could be repeated. There were also some attempts to get the course material and country reports published. Both undertakings unfortunately failed. CHEPS tried to repeat the course in a revised form and the first module took place in March 1996. But without TEMPUS support and on a full cost basis, each module became so expensive that it did not attract a sufficient number of participants. Some thought was also given to developing the course into a distance study programme. That too came to nothing. Maybe it will indeed remain a unique experience, although many still hope that the concept could be revived for future generations of young researchers and administrators in the field of higher education.

Chapter 18

Doctoral Graduates in Higher Education Research: Training and Careers in France

CATHY PERRET
Irédu-CNRS, Université de Bourgogne, France

18.1 Introduction

The topic discussed in this paper is the training of young researchers in the field of higher education and their prospects. In France, there is no specific training of young researchers in the field of higher education. Some higher education subjects can only be the topic of a thesis. In human and social sciences, training for a *doctorat* is similar for those individuals who pursue a career in higher education research. Thus, in this paper, we shall first present *doctorat* training in general and some specific characteristics of training in higher education research. Then, we shall analyse what is required of young researchers for a career in higher education research.

Higher education research is not a discipline in France, only a thematic field. An explanation could be that there is no organization of higher education research. Only some people work in this field in various disciplines and in different universities and laboratories. The Ministry of Education and Research carries out most studies on the French education system. Another reason is that, since the 1980s, policy concerning the training of young researchers lays emphasis on technology. This policy has two characteristics: the growth in the number of *doctorat* graduates in science (recently, in other disciplines) and the public authorities' wish to develop the ties between students and firms.

S. Schwarz and U. Teichler (eds.), The Institutional Basis of Higher Education Research, 239–245.

18.2 The training of young researchers in France

Before 1984, there were three types of doctoral degrees in France (*Doctorat d'État, Diplôme de Docteur Ingénieur, Doctorat de 3ème cycle*). In 1984, they were replaced by a single *doctorat* (*Loi n°84-52 du 26 janvier 1984 sur l'enseignement supérieur*). This reform was implemented to create a degree system that is similar to other European countries, but more especially to the USA (*Direction de la recherche et des études doctorales 1991a*). The *doctorat* is the highest degree in the French system. Two laws have successively governed its organization: 1) the bill of July 5th 1984 modified by the bill of November 23rd 1988; 2) the bill of April 3rd 1992, which concerns the third cycle. Doctoral studies include the DEA (*diplôme d'études approfondies*) and the *doctorat*. The aim of the DEA is to prepare students for the *doctorat*.

Created in 1974, the DEA is the first year of doctoral studies and follows upon four years of study for the *maîtrise*. Admission is based on the results in the *maîtrise*, and, generally, an interview. In the DEA, students spend a training period in a research team or carry out surveys. They attend 150 hours of theoretical and methodological lectures. This degree normally takes one year. But it can take two years, particularly in the case of students who have a full-time job. It is awarded after deliberation by a DEA jury on (art. 18, bill of April 30th 1992): (1) A dissertation which shows the students' research capacities and ability to prepare a thesis; (2) exams or reports covering the theoretical and methodological lectures; (3) an oral examination to evaluate the knowledge of the discipline; (4) if the student undergoes a period of training in a research team, the head gives his opinion on the student.

Usually the DEA is required for admission to the *doctorat*. The prescribed length of study for the *doctorat* is between two and four years. Public authorities recommend three years. It is possible to take longer, particularly in the case of students who have a professional activity. Students work in a research team recognized by the public authorities under the guidance of a supervisor. Requirements for the *doctorat* include the writing of a doctoral thesis which is made available to the public and disseminated[1]. The assessment committee, made up of at least three members, judges the candidate on his research results, his ability to put them into scientific context and his ability to speak in public. The degree is awarded by the committee with different distinctions: *honorable, très honorable, très honorable avec félicitations*. In 1996, 10,963 *doctorat* degrees were conferred in France, and there were 68,426 *doctorat* students in 1997.

Young researchers in higher education research or in education are trained in different disciplines, such as sociology, economics, psychology, management studies, et. and recently in education. The number of DEA graduates in these disciplines has increased, despite the fact that the number of DEA students has decreased since 1994. This reflects the growth in completion rates. In arts, humanities, social sciences, some 50 percent of students obtain their DEA and 50 percent do not finish the course. These figures are respectively 65 percent and 35 percent in law, political sciences, economics and management studies. Some 40 percent of DEA students who graduated in September 1997 enrolled in the *doctorat* at the end of 1997. It seems that the transition rates from DEA to *doctorat* have been decreasing since 1994 in all disciplines. This explains the stagnation in the number of *doctorat* students. As we said above, more than one out of two DEA graduates do not go on to a *doctorat*. In addition to the DEA and the recommendations of the supervisor, other conditions can be required to enrol in doctoral studies (e.g. being a secondary school teacher in the above disciplines). This policy has been developed because of the employment problems of *doctorat* graduates. In addition, DEA graduates can choose not to continue because most of them already have a professional activity or feel that the opportunity costs are too high.

In reality, doctoral studies last between four and five years in all the aforementioned disciplines. Students rarely go abroad during their doctoral studies (only to learn a particular method for a short period). The supervisor decides on this travel period. In general, he considers that the years of doctoral studies are very important for careers because they are part of a learning and socializing period and the prescribed length for the *doctorat* is shorter (Musselin 1997). There are very few institutional incentives (funding, etc.). But we observe a recent evolution with the PRESTIGE programme, which is part of the European Training Mobility Research (TMR) programme.

Most graduates in the aforementioned disciplines study for a *doctorat* without a public grant (80% in arts, humanities, social sciences, and 65% in law, political sciences, economics and management studies). We estimate that most students who are funded in higher education or in education are funded by their research unit with one or more contracts which may or may not be related to the topic of their thesis. One consequence is that the topic of the thesis can depend on the contracts, even if the students choose their topic in the DEA. Some students are funded by the ministry, but they have to obtain a grant in their discipline (economics, sociology, educational sciences, etc.). These grants are attributed according to the results of the DEA and rarely to the topic of the thesis. These students, called *allocataires,* can already be *moniteurs.* The *Monitorat d'initiation à l'enseignement supérieur* was created in 1989 to incite young researchers to integrate higher education after their *doctorat* (*Direction de la recherche et des études doctorales*

1991b). It consists in teaching practices, lecturing at the first level of the university and different lessons about the higher education and research system. A *moniteur* is chosen among the *doctorat* students who are financed by the government. The *monitorat* is a fixed-term contract, but it does not give *moniteur* students an automatic right to teach in higher education.

In fact, in higher education research and in education research, there are different types of doctoral students: a minority of young *allocataires* and sometimes *moniteurs* and a large number of older students who teach in primary and secondary schools. But the former rarely carry out Higher Education Research; and a large number of young *doctorat* students are funded by contracts of their research unit. In the latter case, some students are like *allocataires* students, working only on their thesis, with one or more research contracts. Other students with different levels of funding work on different topics or outside the field of research. The *moniteurs* and other *doctorat* students can teach in the universities during their studies. They represent a very small minority. In general, they teach in their disciplines.

One of the problems of higher education research is that there are no specific French publications. The students must publish in journals that cover each different discipline or in international journals. They carry out their own survey because the data of the ministry are not available or cannot be used in their projects. In addition, there is some reticence on the part of the higher education system and the administration of higher education.

Collaboration between doctoral students in higher education research is not very developed. Students can work with researchers of their laboratories, but they rarely work with students whose thesis is in the same domain. One explanation is the competition between graduates for the posts in research, which contributes to an individual organization of research.

18.3 A career in higher education research

Careers in higher education research are conditioned by the prospects of integrating the university system or the public research organizations, or the public administration of the higher education system.

In order to pursue an academic career, one must have obtained the *doctorat* with the best distinction to obtain a job in the university system or in public research organizations. In academic research, researchers are recruited according to a national selection process, which includes a local examination in the university system. One remark must be made: the modalities of recruitment in the university system change about every two years. Recruitment is based on each discipline, except in educational sciences where the topic of the thesis can be very important. Hence, young researchers in higher education who develop their thesis and their research programme according to the theory and methodology of one discipline (economics, sociology, etc.) have a chance of integrating the university system or public research organizations. *Doctorat* graduates in educational sciences cannot obtain employment in most of the public research organizations (CNRS, National Center of Scientific Research), except in the INRP (National Institute of Pedagogical Research). However, the latter does not develop much research in higher education. In addition to the recruitment by discipline, integrating the CNRS is not easy for doctoral students in the field of higher education because there is preference for basic research on applied fields.

In the public administration of the higher education system you do not need a *doctorat*.

18.4 Young researchers' prospects

There is no source of information about the employment of *doctorat* graduates in higher education research, but we have data on the prospects of *doctorat* graduates in different disciplines.

18.4.1   One year after the doctorat (MRT data)

Arts, humanities, and social sciences
A small number of graduates went on to post-doctoral studies (7.3%, a total of 90 graduates in this subject group in the survey of the Ministry of Research and Technology). 37.4 percent integrated higher education, principally with a permanent job, and 4.1 percent integrated the public research organizations. Only 9.3 percent worked in firms. They were also less unemployed (9.0%) than the latter. But, a greater number occupied a job in the public administration (12.7%) or secondary education (20.0%). Recently, there has been a decrease in the number of *doctorat* holders who integrate higher education and public research organizations, and a growth in the number of unemployed graduates and of those employed by firms.

Law, Political Sciences, Economics and Management Studies
In 1997, one year after the *doctorat*, 41 percent integrated higher education, half of whom were *ATER* (*Attaché temporaire d'enseignement et de recherche*). 4.5 percent integrated public research organizations, 19.9 percent worked in firms, and 11.4 percent were unemployed. The number who went on to post-doctoral studies increased, but represented only 8.5 percent of *doctorat* holders. There seems to have been a growth in the number of unemployed graduates and a rise in the number of those employed by firms.

In addition, the number of *doctorat* holders who integrate higher education or research dropped.

A recent *Céreq* survey gives information about the employment of *doctorat* holders in 1997 (De Lassalle *et al.* 1999), *three years after their degree* (not including foreign graduates). 89.5 percent were employed, 5.9 percent were unemployed and 4.1 percent were in post-doctoral studies. Of the employed graduates, 85 percent integrated the public services (75.8% of the *doctorat* graduates), of which 95 percent were in the higher education sector, public research and secondary schools. 16 percent of the employed *doctorat* holders were employed temporarily.

18.5 Higher education research perspectives in France

The training of *doctorat* students is very much under discussion because of the Attali report (1998). In this report, the authors suggest a transformation of the higher education system. They see two types of training for the *doctorat*. The first is technological training in collaboration with firms, and the second is traditional training for a minority of students. At present, there are two other questions: a placement abroad during doctoral studies and lectures during doctoral studies in economics and management for the majority of students and courses in higher education for the minority who are destined for the universities.

This policy could affect positively the number of doctoral students in higher education and the research on this theme, with the recognition of the students' collaboration with different institutions and administrations, or negatively with a drop in the number of academic theses. On the other hand, courses in higher education for PhD students could offer better university recruitment prospects for young researchers in Higher Education, the latter teaching doctoral students in other fields.

NOTES

1 The dissertation can be disseminated in private, especially when the thesis is centred on industrial topics.

REFERENCES

Attali, J. (ed.) (1998). *Pour un modèle européen d'enseignement supérieur*. Rapport pour le Ministre de l'Éducation nationale, de la Recherche et de la Technologie, Paris.

De Lassale, M., Maillard, D., Martinelli, D., Paul, J. J., Perret, C. (1999). De la compétence universitaire à la qualification professionelle: l'insertion des docteurs. Document Cereq 144, Turin 1999, Marseille.

Direction de la Recherche et des études doctorales (1991a). Observatoire des thèses. Ministère de l'Éducation nationale, avril 1991, Paris.

Direction de la Recherche et des études doctorales (1991b). Le monitorat d'initiation à l'enseignement supérieur. Paris: Ministère de l'Éducation nationale, juin 1991, Paris.

Musselin C. (ed.) (1997). *Mobilité des chercheurs publics en Europe.* Paris: Centre d'analyse, de la formation et de l'intervention, Ministère de l'Éducation nationale, de la recherche et de la technologie, Paris.

Chapter 19

Higher Dead End?

JUSSI VÄLIMAA

Head of Higher Education Research Team, Institute for Educational Research, University of Jyväskylä, Jyväskylä, Finland

19.1 Introduction

One of the main problems of Finnish higher education researcher training is the lack of any systematic training. It seems, however, that it is not only one of the main problems but also a result of a development related to the structure of funding sources and the status of higher education research as an academic field. In this article I will begin by describing how this situation has developed and what are the current problems. Secondly, I will reflect on the future avenues of higher education research and researcher training, which seem to be approaching a (higher) dead end.[1]

The article is based on personal experiences gained as a researcher in several higher education research projects and on relevant research literature and is supported by discussions with my colleagues at the Institute for Educational Research. Following the academic rules of the game I should, however, like to begin with the definition of higher education research that will be applied in this article.

Higher education studies examine practical problems in higher education with the help of various theories and methods with a view to solving these problems. This definition has two elements. First, it admits that higher education research is not an independent discipline but an object-focused field of research which is primarily defined by the object of its analysis, as Teichler (1996) observed. This assumption is supported by theoretical discussions which emphasize that higher education differs from other social systems because it produces new knowledge (Becher & Kogan 1992; Clark 1983). The definition also maintains that higher education research is an applied field of research because it should be able to reveal – or even find so-

S. Schwarz and U. Teichler (eds.), The Institutional Basis of Higher Education Research, 247–258.
© 2000 *Kluwer Academic Publishers. Printed in the Netherlands.*

problem-solving does not, however, mean that the main task of the research-ers is to serve the decision-makers with instrumentally oriented data but with concepts and perspectives that shed light on the functioning of higher educa-tion (Välimaa and Westerheijden 1995).

19.2   The Finnish context

19.2.1   The Years of expansion

In Finland, the development of higher education studies was linked to an expansion of the higher education system between the 1960s and the 1990s, even though these two developments are not necessarily causally related. Finnish higher education policy in a modern sense began in the 1960s, after which it was steered by higher education development laws. The first Act on the Development of Higher Education covered the years from 1967 to 1986. It was followed by two more. The main purpose of the first law was to foster socio-geographic equality by expanding access to the universities and to mobilize talent reserves in the rural areas so as to reach the level of devel-opment of the other industrialized countries as has been pointed out by Pan-helainen and Konttinen (1993). Creating equal educational opportunities – including in higher education – became one of the most important objectives of the welfare state policy. The development law also ensured the growth of resources during an era characterized by the rapid regional expansion of the higher education system. These 20 years saw the creation of six higher edu-cation institutions and increases of 250 percent in student numbers and of 300 percent in the number of teachers (see Välimaa 1994).

The expansion of higher education was supported by a regional policy whereby all the main provinces were allowed to establish universities be-tween the 1960s and the 1980s. Now, there are 20 higher education institu-tions located in every part of Finland. In 1997, they included ten multi-faculty institutions, three schools of economics and four art academies. They offer education to over 140,000 university students. There were also 28 higher vocational education institutions (*Ammattikorkeakoulu (AMK)* insti-tutions) which offered 15,000 first-year places. According to the Govern-ment Plan for the Development of Education, a total of some thirty AMK institutions are expected to be established, all of them multi-faculty institu-tions. The plans include 24,000 places for new students in AMK institutions in the year 2000 (Higher Education Policy 1994). This means that over 60 percent of the age cohort will be offered a place in higher education (Väli-maa 1999).

According to Martin Trow's definition, Finland became a mass higher education system in the early 1970s (Ahola 1995, Trow 1974). Inspired by the ideology of a centrally-steered higher education system, the Finnish Ministry of Education initiated reforms to improve the efficiency of the national higher education system and solve problems caused by the transition to mass higher education. At the system level, the 1970s and the 1980s were periods of major reforms (Välimaa 1994).

The expansion of higher education studies was encouraged by a development strategy based on "learning by experimenting". From the 1960s to 1990s, a common way of initiating reforms in Finnish higher education was to begin with a pilot experimentation at a single institution (or several institutions) and expanding it, within a couple of years, to other institutions. This strategy has emerged gradually. In the 1970s, it was first tested in a reform of university administration (see Marin et al. 1971) and fully utilized in the implementation of the "Great Degree Reform". According to the model of strong state control which prevailed in the 1970s, the Ministry of Education first launched an experimental degree reform at the University of Jyväskylä and then put it into practice in all Finnish universities a few years later. Basically, the same strategy was repeated in all the major reforms, with small variations in the implementation, from the 1970s to the 1990s.

The reforms have been important for the development of Finnish higher education research because there also emerged a need to follow up the changes taking place in the institutions involved. Normally, whenever an experiment was launched, a follow-up study funded by the Ministry of Education was also initiated. When the Reform of Degree System was introduced, the Ministry established and funded the first short-term researchers' posts, mainly to promote the implementation of the reform. The researchers were based at the Institute for Educational Research at the University of Jyväskylä, the largest centre of educational research in Finland. Control of the research activities was firmly in the hands of the Ministry: the researchers reported their main research results every three months.

With the Great Reform of Degree System the position of higher education researchers began to change as a result of there being less need to follow up the outcomes of (the failing) reform. The first short-term contract positions became permanent positions, and in the 1980s researchers began to be able to continue (or start) their post-graduate studies. At the same time, funding for higher education research was stabilized because the Ministry of Education was able to create a special higher education research and development budget. This enabled predictable funding for higher education research at the Institute for Educational Research which was in charge of the majority of the follow-up studies carried out during the 1970s and the 1980s. The establishment of the Research Unit for the Sociology of Education (RUSE) at the University of Turku promoted the use of new sociological frameworks in the late 1980s. It was, however, immediately seen as a competitor by the Institute for Educational Research. The result was a lack of cooperation between the two centres. A positive consequence was, however, that such competition promoted the international orientation of Finnish higher education research in both centres (see Ahola 1995, Hakkarainen et al. 1992; Meek et al. 1996, Välimaa 1995).

In the late 1980s the situation of higher education research was rather favourable because funding was fairly stable and predictable. In addition to permanent researcher positions (six at the Institute for Educational Research and one at the RUSE), the Ministry of Education funded various system-level investigations and follow-up studies, as well as research projects to support pedagogical reforms. It may be estimated that there were 25-30 researchers engaged in various research projects in the two research centres. In addition to these researchers, Finnish academics in other universities also conducted both practical studies related to the problems of higher education and theoretically oriented studies (see Höltta 1995, Koski 1993, Kekäle 1997, Kuoppala & Marttinen 1995).

The Higher Education Development Act of 1986 introduced a new development strategy described by Van Vught (1989) as a strategy of self-regulation. The act and the government decision connected to it secured the basic resources and a ten percent annual growth in appropriations. At the end of the 1980s this was an exceptional trend in Western Europe.

19.2.2 Dramatic changes in Finnish higher education during the 1990s

As we have seen, Finnish higher education research has been closely connected with the changes in higher education policy. The relationship between higher education research and the central authorities has been and is more sensitive than in the established academic disciplines because practically all research projects have been initiated as a reaction to problems in higher education. The rather favourable situation of higher education research began to change when the expansion of the Finnish university system was completed in the late 1980s. Simultaneously, an economic recession hit Finland in the beginning of the 1990s, resulting in high unemployment rates and cuts in the higher education budget (Välimaa 1994, 1999). Consequently, state expenditure on higher education (universities) fell by 4.9 percent between 1991 and 1994, after which it increased again, reaching the level of the 1991 budget in 1998. In 1995, the new Government fixed guidelines for higher education up to the year 2000: education and research were and are seen as a crucial aspect of Finland's strategy for the future. Furthermore, higher education institutions are seen as a part of a national innovation strategy to help the national economy on the world market (Higher Education Policy 1998). A new Universities Act (1997) was implemented in 1998.

In the new Universities Act, Finnish universities were given internal autonomy in all important matters. These include the right to allocate their internal resources independently of the Ministry of Education, the right to design their own institutional regulations and decision-making procedures, and the right to appoint professors and other academic staff. These are significant changes in a public higher education system rooted in the traditions of the continental model because now universities have the opportunity to decide on institutional policy-making. Before the Universities Act, the dynamics of the Finnish higher education system were changed with the introduction of a set of steering instruments called "management by results" in the 1990s. These include budgeting by results, lump-sum budgeting, and results agreements between the Ministry of Education and the universities. The policy goal of management by results is to reward performance and effectiveness (Higher Education Policy 1998). Furthermore, the trend of the 1990s has been towards increasing the power of the academic leaders (rectors and deans and the heads of departments) at the expense of the collegial bodies.

The structure of higher education financing has also changed. Between 1991 and 1997 the proportion of public funding for higher education provided by the Ministry of Education decreased by eight percent (from 77% to 69%), while external funding from both private and public sources almost doubled. In terms of real income, between 1991 and 1997 the total income from chargeable services and other external funding (European Social Fund, The Academy of Finland, other public and private sources) grew by FIM 1,260 million, whereas funding from the Ministry of Education remained about the same (FIM 4,100 million) (see Välimaa 1999). As a result, competition for outside funding has increased competition between institutions and between faculties and departments within institutions. Hence, it is not an exaggeration to say that the implementation of the Universities Act took place in the context of a "marketization" of higher education as described by Bargh et al. (1996).

19.2.3 The problems of higher education research and career perspectives

The position of higher education research and researchers has been closely associated with their main funding source, the Ministry of Education. This has been reinforced by the lack of institutional policy analysis. There was no need for such analyses in the centralized Finnish higher education system during the 1970s and 1980s. Higher education institutions did not have opportunities to establish their own policy-making because everything was regulated by the Ministry of Education. For this reason also, there was no need for institutionally-based utilization of higher education research, and consequently, no need to hire people who were specialized in higher education or higher education research. The central administration in universities put more emphasis on bureaucratic procedures than on efficient management. This has been reinforced by the statistical database, KOTA,[2] which provides information on students, university teachers and other staff, expenditure, degrees conferred, etc. according to institutions and disciplines from 1981 onwards. Thus, the institutions have access to their basic data even though the criteria observed in gathering the information are sometimes problematic because they stem from the needs of the central authorities (Välimaa 1993).

The position of higher education research also changed during the 1990s. In 1996, the Ministry of Education decided to abandon its higher education research and development budget and give the money to the universities of Jyväskylä and Turku where the majority of the relevant studies had been conducted. The Ministry wanted to increase the autonomy of the universities in the spirit of self-regulation. But it failed to see (or refused to see) that as a result it gave up its power to negotiate the contents of higher education development projects supported by research. From the perspective of researchers this means that there is no longer a national funding body which is interested in the contents of research, but two local agents with their local interests instead. This means that we, as higher education researchers, must compete for funding with the established disciplines and with our local colleagues. Hence, higher education research faces the problems of justification. First, we need to justify the subject of our research (higher education) in a local context where our colleagues are (potential) subjects of our research. Secondly, we need to justify our methods of enquiry and the tradition of higher education research in competition with many institutionalized disciplinary traditions.

In this situation higher education researchers' lack of regular career prospects in higher education is especially problematic because, with the exception of pedagogical development projects in a few Finnish universities, there are no clients who are interested in "buying" our research findings. This also affects the training of junior academics in two ways. First, there is no longer a predictable funding source. Therefore, we can only recruit junior researchers on short-term contracts (from three to six months) for a specific research project. Secondly, after having been trained as a researcher in the field of higher education studies – as some of us have been – one has quite limited career perspectives because there are no academic positions or administrative posts available for a higher education specialist.

19.3 Discussion

It may seem paradoxical that the quantity of research publications on topics linked to higher education has increased, even in the 1990s. The variety of approaches and topics is seen every third year at the National Higher Education Symposium organized by the Higher Education Research Team of the Institute for Educational Research. In 1996, there were more participants (over 160 people) and presentations (52 research papers, panels or posters) than ever before in the 20-year history of National Higher Education Symposia. The presenters' academic backgrounds covered the following disciplines: education, economics, history, political science, the sociology of education (Liljander 1996).

The number of researchers who are active in the field of higher education research has not, however, led to any strengthening of higher education studies as an independent field of research. Three main reasons can be found for this. First, Finnish researchers have been oriented towards their own academic disciplines (psychology, social sciences, education) rather than towards establishing contacts with European or American scholars in the field of higher education studies (Fulton 1992). Thus, we have many researchers who made forays into higher education topics but who have not been able or willing to communicate with other researchers before returning to their own disciplines. It has been difficult to accumulate academic knowledge about or understanding of higher education because we lack a means of communication: a common language with established concepts which involve an acceptance of the social dynamics of higher education institutions based on a process of knowledge production. Secondly, new researchers have been recruited only for specific research projects on short-term contracts. In the 1980s, it was difficult to plan researcher training because funding followed the rhythm of the state budget, even though research projects often lasted several years. Recently, the situation has become worse because research projects are very short. Thirdly, if and when young researchers wanted to continue their post-graduate studies they had to defend their postgraduate theses within established disciplines (normally the social sciences, education and psychology) following the rules of the disciplines concerned. Consequently, Finnish higher education researchers have not developed any distinct identity as researchers of higher education. The lack of chairs in higher education studies strongly reinforces the unstructured character of the field.

From the perspective of junior academics, it can be said that there are no career prospects for those who are qualified in the field of higher education studies. The situation resembles the position of other junior academics in Finnish higher education. Today, now that there is no longer any expansion, the Finnish higher education system offers university teachers and researchers only a limited market. Hence, there are few posts available to junior academics. This is, in turn, related to the funding structure of Finnish higher education. Most of the funding for junior academics comes from external sources which have created a market for short-term research contracts. I have analysed the current situation in another paper (Välimaa 1999) with the help of two career fields linked with each other: permanent positions and temporary positions.[3]

In the temporary field, the essential question is how to find one's first job and make it last. In the field of higher education studies, the first job also depends on one's personal networks because project researchers (the most probable first job) are appointed by a project manager without the involvement of any collegial body. The field of permanent positions follows a different logic. There, one may speak about an academic career. The development of one's career greatly depends on research activities. Reputation is the currency. As to higher education studies, however, there is no real field of permanent positions. One of the alternatives would be to choose the administrative track. The problem is that there is no need for specialised knowledge of higher education in university administration or management because other administrative qualifications have been sufficient so far. Normally, the qualification needed for a public office in a university's central administration (and also in the Ministry of Education) has been an MA degree. Because of the lack of demand, no courses or study programmes on higher education have been offered or organized in the Finnish universities. Furthermore, the Finnish universities have not needed institutional policy analysis or research-based data gathering because they have had no real opportunities for any institutional policy-making. In addition, the funding of higher education research has been based on projects and contract research which makes it very difficult to train young researchers in higher education studies as a field of research with its own traditions and methodological perspectives. Therefore, it seems that the Finnish situation is approaching a (higher) dead end.

The current situation can be interpreted, however, also as a challenge. The new University Act has the potential to significantly change the situation described above because the Finnish universities' increasing institutional autonomy may create a need for institutional policy-making and institutional policy analysis.[4] I am speaking not only about data gathering, which is well organized, but also about a need to analyse the data from a critical perspective. This is also supported by the greater marketization of higher education because institutional analysis may increase higher education institutions' ability to adapt to various societal and economic needs. More institutional autonomy also creates a demand for more efficient managerial tools.

tion institutions' ability to adapt to various societal and economic needs. More institutional autonomy also creates a demand for more efficient managerial tools.

These developments open three possible avenues to develop research on higher education in Finland. First, the emergence of institutional policy-making supported by institutional policy analysis opens an avenue leading to institutional research. I am not saying that we should copy the American model of institutional research (Terenzini 1993). Such copying is not possible because the dynamics of the system and that of its institutions are different in Finland. I assume, however, that American institutional research with its instrumental use of knowledge may provide examples that could be considered in the Finnish universities. It is therefore a possibility that new challenges create a demand for (a Finnish type of) institutional research resulting in a demand for training administrators who are specialized in higher education.

The second avenue is related to the strengthening of national-level higher education policy-making. Because of the increasingly autonomous universities, the Ministry of Education may need analyses of current trends and developments in the higher education system because higher education institutions are more than willing to give a politically correct picture of their activities. This alternative would create a need for national system-level analyses of higher education and a demand for higher education studies.

Both these avenues presuppose a greater need for analyses of Finnish higher education at the institutional and the national level. These requirements may help to create new funding sources and may also promote the emergence of careers in higher education studies. This requires a systematic way of training not only higher education researchers but also persons capable of understanding the dynamics of higher education institutions and higher education systems. It also requires the development of higher education studies as an academic field with its courses, programmes and degrees. These assumptions are based on a conviction that the management of higher education institutions will have to be developed within a marketized system of higher education. The development of management should not be taken, however, as a value statement in favour of more efficient administration. It seems, nevertheless, that the development of higher education research and researcher training is related to the changes that are taking place in the management and steering of the Finnish higher education system.

A third avenue is related to the academic status of higher education studies. At the moment we may easily find ourselves in a legitimation crisis, obliged to justify our existence alongside the established academic fields and disciplines. Higher education studies are not necessarily recognized as an academic field of research, but may be seen as a semi-administrative activity, at least in the Institute for Educational Research. We should therefore pay attention to the quality of higher education research as an academic endeavour. It is evident that we will be better able to increase the attractiveness of higher education studies when we improve the academic standard of our research. This goal will challenge us to improve communication between different disciplinary traditions in the study of higher education and to become more aware of the international traditions of higher education studies. We also need more cooperation with established disciplines. There are also practical and academic problems related to the fact that there are no professors of higher education studies in Finland, and, therefore, no institutional support for developing study programmes in the field. We need chairs in higher education research.

The question addressed in this article is: what is the future of higher studies and higher education researcher training in Finland? The title suggests that we are approaching a crossroads where a dead end is one of the alternatives. The aim of the article is to show that the alternatives are many. It seems that we must build our roads ourselves.

NOTES

1   I wish to thank Professor Marcela Mollis (UBA), whose Freudian slip – "Higher Dead" when she meant to say "Higher Ed." at the ASHE conference in 1998 – inspired the writing of this article.
2   The KOTA (Korkeakoulujen tietokanta) data base was developed by the Ministry of Education which is also responsible for updating it. See http://www.csc.fi/kota/facts/html.
3   "Field" is used here as a metaphor derived from arcade and computer games: one needs to gain a certain number of credits to be able to move from a lower to an upper level. In this case one needs research credits to advance from the field of temporary academic positions to the field of permanent positions.
4   This seems to be taking place at least at the University of Jyväskylä. The writing of this article was delayed by an ad hoc policy analysis.

REFERENCES

Ahola, S. (1995). *Eliitin yliopistosta massojen korkeakoulutukseen.* (From Elite to Mass Higher Education. Changing Structures of Selection in Finnish Higher Education). Turku: Research Unit for the Sociology of Education, Report 30.
Bargh, C., Scott, P. and Smith, D. (1996). *Governing Universities. Changing the Culture?* Bury St Edmunds: SRHE and Open University Press.
Becher, T. and Kogan, M. (1992). *Process and Structure in Higher Education.* London and New York: Routledge.

Clark, B. R. (1983). *The Higher Education System. Academic Organization in Cross-National Perspective.* Berkeley: University of California Press.

Fulton, O. (1992). 'Higher Education Studies', in Clark, B. R. and Neave, G. (eds.) *The Encyclopedia of Higher Education,* vol. 3. Oxford: Pergamon Press, 1810-1821.

Hakkarainen, P., Jalkanen, H. and Määttä, P. (eds.) (1992). *Current Visions and Analyses on Finnish Higher Education System.* Jyväskylä: University of Jyväskylä. Institute for Educational Research. Publications Series B 75. Theory into Practice.

Higher Education Policy (1994). *Higher Education Policy in Finland.* Helsinki: Ministry of Education.

Higher Education Policy (1998). *Higher Education Policy in Finland.* Helsinki: Ministry of Education.

Hölttä, S. (1995). *Towards Self-Regulative University.* Joensuu: University of Joensuu. Publications in Social Sciences, no 23.

Kekäle, J. (1997). *Leadership Cultures in Academic Departments.* Joensuu: University of Joensuu. Publications in Social Sciences, no. 26.

Koski, L. (1993). *Tieteen tahtomana, yliopiston tekemänä. Yliopiston sisäiset symboliset järjestykset.* (Required by Science, Created by Universities. The Internal Symbolic Orders of Universities). Joensuu: University of Joensuu. Publications in Social Sciences, no. 17.

Kuoppala, K. and Marttinen, K. (1995). *Suomen tiedehallinnon määräytyminen osana eurooppalaista korkeakoulujärjestelmää.* (Determination of science administration in Finland as part of the European higher education system) Vaasa: Vaasan yliopisto. Länsi-Suomen taloudellinen tutkimuslaitos. Julkaisuja, no. 60.

KOTA. Data base organized and coordinated by Finnish Ministry of Education.

Liljander, J.-P. (ed.) (1996). *Erilaistuva korkeakoulutus.* Artikkelikokoelma Jyväskylässä 15.-16.8. 1996 järjestetystä korkeakoulutuksen VI symposiumista. (Higher Education in Differentiation. Collected papers from the VI Symposium on Higher Education in Jyväskylä, 15-16 August 1996). Jyväskylä: The Institute for Educational Research. University of Jyväskylä.

Marin, M., Määttä, P., Lillberg, J. and Jalkanen, H. (1971). *Korkeakoulujen sisäisen hallinnon uudistaminen* (Reform of Administration in Higher Education). Institute for Educational Research 89/1971.

Meek, V.L., Goedegebuure, L., Kivinen, O. and Rinne, R. (1996). *The Mockers and Mocked: Comparative Perspectives on Differentiation, Convergence and Diversity in Higher Education.* Guildford: IAU Press and Pergamon.

Panhelainen, M. & Konttinen, R. (1993). 'Creating New Strategies: Self-Evaluation in Finnish Higher Education'. *General Conference of International Network of Quality Assurance Agencies in Higher Education. Quality Assurance in a Changing World, Higher Education at a Crossroads,* Montreal, 26-28 May 1993.

Teichler, U. (1996). 'Comparative higher education: Potentials and limits'. *Higher Education,* pp. 431-465.

Terenzini, P. (1993). 'On the Nature of Institutional Research and the Knowledge Skills It Requires'. *Research in Higher Education,* vol. 34, pp. 1-10.

Trow, M. (1974). 'Problems in the Transition from Elite to Mass Higher Education'. *Policies for Higher Education. Conference on Future Structures of Post-Secondary Education.* Paris.

Välimaa, J. and Westerheijden, D. F. (1995). 'Two discourses: Researchers and policymaking in higher education'. *Higher Education,* vol. 29, pp. 385-403.

Välimaa, J. (1993). KOTA-todellisuus (KOTA Reality). *Korkeakoulutieto* 2, 54-58.

Välimaa, J. (1994). 'A Trying Game: experiments and reforms in Finnish higher education'. *European Journal of Education,* vol. 29, no. 2, 149-163.

Välimaa, J. (1999). *The Changing Nature of Academic Employment in Finnish Higher Education*. Manuscript.

Van Vught, F. A. (1989). 'Creating Innovations in Higher Education'. *European Journal of Education*, vol. 24, no. 3, 249-270.

Chapter 20

A Portrait of the Researcher as a Young (Wo)Man[*]

JEROEN BARTELSE & JEROEN HUISMAN
Centre for Higher Education Policy Studies, University of Twente, The Netherlands

20.1 Introduction

One of the themes of the 1998 International Symposium in Kassel was "Training of Young Researchers and Careers in Higher Education". In this paper, we shall address the place of the young researcher in the context of the Dutch doctoral system and of higher education research. We shall formulate a few survival rules for those who wish to pursue a career in higher education research and make some suggestions as to how research training could be organised to transform survival into a rewarding career.

First, we shall place young researchers in the Netherlands in a historical context. Then, we shall address the specific context of higher education research that young researchers are confronted with. A dilemma regarding career options appears. We shall conclude by making some suggestions as to how to deal with this dilemma.

20.2 Research training in the Netherlands, a brief history

Today, to be accepted in the Dutch research community one must normally hold a PhD. The experienced researcher who has a long publication record and an established academic status may avoid the doctorate, but the young university graduate typically starts his career as a PhD student. The history of the doctorate deserves a few comments to understand the current situation of young researchers' early career moves.

In 1644, the University of Utrecht was the first in the Netherlands to use the title '*Philosophiae Doctor et Liberalium Artium Magister*' (Hesseling 1986, p. 25). The dissertation could be a set of propositions which became a

259

S. Schwarz and U. Teichler (eds.), The Institutional Basis of Higher Education Research, 259–269.
© 2000 *Kluwer Academic Publishers. Printed in the Netherlands.*

short essay that had to be defended before students, doctors and *magisters*. This often involved an extensive ritual. Many of these rituals still exist. In the 17th and 18th century, "doctorate" meant a "vocational" rather than a research degree. Its holder was entitled to teach. Little has been recorded about the process to obtain the degree at that time. It seems to have been an individual pursuit that was not structured or prescribed, except for the dissertation. In the 19th and early 20th century, the procedure gradually changed. Although the Dutch universities were still institutions of education (Wachelder 1992, p. 28), a research ethos gained in importance. The functions of the degree changed under the influence of the research imperative of German universities and laboratories. The doctorate became a proof of one's ability to conduct independent research. In the sciences, renowned scholars formed research groups where research was conducted through master-apprentice relationships. Although inspired by practices in German universities, the Dutch doctoral system has developed within its own distinct societal and academic context.[1]

After World War II, and until the 1980s, PhD students were usually employed as faculty staff – sometimes as research-assistants, but also as regular (senior) staff. Apart from the ceremonial rites of passage, the writing of a doctoral dissertation was an informal endeavour. There were no fixed tasks dictated by (university or government) standards. It usually resembled the apprenticeship model, with the candidate working under the guidance of a professor. Yet, in comparison to Germany, the role of the supervisor or chairholder was less authoritarian. The writing of a dissertation was primarily the responsibility of the student. But, obviously, there were great disciplinary differences.

In the natural sciences, research took place in laboratories and was conducted in teams. Already in the 1950s, the preparation of a dissertation no longer consisted in individual work. It was supervised by senior staff and the supervisor. This, together with a clear demand from outside academia for qualified researchers, led to the concentration of larger groups of doctoral candidates in university laboratories (Beenakker 1990, pp. 321-322). A research team controlled the quality and proceeding of those working on a dissertation. The role of the professor should be seen as that of a mentor.

Unlike in the natural sciences, a structured process leading to the dissertation was less prominent in the social sciences and humanities. This stimulated individual work. The dissertation was written in relative isolation, in addition to teaching and research responsibilities. It was often a lifelong *opus magnum*. Besides, a clear labour market demand for doctors in the social sciences never developed. Hence, these fields did not have an external structuring influence on the doctoral process. The role of the supervisor was also different. He was more like a colleague who commented on the work in progress.

Since the 1960s, the Dutch government has become involved in research training. In a series of policy statements and laws, attempts have been made to adjust or reform doctoral training. Important points of discussion concerned (see also Bartelse 1999):

20.3 The function of doctoral training and the doctorate

As mass higher education developed and began to cater for a wide range of professions, a discussion emerged to include research training in a separate programme. This implies a break with the tradition, particularly present in the social sciences and humanities, of the doctorate as a lifelong work. Instead, it becomes a proof of one's ability to conduct independent research. The criteria used to judge a doctorate (an original piece of research usually published as a monograph), are closer to the early tradition than to this new concept.

20.4 The structure and duration of the training

Two different models seem to have underlain policy discussions on doctoral training since the 1960s (Van Hout 1988). The first is a three to four years period of work on a dissertation as a temporary staff member at a university. The second consists of two stages, a one year student assistantship and a two to three years assignment to write a dissertation. There were diverging opinions as to the time to obtain the degree. Until the introduction of the AiO-system in 1986 (see below), this was not reduced considerably, although the sciences were better able to limit the time to obtain the degree than the social sciences and humanities.

20.5 The employed educational concept

Two educational models can be distinguished in the history of Dutch doctoral education. The idea of learning by doing (the apprenticeship model) prevails in the early policy documents and laws. The professional model (which includes a more substantial course-work component) prevails in the policy documents of the 1980s. The idea behind incorporating course-work elements was to shorten the period of study to obtain one's degree, to lower attrition and to be attuned with international developments.

It is beyond the scope of this paper to reflect the (policy) discussions in full, but the current system is the outcome of and at the same time still subject to the issues mentioned.

20.6 The current Dutch doctoral system

Doctoral training in the Netherlands was given shape in the 'AiO system', which provides advanced research training to doctoral candidates (research trainees, abbreviated in Dutch as AiO) by active participation in university research and, to a limited extent (<25%), in teaching and administration. In the 'Adjustment of the second tier' act (1985), the AiO was introduced as a distinct academic position.

Dutch PhD candidates are appointed for a four-year period during which they must write their thesis. During that period, they may attend classes that relate to the subject of their thesis. They can also be called in for teaching activities in the department or faculty that appointed them. The AiOs receive salaries that are calculated according to a special scale. In the first years of their appointment, the salaries are cut back to compensate for the training students receive. The table below shows the monthly income for each year of the appointment (as per 01-01-1999):

Table 1: Monthly incomes of AiOs

Year of appointment	Salary
1st year	DFL 2.195,--
2nd year	DFL 2.507,--
3rd year	DFL 3.068,--
4th year	DFL 3.919,--

Recently, the labour market situation forced universities to change their AiO financial support system. In 1995, many PhD holders from the AiO system could no longer be absorbed by the (academic) labour market. But the universities were obliged to offer them unemployment payment, which meant an important financial 'loss'. Some universities decided to introduce PhD-grants instead of employment. One can easily imagine the resistance of the doctoral candidates: lower incomes, worse secondary conditions of employment and a feeling that their work was not valued.

More recently, however, the labour market situation for academics improved considerably. Almost all the universities abandoned the grant-system. It only exists now for PhD programmes that aim to attract international candidates. Instead, universities have started to complement AiO salaries to a level comparable to other academic staff members. This phenomenon is a now common feature of the universities of technology.

The recent developments of the means of support illustrate the ambiguity surrounding this issue. The doctoral candidates (AiOs) occupy a hybrid position in Dutch universities. On the one hand, they are students who receive training and supervision. On the other, they are seen as the engine of academic work. The financial support structure that was introduced in the framework of the AiO system reflects this. But there is increasing pressure from the labour market and the internationalisation of postgraduate training.

A recent development in the Dutch research landscape should improve the somewhat unappealing image of the first years of the research career: the graduate school. As the AiO-system did not provide adequate mechanisms to shape research training satisfactorily, the Dutch Minister introduced graduate schools at the beginning of the 1990s (referred to as 'research schools' in Dutch). They are defined as centres of high quality research where young researchers are offered structured training (Parliamentary Proceedings 1991). By March 1998, 119 were registered in virtually all disciplines (VSNU 1998, p. 6). Although they are meant to include all doctoral candidates, participation rates differ among the disciplines. Also, their level of development differs according to the field and in how far they have given shape to a structured doctoral process.

What happens after the young researchers obtain their doctorate? What are their prospects in the (academic) labour market? This issue has been the subject of heated debate since the mid-1990s. The academic labour market was seen as being unable to absorb the growing number of young doctoral degree holders who wished to pursue an academic career. At discussion seminars on this topic, doctoral candidates tend to refer to themselves as a 'lost generation'. In 1996, the Ministry of Education, Culture and Science commissioned a study on their situation in the labour market (Hulshof, Verrijt and Kruijthoff 1996).

There seemed to be fewer unemployed doctors than non-PhD holders: six percent versus 14 percent. For PhD holders who obtained their degree through an AiO position, the unemployment figure is slightly higher: nine percent (Hulshof, Verrijt and Kruijthoff 1996, p. 51). Overall, this picture is not negative, compared to the rest of the Dutch labour force. However, the employment conditions – in terms of salaries and job security – are generally less favourable for PhD holders.

Figure 1 shows the labour market destination of PhD holders as compared to non-PhD holders. Clearly, most PhD holders find work in research and teaching positions in the universities or research institutes (54%), or in industry (16%). There is, however, a move out of academia into other positions. In 1983, 70 percent of the PhD holders worked at universities, whereas in 1995, only 38 percent were employed by a university. Although 70 per-

cent have a research job – a figure that has remained fairly stable since 1983
– most doctors change jobs during their career.

Figure 1: Labour market destination of PhD holders

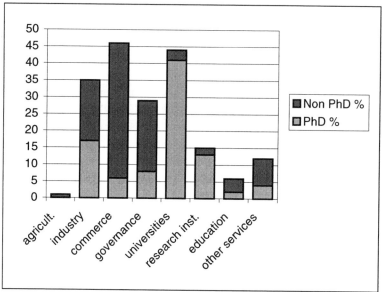

Source: Hulshof, Verrijt and Kruijthoff 1996, pp. 65-66

The current discussions on the labour market for PhD holders are no
longer dictated by pressing labour market issues. There is a move to discuss
the consequences of a broader labour market orientation for doctoral education. If replenishment of the professoriate is not the main objective for PhDs,
then how should doctoral education (which is still very much focused on academic work after the doctorate) meet the societal needs for highly educated
professionals? This issue greatly influences the orientation of doctoral education: towards the market or academia? Subsequently, the question that is being asked is the implications this changing orientation have for obtaining the
doctor's degree. If a broader labour market orientation is accepted, then the
required qualifications of the PhD graduate may need to be reconsidered.
There are a few experiments with the professional doctorate, but the issue is
still sensitive.

Let us formulate a few tentative conclusions on the position of the young
researcher in the light of the Dutch doctoral system described above:

Obtaining a research position is not always easy. Typically, one must apply for a job and not just enrol in a doctoral programme.

Working conditions and salaries are relatively unattractive. There must be a strong motivation to pursue an academic career. Talented students might be discouraged to choose a career in higher education research.

Supervision still very much depends on the commitment and skills of the professor, or a favourable research culture. Dropout rates and the time taken to obtain the degree are greatly influenced by the nature of the supervision and the (institutional) research environment. The graduate school may offer an opportunity to create such an environment.

There are not many job prospects for young doctorates in the academic world (we assume that young researchers wish to pursue an academic career). They are often in junior or temporary post-doctoral positions and must compete with the growing opportunities for young doctors to find employment elsewhere. The danger is to lose trained and talented researchers for the academic profession and to marginalise academic work.

This description of the Dutch doctoral system concerns the national context of the Dutch PhD candidate in higher education research who is also subject to the habits and structures that characterise higher education research itself. The institutional context of higher education is much less nationally based than the typically Dutch doctoral system, but it certainly forms another important frame of reference to understand the whereabouts of our young researcher.

20.7 The institutional context of higher education research

Like Teichler (1996), we maintain that higher education is an object-focused area of research. It is not a discipline, although it is accepted as a sub-discipline of education in certain countries. The object defines the boundaries of research (e.g. higher education versus secondary education), not the scientific principles and methods. Such areas of knowledge, especially higher education, are characterised as follows (Teichler 1996, p. 433):
- They are strongly driven by the social relevance of the core theme, thus implying a close link between research and problem-solving;
- they require substantial knowledge of the field; and
- they cut across disciplines and their favoured thematic areas.

These important features (notably the first and last) have considerable implications for the (young) researcher in higher education. First of all, not so much scientific curiosity, but practical and societal relevance is seen as an important feature. Second, to be able to carry out research in the field of higher education, knowledge of this field is a prerequisite. But it could be maintained that for empirical research knowledge of and insight into the object of investigation is also a prerequisite. In this respect, higher education as a field of research does not differ very much from disciplinary research. Third, the fact that there is no exclusive discipline overarching research in higher education raises the problem of disciplinary embeddedness. There is no common theory and methodology in the field. The disciplinary spectrum ranges from behavioural and social sciences to the humanities, together with its great variety of theoretical and methodological approaches.

Given the context of doctoral training in the Netherlands and the context of higher education research described above, a dilemma for young researchers looms ahead. On the one hand, those who are interested in an academic career are 'forced' to take up a PhD. On the other, interest in a career in higher education research implies a 'feeling' for societal relevance, an interdisciplinary perspective and a sense for practical problem solving (not only by doing research but also by transferring knowledge through training and consultancy activities). This part of the career is not driven by theoretical questions, but by practical policy problems. The disciplinary education and the object-focused characteristics of the field of higher education seem to be at odds. The dilemma is also recognisable for higher education researchers in general, but notably for young researchers: which career option is suitable for them?

20.8 A career in higher education research

The Dutch context of doctoral education and the characteristics of the field of higher education impose specific pressures on young researchers and their ambition to develop as a researcher. What can we say about research training in our field of study in order to improve the chances of a favourable career and hence to ensure the continued existence of academic work by preparing new generations of scholars?

Following Maassen (1997), the main concerns of the field of higher education relate to its legitimacy (in the short and long run). To legitimise its existence as an autonomous object-based area of research, the outcomes of higher education research should ideally: (1) contribute to the theoretical and conceptual state of the art in the disciplines; (2) add to the knowledge on higher education (improving steering, policy making, strategic management, quality, etc.); and (3) allow for connections with fields which focus on related domains (educational sciences, science studies). Maassen states that this ideal situation is far from being achieved. The low status – the field is disconnected from the disciplines – and the non-optimal relation with institutional and governmental stakeholders (which threatens the financial viability of higher education research in the long run) are of critical concern.

To reach the ideal situation, an hourglass structure is proposed. The core of the hourglass consists of broad research programmes in higher education with a theoretical and an applied focus. At the top of the hourglass, disciplinary-based scholars should contribute to the development of theoretical/conceptual frameworks that relate to the basic problems in the field of higher education (e.g. concepts and theories that improve the understanding and effects of governmental steering approaches). These concepts and frameworks must be applied by higher education researchers – at the lower side of the hourglass. One of the underlying assumptions of the hourglass structure is that the functions of higher education researchers and disciplinary-based scholars, both of some status in their field/discipline, are difficult to combine in one person (there are, however, notable exceptions). The outcomes of higher education research should be fed back to the disciplinary scholars. The application should be based on higher education scholars' specific knowledge of their domain. The relevance of higher education research should be improved by involving stakeholders in the development and adjustment of the research programmes and agenda.

The hourglass 'solution' helps to remove the pressure on the young researcher in higher education. Instead of ambiguous demands – driven by disciplinary and societal requirements – young researchers may choose their position in the hourglass, provided that the connection to the 'other' part does not silt up. If the researchers choose to write a PhD in the lower part of the hourglass, they should have an open interaction with the disciplinary-based scholars in the upper part. However the requirements of the dissertation mainly concern applied research and research methodologies. If, on the other hand, researchers choose to write a PhD in the upper part of the hourglass, they should be able to communicate and reflect with scholars with an applied orientation. But the yardstick for quality lies in the ability to make an original contribution to theory.

The hourglass structure in its ultimate form allows for a differentiation of doctoral research. Different requirements for the dissertation imply different doctoral processes. But, at the same time, continued and open communication among scholars is necessary to maintain an identifiable and integrated field of study. How should such an idea be set up organisationally, given the Dutch (or for that matter: country-specific) institutional context of doctoral training?

We argue that, despite the almost unlimited possibilities of present-day communication technologies, a certain critical mass within a single organisation is the best solution. This critical mass relates both to the size of the disciplinary-based group of scholars and the size of the applied higher education research group. The presence of a larger group of young researchers, senior researchers and academic leadership could provide an environment that includes both compartments of the hourglass. In addition, larger research centres may more easily attract funds from research councils or contract research to offer attractive facilities and contracts. Furthermore these centres may provide a career perspective that is attractive enough to keep talented scholars in the field. This option would reduce some of the tensions that were outlined in the tentative conclusions on the position of the young higher education researcher in the light of the Dutch doctoral system.

A second-best option, which is more viable and important for those researchers in higher education that are not connected to these larger research groups, is to create international programmes of doctoral training. Typically these should be designed as a comprehensive, high quality programme leading to the award of a PhD. These programmes would encompass doctoral candidates of both sides of the hourglass and would enable participants to:
– understand the nature and use of social science theories;
– undertake original independent research and disseminate the results;
– analyse professional situations and issues in higher education policy and management with the help of insights from theory, and through empirical research.

Currently, CHEPS is designing a doctoral programme in cooperation with other partners in higher education research. It consists of course work (typically one year) and doctoral research (typically two to three years). The length and balance of these components may vary depending on the research project undertaken and the educational background and experience of the candidate. At the outset of a doctoral project, the candidate and his/her supervisor will design an appropriate work plan within the framework of the general programme structure. The programme can be followed on a full time or part time basis.

The course work component includes advanced modules on issues in higher education policy and management, as well as in research methodology, philosophy of science, and the history of higher education. In addition, a number of specialised modules will be offered by the various partner institutions of the programme. CHEPS will develop modules in the areas of higher education governance and management, finance and economics, and quality. Other topics to be covered by partner institutions include research policy and management, and higher education human resources management.

The course work components will be offered either as distance learning modules, or as summer schools and seminars at the various participating universities. Participants will have ample opportunities to discuss their work with internationally renowned experts in the field of higher education and with other doctoral candidates in the programme.

The research component consists of the preparation of a dissertation. The work on a dissertation is supervised by a supervisor at the candidate's 'home' university and a co-supervisor at a partner institution. Candidates will be offered the opportunity to conduct research at a university other than their home institution for a period of at least three months.

The two options discussed here, i.e. the research institute of a critical mass and the international doctoral programme, may offer research environments that guide our researcher as a young (wo)man through the dilemma put forward in the previous section. In addition they might contribute to an attractive career perspective for young talented researchers – those who in the long run should warrant a flourishing field of study.

NOTES

* Inspired by the title of James Joyce's 1916 novel 'A portrait of the artist as a young man'.

1 The German 19th century university system provided a clear example upon which to model a uniform research and doctoral system. For an elaboration of this point see Wachelder 1992, pp. 27-33 and Clark 1995.

REFERENCES

Bartelse, J. A. (1999). *Concentrating the Minds: the institutionalisation of the graduate school innovation in Dutch and German higher education.* Utrecht: Lemma.

Beenakker, J . J. M. (1990). 'Randvoorwaarden voor de onderzoekersopleiding', *Universiteit & Hogeschool* 36(6), 321-329.

Clark, B. R. (1995). *Places of Inquiry.* Berkeley: University of California Press.

Hesseling, P. (1986). *Frontiers of Learning: The PhD octopus.* Dordrecht: Floris publications.

Hout, J. F. M. J. van (1988). *Onderzoekers in opleiding.* Nijmegen: IOWO.

Hulshof, M. J. F., Verrijt, A. H. M. and Krijthoff, A. (1996). *Promoveren en de arbeidsmarkt: ervaringen van de lost generation.* Nijmegen: IOWO.

Maassen, P. A. M. (1997). The hourglass structure and its implications. Presented to the round-table on "The relationship among research, policy and practice in higher education", Tokyo, Japan.

Parliamentary Proceedings (1991). Onderzoekschool, 21 839, nr. 3, vergaderjaar 1990-1991.

Teichler, U. (1996). 'Comparative higher education: Potentials and limits', *Higher Education* 32(4), 431-465.

VSNU (1998). *BIOS: Bestuurlijke Informatie Onderzoekscholen.* Utrecht: VSNU.

Wachelder, J. C. M. (1992). *Universiteit tussen vorming en opleiding: de modernisering van de Nederlandse universiteiten in de negentiende eeuw.* Hilversum: Verloren.